WOMEN ON THE
BRINK OF DIVORCE

WOMEN ON THE BRINK OF DIVORCE

A GUIDE TO SELF-HELP BOOKS

By Cynthia David

ATHENS REGIONAL LIBRARY
2025 BAXTER STREET
ATHENS, GA 30606

Highsmith PRESS
Fort Atkinson, Wisconsin

Published by Highsmith Press LLC
W5527 Highway 106
P.O. Box 800
Fort Atkinson, Wisconsin 53538-0800

1-800-558-2110
© Cynthia David, 1995

Cover Design: Frank Neu
All rights reserved. Printed in the United States of America.
Except as permitted under the United States Copyright Act of 1976, no part of
this publication may be reproduced or distributed in any form or by any means,
or stored in a database or retrieval system, without the prior written permission

The paper used in this publication meets the minimum requirements of
American National Standard for Information Science —
Permanence of Paper for Printed Library Material.
ANSI/NISO Z39.48-1992.

Library of Congress Cataloging in Publication

David, Cynthia
  Women on the brink of divorce: a guide to self-help
books / by Cynthia David.
      p.   cm.
  Includes bibliographical references and index.
  ISBN 0-917846-54-0 (alk. paper)
  1. Marriage--Psychological aspects--Bibliography. 2.
Divorce--Psychological aspects--Bibliography. 3. Self-
help techniques--Bibliography. I. Title
Z7164.M2D38 1995
[HQ734]
016.6467'8--dc20   95-15693

ISBN 0-917846-54-0

To Dr. Bernie Siegel, the highly competent physician, lecturer, and author of Love, Medicine and Miracles *and numerous other books. During my 1981 office visit for a suspicious condition, this man recognized more than physical symptoms in me. Taking time from an already over-booked schedule, he intuitively questioned until I confessed (for the very first time to anyone) that indeed my marriage was in trouble. As I left, Dr. Siegel gave me my first self-help book,* Love Is Letting Go of Fear *by Gerold Jampolsky. With his gift, I began my first small step on the road to recovery, a new life, and ultimately the writing of this guide.*

Contents

Foreword   *ix*

Preface   *xi*

Acknowledgments   *xv*

1. Understanding Ourselves First   *1*
   Slay Your Own Dragons

2. Understanding the Men in Our Lives   *29*
   The Secrets Men Keep

3. An Overview of Marriage, Love and Divorce   *49*
   Husbands and Wives

4. Trying to Save the Marriage First   *53*
   I Love You, Let's Work It Out

5. Problem Areas in Marriages   *93*
   When Love Goes Wrong

6. Preventing and Surviving Affairs   *117*
   Sex, Lies and Forgiveness

7. Breaking Up   *131*
   Between Marriage and Divorce

8. The Impact of Divorce on Children   *147*
   A Hole in My Heart

9. Legal and Financial Aspects of Divorce   *165*
   The Survival Guide

10. Recovering from Divorce *185*
       Smart Cookies Don't Crumble

11. Living Alone *205*
       Formerly Married: Learning to Live With Yourself

12. Finding a New Relationship *221*
       When It's Time to Love Again

   Epilogue: Remarriage and Stepfamilies *239*

   About the Author *241*

   Title Index *243*

   Author Index *251*

   Subject Index *259*

Foreword

I had no idea, when asked by Cynthia David to write an introduction to her self-help book on mending or ending a marriage, that the book was dedicated to me. I say that so you will not think I am recommending this book or writing the introduction because of the dedication.

I am recommending this book to all of you so you can learn from it, avoid many traumas, find enlightenment and not need to write another self-help book.

I receive many self-help books written by people who have been through one of life's difficulties and want to share what they have learned from it.

My comment is to not write another book but to learn from those who have preceded you. Cynthia David's book is an excellent source of empowerment. Remember the key is self-help not the book. A book cannot change you.

In a Calvin and Hobbes cartoon, Calvin tells Hobbes he is planning to get rich writing a self-help book to help people solve their addiction to self-help books. In the last scene Calvin is saying, "The trouble is…if my program works, I won't be able to write a sequel!"

That's my point. Use what is here to guide and teach you. You are the power, not the book. The book is a resource.

I do a great deal of counseling for people with life threatening illnesses. If they come to me and say, "After reading your work or listening to you I am inspired," or "Here's the man who cured me," or "Your book healed me," I disagree with them. I tell them they are inspiring and the one who created the cure or healing. I can only guide and teach.

I might also add that I don't accept responsibility for their guilt, shame or blame but ask them again to look inside themselves for the source of those feelings.

What I appreciate about this book is that it offers itself as a guide. Each of us is on a path and what we often require is guidance. Too often our intellect thinks it knows the way only to lead us on a path-o-logical course.

Who are the best guides? The people native to the territory. This book contains a list of guidebooks by natives. People who have been where you are now or have been where you are going. By reading what they know you will save yourself a great deal of pain and doubt, and they can be war-buddies for you during the period of conflict and turmoil.

I have often said that we need a book with a chapter on every problem life can present to us. Each child would be issued a copy on the day of his or her birth. That book hasn't been completed yet, but Cynthia David's resource book and guide could certainly fulfill the needs for the chapter on marriage and how to survive in it or after it.

I write this on July 11, 1994, our 40th wedding anniversary. My wife has on occasion described our marriage as a struggle. Joseph Campbell has described marriage as an ordeal. Why these words? Because any relationship takes work and this book will help you get the work done.

BERNIE S. SIEGEL, M.D.

Preface

Something's wrong. Very wrong. I feel it everywhere. Like a silent ever growing cancer, it's slowing killing our whole family. Sometimes I think I'm going crazy! I don't want a divorce, but I just can't live like this much longer. Can we save the marriage or should I leave? I don't know if the effort and pain are worth it anymore. We used to love each other so much. Now we can't talk about anything. If we don't pull it together, what will happen to the children? Will we have enough money to survive? I'm so afraid. What will our families and friends think? I can't eat...or sleep...or work. Could there be another woman? Where can I turn for help? I just want to be happy again and pretend all of this never happened. How will I cope with being all alone? I'm too young to have failed... I'm too old to start over... Maybe we can just live separate lives and keep things together for the kids. Maybe it's all in my mind. Maybe... Maybe it's time for a lawyer.

Some of your feelings may resemble the kinds of conflicted thoughts I once had. You will probably choose to keep them all to yourself at first. Then one day, you'll finally confide in a friend. The secret is out. It must be real after all. Your marriage *is* in trouble. Although talking helps, the problem doesn't go away. Perhaps professional help is the answer. You seek out a therapist. At last! Someone who listens, understands, and has counseled others in the same predicament. But this kind of support is expensive and you can only afford it once or twice a week, if that. What about the moments in between? How can you better understand what is happening, what options you have, and what steps you should be taking?

Purpose & audience

I hope *Women on the Brink of Divorce* is your answer. It is designed to be an indispensable reference and guide, first and foremost, for readers who want to salvage their marriages. If the marriage is beyond salvation, then the book is for those of you who are trying to find your way through the confusing divorce and recovery process. While women are the primary audience, the vast majority of selections will be very helpful to male readers as well. In addition, *Women on the Brink of Divorce* will be of great value to counselors, clergy, women's studies centers, libraries, and bookstores. A lay person's annotated bibliography, it summarizes 553 noteworthy self-help books. Old classics as well as unusual and new releases are here. It contains a wide variety of sources that focus on the whole gamut of issues involved in the mending or ending of marriages—whether they be emotional, legal, or financial questions. Each topic has its own chapter. The chapters then fall into the logical stages that are inevitable in this traumatic life passage, for example understanding yourself, dealing with the children or the legal process, or learning how to live alone. The result is an easy-to-use, logically organized handbook that filters the options and a sourcebook that complements and enhances all the others types of valuable support you may already be receiving.

Need for *Women on the Brink of Divorce*

In my own personal experience with divorce, I found that books, more than anything, were my salvation. During the many hours I spent alone trying to understand what was really happening or what steps I should take, they were my constant companions. I read, underlined, and took notes. Friends and counselors would often chuckle as I referred to my most recent self-help reading. Could there be any books left that I had not tackled? Some, admittedly, were a waste of time. Others made a noteworthy point or two. A large number of books, however, provided new insights into the self, men, marriage, divorce, independence, and life. These are the ones I discussed at length with my therapists and recommended time and time again to friends in need.

During my visits to countless bookstores and libraries, I was always amazed with the huge variety of self-help books available. Interestingly, however, the selection was never the same. While every facility seemed to stock at least some of the basics, each one had titles that none before had offered. What I saw on the shelves of one store or library was not at all what appeared in the next. How could a woman know what was really out there? It was this problem that helped pinpoint a need. A comprehensive catalog or bibliography of books focussed on the problems related to marriage and relationships did not seem to exist. Authors had written very successful guides to a wide variety of books for children, but no one had specifically tackled the enormous arena of adult self-help literature, especially as it related to women and the prospect of divorce.

Thus, *Women on the Brink of Divorce* was born. The objective was not to evaluate the books selected for the guide nor to pass any type of judgment on them. It was, rather, to summarize them briefly and concisely according to what the authors stated as their goals, their subject matter, and their theories. The interpretation of their objectives was completely the result of my own review of each author's work. To the best of my knowledge, each synopsis reflects the book's content and intended purpose. Obviously, a nine to twelve-line summary is unable to deliver a complete overview of any book. Yet it was clear that brevity would be critical to the user—the professional counselor, the women's studies professor, the clergyperson, the librarian, the bookstore, the health center, and most of all to the woman in need.

Subjective judgments are absent for many reasons. First of all, evaluations are useful only if the intended audience is similar to the author in age, psyche, intellect, background, and life experience. Countless factors can influence a woman's reaction to a book. It is simply not possible to determine whether a particular piece will be as good for the 40-year-old, white, Midwestern housewife as it might be for the 25-year-old, black, New York career woman. Secondly, in the area of self-help, there are no "right answers." Instead, there are insights that work well for one set of problems and very different but valid pieces of advice that might prove to be breakthroughs for another. An objective summary points us to the possibilities and then allows each of us to pass our own judgments.

Selection criteria

Thousands of self-help books have been published, and new ones continue to appear everyday. Understandably, *Women On the Brink* could not include them all. The selection criteria were therefore multifaceted. Old, new, and interesting or unique perspectives were necessary to give a full picture and to achieve balance. Bookstores will offer the newer selections, whereas libraries may need to be relied on for the older and classic selections. The vast majority of books included were written in the 1980s and 1990s. The overriding belief here was that readers would gravitate toward more current books, especially in legal and financial areas where an understanding of such areas as recent tax laws would be crucially important. Some older or classic pieces as far back as the 1960s, however, were included either because their concepts were unique, their message universal, or because they were simply too well-known to pass by.

Balance was very important in the writing of this book. It seemed that there should be sufficient reference material for each stage of the process without becoming encyclopedic or overwhelming. In this regard, some fine books were omitted simply because of excessive overlap of subject matter. Others, on the contrary, found a place primarily because they covered a topic none other had touched. In order to achieve balance, there had to be the really well-known classics as well as some controversial eye openers, some traditional views and some fresh, new approaches. Ideally, there would be a blend of scholarly studies, current research, surveys, musings, personal accounts, and popular advice. The idea was to try to provide some of everything so that any type of reader would be able to find a suitable resource for any given problem in the field.

To those of you who feel a favorite or especially significant book is missing or to authors who have, without intention, had their works excluded, I apologize. If you wish to bring these to my attention, please write me in care of my publisher, Highsmith Press. Since it is our intent to publish periodic updated revisions of *Women on the Brink*, we would welcome your suggestions.

Where can you find the books in the guide? Don't underestimate the value of your library. Even the smallest facility can probably obtain any book you want through interlibrary loan. Should you wish to buy, most bookstores can order any type of book.

Structure

A word about the structure of the book. Having lived through the troubled marriage/divorce process myself and having studied it extensively, it became clear that there is a logical progression or pattern that occurs. One step often leads naturally to the next. This guide is structured according to this pattern. Initially, the focus is likely to be on the other person, the husband or the "bad guy." Gradually it comes around to the woman herself and how she may be less-than-perfect also. Once there is greater insight into the inner feelings and problems of women as well as men, the focus changes to trying to save the marriage and solve specific problems. If separation and divorce finally prove inevitable, it is time to explore legal, psychological, and financial matters as well as how to protect the children whose welfare is so important. Emotional healing needs to be addressed when the divorce is over, as do the final phases of learning to live all alone and allowing a place for new romance to flourish.

The process of mending or ending a marriage, the cycle or pattern described above, can be divided into twelve stages. These twelve stages create the twelve chapters of *Women on the Brink*. Each of the 553 books was placed in one of these chapters. It was frequently difficult to categorize particular books since many examined a wide range of important issues treated in more than one chapter. Nevertheless, one section always seemed more appropriate for each title. An important feature of this book, however, is the cross-referencing. Each chapter has a list of books from other chapters that relate to the same topic. Thus, the reader can appreciate the full value of each book. In addition, the subject index also provides more specific help.

Your decision to mend or end your marriage is one that will have a lasting effect upon your life. *Women on the Brink of Divorce* will have succeeded if it helps guide you to at least some of the answers that are right for you.

Acknowledgments

It would never have been possible to write this book without the assistance of a long list of terrific people. To all of them, I offer my special thanks and a promise to help them realize their own dreams in whatever ways I can.

I especially thank Kimberly and Miles David, my children, for supporting my many hours of labor, my stacks of books, and my mission to get this book published. I'm sure there were times when the pressures of deadlines meant denying many of their wishes, and I truly appreciate their understanding.

Many thanks to my friend, Mike Sulzbach, for reviewing my publishing contract; to Dr. Bernie Siegel, for agreeing to write the preface; to Karen Letterman, for knowing the answers to thousands of questions and helping me network; to Steve Lauri, for his work in developing a cover design for the pre-publication printing; to John Greenwald, for his assistance in editing and proofreading the original manuscript; to Linda Wilson, for converting the manuscript and helping me understand my software; to my sister, Andrea Hricko, for helping to edit chapter introductions and offering to introduce the work to others; to Nora Gluck, for supporting the general concept of the book early on and then writing an endorsement; to Linda Fuller, for advising me on the ins and outs of publishing contracts and writing an endorsement; to Rabbi Laura Geller, Slane Holland, Sherry King-Rockman, and Kathy Wexler for finding time in their very busy schedules to review the book and endorse it; to Roxanne Coady, for letting me use her Madison bookstore to update some literature; to Carol Christensen, for being a bosom buddy to a lonely writer; and to my old friends, Susan Johnson, Sherry Craig, Nancy Hurley, and Ann Erda for their nurturing during my own separation and divorce. Without that help long ago, I might not be in this place today.

Finally, I need give my deepest gratitude to my best friend and partner, Bill Junkin, whose love for me and belief in me have been unflagging.

In addition, I must pay tribute to the dozens of bookstore employees and librarians from Southern Connecticut (especially Madison) to Southern California who gave me hours of their time as they searched for the books I needed. The advice and guidance these individuals provided was invaluable.

1

Understanding Ourselves First

Slay Your Own Dragons

In a marriage crisis, the very first place we must direct our attention is to understanding ourselves better. While it may appear to women that husbands are the problem, it is entirely possible that their own personal female issues may really be the culprit. Changing others is very difficult at best; changing ourselves may truly be the only solution.

If there are problems in a woman's childhood that have been left unresolved, they may linger into adulthood and cause her to act out unhealthy behavior patterns such as mothering or controlling the man in her life. Women also may have developed very dependent personalities which prevent them from being assertive and able to state clearly what they want from others. Issues of low self-esteem can spawn jealousy and affect their ability to be open to love. Some women may suffer from misconceptions about romance which give rise to unrealistic expectations of their marriage partners. On the other hand, women may find themselves losing interest in sex. Perfectionism, worry, and stress from the overwhelming demands of their families and jobs often create an overall dissatisfaction with the quality of their lives. Sometimes there is also a strong need for financial independence that perhaps a new career, rather than a new husband, might cure.

The books in this chapter address a wide array of challenges facing women in today's rapidly changing world. Learning to meet them with appropriate responses can improve a woman's self-knowledge, personal happiness, and consequently her relationships.

1. *The Agony of It All: The Drive for Drama and Excitement in Women's Lives.* **Joy Davidson, Ph.D. Los Angeles, CA: Jeremy P. Tarcher, Inc., 1988. Hardcover. 270 pp.**

   The Agony of It All provides an in-depth look at how conforming to the subconscious expectations of a female's traditional role in society convolutes some women's positive sense of adventure and "sensation-seeking" into negative patterns of acting out. Davidson talks about potentially destructive results such as constant turmoil, arguments, crises, career failures, affairs, excessive behaviors and addictions, instability, and unsatisfactory relationships. She offers advice on how to redirect what she views as a genuinely positive attribute away from the pursuit of a "melodramatic" lifestyle toward the creation of more fulfilling relationships and life-enriching goals. The book studies three types of victims: "the fighter," "the challenger," and "the rebel."

2. *Being a Woman: Fulfilling Your Femininity and Finding Love.* **Dr. Toni Grant. New York: Avon Books, 1988. Paperback. 233 pp.**

   In this controversial best seller, Dr. Grant advocates a return to the kind of femininity that she feels the recent advances of feminism and the women's movement all but destroyed. Specifically, a woman must put aside the modern "Amazon Woman" interested primarily in achievement and restore the "Mother, Madonna and Courtesan aspects of her personality." The author feels that this will provide women the serenity and love that are truly the rewards of femininity. Grant states that prioritizing love as a woman's primary objective can affect amazing changes in their lives. Most importantly, it can facilitate self-understanding, the rediscovery of feminine strengths, and the building of better relationships.

3. *Bitches and Abdicators.* **Toni Scalia. New York: M. Evans & Co., 1985. Hardcover. 225 pp.**

   Scalia contrasts two types of behaviors that determine the degree to which women get what they want: "abdicators and bitches." She defines the "abdicator" as one who "relinquishes control" of her life by weakly rearing her children, acting unassertively in the work world, and stagnating in bad relationships. Society wrongly labels women "bitches," she states, when they choose to use their strengths to "take control of their lives" and meet their legitimate needs. According to Scalia, passivity is far more acceptable to men and a culture that is clearly more comfortable with subordinate women. Based on interviews and personal experience, the book guides women in changing their behavior, ridding themselves of "self-defeating responses," and becoming goal-oriented "bitches" in the best sense of the word.

4. ***Bradshaw On: The Family. A Revolutionary Way of Self-Discovery.*** **John Bradshaw. Deerfield Beach, FL: Health Communications, Inc., 1993. Paperback. 242 pp.**

This is a 12-step workbook for "spiritual awakening and empowerment" with charts, checklists and guidelines. Using it, readers can gain an understanding of the dynamics of both functional and dysfunctional family systems. Based on his TV series, Bradshaw's best seller shows how family rules can unknowingly perpetuate serious problems and addictions. If we fail to discover our "true selves," he says, we can carry with us the baggage that our family script recites to us deep within; thus problems we have with ourselves and the world really take root in our family. The author's positive news is that we *can* alter all of that and find wholeness, regardless of how unhappy our history. Topics include: shame and guilt, compulsive/addictive behavior, birth order, effective communication, fair fighting, obedience, power, control, violence, and eating disorders.

5. ***Career & Conflict: A Woman's Guide to Making Life's Choices.*** **Anne Russell and Patricia Fitzgibbons. Englewood Cliffs, NJ: Prentice-Hall, Inc., 1982. Paperback. 211 pp.**

Two working women, one single and one married, write in practical terms about the challenges career women face when it comes to questions of marriage and family. Traditional roles for women have changed drastically, opening up numerous new alternatives, they say. This book examines the major challenges and questions women might face, namely: whether or not to marry; if and when they should have children; if and when they should go back to work after childbirth; and how to best combine marriage, career, and children. Actual case histories and personal experiences help to develop greater self-awareness and strengthen decision-making skills. Numerous examples illustrate the practical and emotional results of their solutions.

6. ***The Cinderella Complex: Women's Hidden Fear of Independence.*** **Colette Dowling. New York: A Pocket Book, Simon & Schuster, 1981. Paperback. 289 pp.**

Based on personal experience and interviews with experts and women of all types, this book studies how females have been raised to expect that someone else (especially a male) will be responsible for them. This man will "save" a woman from the harsh realities of life. Dowling's premise is that such a dependent outlook disables women and prevents them from realizing their full potential. She says that it instills feelings of inferiority as well as discontent that impact women's lives negatively. The author's goal is to study the origins of this problem and to help women develop healthy

3

independence. Topics also include: early childhood "orientation," escaping through marriage, the results of ignoring one's ambitions, and busy work as a cover for unhappiness.

7. *Codependent No More: How to Stop Controlling Others and Start Caring for Yourself.* **Melody Beattie. New York: Harper & Row Publishers, 1987. Paperback. 229 pp.**

This best seller is primarily for people whose partners are afflicted with alcoholism or other compulsive disorders. It may also be useful to those who focus excessively on others rather than caring for themselves and living their own productive lives. Codependents feel excessive responsibility for those around them, a trait that often results in attempts to control other people and events. Beattie, an ex-alcoholic, looks at the way substance and other abuse victimize families. She describes the caretaker's resulting codependent behavior, traces its developmental origins, and discusses its potentially negative effects. The book suggests healthier alternative behaviors as ways to "let go," grow, and "set ourselves free."

8. *The Crisis of the Working Mother: Resolving Conflict Between Family and Work.* **Barbara J. Berg. New York: Summit Books, 1986. Hardcover. 249 pp.**

Berg interviewed a thousand working mothers nationwide and discovered a recurrent pattern. Although she says that 52 percent of those with preschool children work, there is still a prevailing sense of guilt about the quality of their mothering. Performing all of their duties well leaves them "torn in half" and "fragmented," she notes. Even if working is mandatory, Berg claims that the "corrosive ingredient" in their disturbed feelings is a sense of guilt based on not caring for their families as their mothers did. Unlike fathers who never question their role as career person, some mothers see home and work as entirely separate. Berg offers solutions for child rearing, lessening work demands, sharing the load with families, and saving time for both the self and the marriage.

9. *Don't Say Yes When You Want to Say No: The Assertiveness Training Book.* **Herbert Fensterheim, Ph.D. and Jean Baer. New York: A Dell Book, Dell Publishing Co., 1975. Paperback. 304 pp.**

These authors instruct women on how to assert their rights in all aspects of their lives: marriage and sex, family, careers, and social life. They carefully differentiate assertiveness from aggressive "pushiness." To be assertive, they say, is "to take an active approach" to one's life, to set one's own clear goals, acknowledge one's own value, defend it, and insure that others recognize it also. Fensterheim and Baer employ case studies and assignments in this "guide to changing habits." Topics include: how and when to communicate anger and resentment, expressing oneself more clearly, accepting success without guilt, saying "no" when necessary, avoiding neurotic behavior, bodies and weight loss, and developing a satisfactory social network.

10. *The Emotionally Abused Woman: Overcoming Destructive Patterns and Reclaiming Yourself.* **Beverly Engel, M.F.C.C. New York: A Fawcett Columbine Book, Ballantine Books, 1990. Paperback. 244 pp.**

Engel writes for women whose past histories often make them gravitate unconsciously toward destructive and abusive relationships. The book offers systematic advice for survival and recovery and is illustrated with a multitude of case studies. It aspires to help victims do away with bad habits introduced during childhood, thereby stopping the continuing cycle of abuse. Topics discussed include: identifying and understanding exactly how women are being abused, recognizing patterns that keep them emotionally blocked and locked into abuse, resolving remaining problems from the past, dealing with the abusive individual, and learning how to develop more fulfilling relationships.

11. *Fascinating Womanhood.* **Helen Andelin. Santa Barbara, CA: Pacific Press, 1992. Paperback. 309 pp.**

Updated for the 90s, this controversial best seller offers practical guidelines on how to strengthen marriages. It suggests that women can enrich their lives using the "old-fashioned values" of traditional femininity. If women know what men really think and what they "find irresistible," women will be able to revive their love life, while encouraging a man to be his gallant best, they propose. The book gives eight guidelines for achieving fulfilling relationships. Andelin's fascinating woman thrives on being the ideal wife, unselfishly loving though not a slave. Cherishing her femininity, her major career focus is on the home where her husband and children are of primary importance. Working women will find suggestions here as well.

12. *The Female Stress Syndrome: How to Become Stress-Wise in the 90's.* **Georgia Witkin, Ph.D. New York: Newmarket Press, 1984, 1990. Hardcover. 320 pp.**

This updated version has workable solutions for the stress problems of modern women. While society continually spotlights male stress, Witkin suggests that women must be seen as suffering at least equally. As evidence, she cites high female death rates due to heart disease and hypertension. The book urges women to work seriously on stress reduction and gaining control of their lives. Greater happiness, more satisfying relationships, and improved health will result, Witkin believes. As a basis for resolving feelings of overload, the book studies the nature and causes of these problems as well as the need to adopt new ways of dealing with responsibilities. Charts, lists, quizzes, and examples teach women to "give up some control" in numerous areas of their lives.

13. ***Getting Unstuck*: *Breaking through the Barriers to Change*. Dr. Sidney B. Simon. New York: Warner Books Inc., 1988. Hardcover. 296 pp.**

Simon believes we all get "stuck" occasionally in our lives, especially when difficult choices or problems face us. Failing marriages, bad career choices, weight problems, abuse, and the like tend to paralyze people, affect reasoning, create self-doubt, and keep them from reaching their goals, he feels. This book helps readers understand the various "psychological and emotional barriers" in their way. Simon says that more fulfilling lives await if people have skills to identify the problems and begin to work toward productive change. He views "taking no action" as deadly. A variety of "stuck," helpless, or trapped individuals are profiled as examples. Exercises, quizzes, and methodical techniques assist readers in recognizing the "Eight Basic Barriers to Change," building self-esteem, and creating goals.

14. ***Golden Handcuffs*: *How Women Can Break Free of Financial Dependence in Their Intimate Relationships*. Dr. Neal H. Olshan. New York: Birch Lane Press, 1994. Hardcover. 149 pp.**

A psychologist for 20 years, Dr. Olshan shares actual stories of members of his Golden Handcuffs Group. These women feel trapped in marriages where financial dependence on men creates a barrier to leading independent lives. Being unable to support themselves or fearing they lack the necessary skills holds them hostage to unhappiness. Olshan provides a step-by-step guide to his "proven techniques" for: identifying the danger signs of this problem, taking steps toward understanding the part both spouses play in this "money trap," and learning to develop individual dreams. By increasing their level of self-awareness, realizing how their state of mind plays into the game, and then becoming more assertive in making the necessary changes, women can win freedom and self-esteem. A checklist allows readers to test themselves.

15. ***The Good Girl Syndrome: How Women Are Programmed to Fail in a Man's World—and How to Stop It*. William Fezler, Ph.D. and Eleanor S. Field, Ph.D. New York: Macmillan Publishing Co., 1985. Hardcover. 313 pp.**

This book is an examination of the "Good Girl Syndrome," a major problem composed of 12 different areas termed "programs." In separate chapters, it exposes the specific "myths" of these areas, which have been ingrained in women from childhood. Fezler and Field say that a central aspect of the syndrome is the self-defeating need of women to live according to the numerous expectations of others, especially men. According to the authors, women often see themselves as inferior and as "good" only if others (usually men) are pleased. They warn that such pressure and lack of personal need fulfillment create suppressed feelings of anger that can suddenly flare up. Fezler and Field give tested daily exercises to help women learn to: initiate change, obey their own needs and rules, eliminate guilt, and bear responsibility for themselves.

16. *Growing Up Firstborn: The Pressures and Privileges of Being Number One*. **Dr. Kevin Leman. New York: Dell Publishing Co., a Div. of Bantam Doubleday Dell, 1989. Paperback. 309 pp.**

Leman writes for readers who are bringing up a firstborn, working under one, married to one, or are one themselves. He asserts that this difficult family position has an impact on everything firstborns do and all the choices they make. Negative qualities such as an exaggerated sense of responsibility, excessive organization and discipline, perfectionism, and low self-esteem may plague these individuals. Leman does agree, however, that this privileged position can encourage leadership and achievement as well. He describes the traits of firstborns so that readers can solve potential or actual problems and improve relationships. His book shows how to: eliminate "sibling rivalry," develop confidence, avoid overachievement, deal with failure, and alter unhealthy behavior patterns.

17. *Having It All: Love Success • Sex • Money ...Even if You're Starting with Nothing*. **Helen Gurley Brown. New York: Simon & Schuster/Linden Press, 1982. Hardcover. 462 pp.**

As the creator of *Cosmopolitan* magazine, Brown has achieved success both professionally and personally. In this book, she uses her own personal ascent from "mouseburger" to "having it all" as practical inspiration for other women. The author defines a "mouseburger" as an ordinary woman, physically and intellectually, who has a strong desire for "better things." Brown's purpose is to be a comprehensive, personal "24-hour-a-day advisor" on over 200 topics ranging from diet, exercise, beauty, dress, chic, sex, love, and marriage to friends, money, and career. She includes a "mouseburger" self-test and stresses setting goals and working diligently toward achieving them. With frankness and humor, Brown gives detailed advice that she believes can change women's lives.

18. *Homecoming: Reclaiming and Championing Your Inner Child.* John Bradshaw. New York: Bantam Books, 1990. Hardcover. 288 pp.

For this book, Bradshaw draws on personal experience and on "Inner Child Workshops" which he conducts for people who are victims of substance abuse, unhappiness, or dysfunctional relationships. He believes that the pain we suffered in our childhood through various kinds of mistreatment or hurt, if left unresolved, can reside in us forever, causing continued problems in our later adult lives. In this book, he allows us to reconnect with that "child," give ourselves what we never received, grow up again, and heal. The book offers practical strategies along with questionnaires to allow our child to look at the original causes of problems, "to break destructive family rules and roles," handle anger, and listen to our own deepest needs.

19. *How to Be an Assertive (Not Aggressive) Woman in Life, Love and On the Job: The Classic Guide to Becoming a Self-Assured Person.* Jean Baer. New York: Penguin Books, 1976. Paperback. 311 pp.

Baer's specific intent in this guidebook is to teach women how to stand up for themselves and thereby improve the quality of their intimate, social, and work relationships. She encourages women to be dynamic rather than passive participants in their own lives, to develop and communicate their own opinions and goals, and to become more comfortable with risk, conflict, anger, resentment, and criticism. The author substantiates her opinions with numerous case studies and offers women assignments for taking an active role in changing their lives. Her book addresses: why women lack assertiveness, the positive impact of being able to say "no," and the need for assertiveness in the realms of child-rearing and sexuality.

20. *I'm OK—You're OK: The Transactional Analysis Breakthrough That's Changing the Consciousness and Behavior of People Who Never Before Felt OK About Themselves.* Thomas A. Harris, M.D. New York: Avon Books, a Div. of Hearst Publications, 1967. Paperback. 317 pp.

Seen by many as a "breakthrough" when introduced in 1967, transactional analysis aims to constructively assist individuals in solving problems in their marriages and personal lives. Harris sees its primary benefit as enabling adults to move forward positively, bearing full responsibility for their actions regardless of past events. He bases his "PAC System" on identifying three aspects in a personality: "The Parent" giving out orders, "The Child" personifying spontaneous feelings, and "The Adult" who keeps the other two in balance by making necessary reality decisions. The book discusses how freeing the adult from the parent/child messages of the past is critical to personal growth.

21. *In a Different Voice: Psychological Theory and Women's Development.* **Carol Gilligan. Cambridge, MA: Harvard University Press, 1982. Paperback. 184 pp.**

Gilligan's thesis is that experts have "systematically misunderstood women" and that they have historically based their theories on human development on "observations of men's lives." Men and women speak about their lives in dissimilar ways and form moral judgements differently as well, she says. Thus it is the author's goal to analyze human development from the perspective of the female personality. Gilligan analyzes the ways women grow, think, form opinions, and act in two studies on college students and abortion. This examination of moral dilemmas facing women adds to the overall understanding of their upbringing, their differences from men, what women see as important, what strengths are unique to women, and how these affect their relationships.

22. *In Transition: How Feminism, Sexual Liberation, and the Search for Self-Fulfillment Have Altered Our Lives.* **Judith M. Bardwick. New York: Holt, Rinehart and Winston, 1979. Hardcover. 203 pp.**

The belief here is that feminism and sexual liberation have drastically altered the view of women's roles for advocates as well as opponents. Bardwick helps readers understand the effects of these changes, which she says have promoted a new focus on self-gratification. This "me" emphasis has led women to rethink their notions of faithfulness, obligation, concern for others, and commitment. The book assesses both negative and positive effects of feminism and their impact on the areas of domestic matters, careers, and sexual relationships. Topics include: anxiety, the breakdown of commitment, women's feelings about women, maternity, "duty vs. choice," new definitions of masculinity and femininity, and their relationship to a woman's demands on her partner.

23. *The Late Show: A Semiwild But Practical Survival Plan for Women Over 50.* **Helen Gurley Brown. New York: Wm. Morrow, 1993. Hardcover. 384 pp.**

In her own humorous and down-to-earth fashion, Brown, the editor in chief of *Cosmopolitan*, writes to help us grow old "resourcefully and energetically." There is no giving up for Brown; she believes passionately in women caring for themselves, maintaining their beauty, tending to their health and diet, feeding their brains and enjoying their sex lives. Her 12 chapters are full of personal anecdotes as well as research. They contain tips about all sorts of subjects: beauty, exercise, food, clothes, health, doctors, cosmetic surgery, work, money, marriage, "joys, sorrows and compensations." Even recipes appear. Brown shows women what they can look forward to and what they must watch out for. Her tone is positive and she hopes what she says will "ring true" for her readers. "Age is a careless jailer," she says. Women *can* fool it now and then.

24. ***Letters from Women Who Love Too Much: A Closer Look at Relationship Addiction and Recovery*. Robin Norwood. New York: Pocket Books, Simon & Schuster, 1988. Paperback. 425 pp.**

Based on letters and questions Norwood received from her previous very popular book, *Women Who Love Too Much*, this work provides answers and in-depth analyses for understanding "cross addictions." These include such disorders as drug and alcohol abuse, sex addiction, eating disorders, and especially relationship addiction. Norwood sees romantic obsession as a disease that can be cured by using the step-by-step concrete help and tools developed in her work with successful recovery groups. She looks at a wide variety of letters from women and comments on: relationships between addicted women and their children, battered women, forgiveness of past hurts, and the benefits of support groups.

25. ***Light His Fire: How to Keep Your Man Passionately and Hopelessly in Love with You*. Ellen Kreidman. New York: Dell Publishing, a Div. of Bantam Doubleday Group, Inc., 1989. Paperback. 204 pp.**

Written for single or married women, Kreidman's book is a seven-step guide on how to maintain a long-term, exciting romance with a chosen man and how to "star in our own love story." The book is quick reading with concrete examples and easy-to-understand principles for achieving immediate results. Kreidman suggests 51 ways to "light" a lover's "fire" along with advice on how to put more "fun, growth, thrills, and communication" back into a woman's sex-life and relationships. The book's audience is those women who want to charm their men, continue to feel the "butterflies" they felt in the beginning, turn around a failing marriage, or successfully enter a new relationship.

26. ***Looking Out for #1*. Robert J. Ringer. Beverly Hills, CA: Los Angeles Book Corp., 1977. Hardcover. 320 pp.**

Ringer suggests that the best route to personal satisfaction in life is to act according to our own personal desires. To learn to live by this rule, he asks us to raise our "level of awareness" so that we can consciously identify exactly what we are doing and why. Ringer proposes that resisting the temptation to let others judge and control us and standing firm in making our own individual choices will: simplify our lives, reduce fatigue, put us in control, raise self-esteem, and bring us happiness. The controversial book presents practical suggestions for combating guilt, for learning to "clear the hurdles" that prevent us from doing what we really enjoy, and for eliminating in our lives what we don't like. A prerequisite to the theory is respecting the rights of others, Ringer asserts.

27. *Lovesick: The Marilyn Syndrome. Why Women Become Addicted to the Wrong Men – And What to Do About It.* **Elizabeth Macavoy, Ph.D. and Susan Israelson. New York: Donald I. Fine, Inc., 1991. Hardcover. 248 pp.**

This workbook contains numerous "exercises, visualizations, and affirmations" for women who, like Marilyn Monroe, suffer from the inherited disorder of "lovesickness." The authors define the syndrome as an inability to love or receive love due to a "dysfunctional upbringing" that deprived women of nurturing and "unconditional love." They claim that the consequent tendency is to recreate the past by repeatedly seeking destructive, unloving partners. Because the victim suffers from low self-esteem, such ill-fated unions usually end in rejection, the book notes. Part I shows how to identify the signs and excessive tendencies, while Part II outlines action-oriented recovery strategies. Macavoy and Israelson emphasize that changing patterns is possible if women learn the necessary skills.

28. *Men Are Just Desserts: How Learning to Be a Woman with a Life of Your Own Can Enrich the Life You Share with a Man.* **Sonya Friedman. New York: Warner Books, 1983. Paperback. 302 pp.**

In this best seller, Friedman tells women to consider themselves the "main course" and to regard men purely as "desserts." Women must realize, she proposes, that they can exist alone and nurture themselves, that happiness comes from within, and therefore a man alone cannot bring contentment or provide a woman with her only reason for being. The author proposes that once woman master this concept, they will relate to the men in their lives far more successfully on all levels. Topics include: studying the past and family relationships, liberation from the "dictums" of our mothers, developing a personal identity, establishing a genuine partnership with a man, and realizing "true intimacy."

29. *My Enemy, My Love: Man Hating and Ambivalence in Women's Lives.* **Judith Levine. New York: Doubleday, 1992. Hardcover. 416 pp.**

Levine researched what she calls a major problem in American society: the often camouflaged or hidden yet very pervasive hatred of men by women. This book claims that if overt man-hating is absent, its "milder, more diplomatic...twin," ambivalence, is often present. It states that while women may love, need, and desire men, women (as a group) can be simultaneously hostile, fearful, envious, or alienated from them. In three sections, Levine examines actual illustrations of man-hating, describes the underlying causes in family life, and provides interviews with 80 women that reflect the way they live with these contradictory emotions. Levine's book examines male stereotypical behavior that can propagate the problem but states that women are "perpetuating their own oppression" as well.

30. *My Mother/My Self: The Daughter's Search for Identity.* **Nancy Friday. New York: A Dell Book, Delacorte Press, 1977. Paperback. 475 pp.**

Friday's book comprehensively investigates what it calls the "first, most lasting…tie of every woman's life," the bond with her mother. A best seller, it examines how this tie has a continuing direct effect upon women's psychological lives and thus, ultimately, upon their relationships with everyone else. The book explores the positive and negative aspects of the bond including: behavior modeling, repressed anger, lies each has told the other, and harmful, unwritten sexual "admonitions." Friday analyzes her own life and a variety of women in their daily interactions with men, jobs, children (especially daughters), and other females. She shows how women can begin to understand themselves better, change potentially undesirable behavior, and become "independent, fully sexual women."

31. *The New Suburban Woman: Beyond Myth & Motherhood.* **Nancy Rubin. New York: Coward, McCann & Geoghegan, 1982. Hardcover. 320 pp.**

Rubin covers a topic largely untouched: drastic changes in suburban populations and the resulting effects upon women. She claims that women cherish a "utopian" view of the suburbs as the "idyllic place" of childhood that waits, unchanged, for their return. Her book debunks this myth, revealing that the suburbs are full of women who do not fit the dream; they are divorced, full-time workers rarely at home, minorities, single and childless, or even victims of financial tragedies. Those who fit the stereotype, Rubin notes, can find themselves "caught between two different time zones" and often "paralyzed" in an environment where they have few outlets. One goal here in analyzing suburban life is to determine its impact on the "future of the family."

32. *Opening Our Hearts to Men: Transform Pain, Loneliness and Anger into Trust, Intimacy and Love.* **Susan Jeffers, Ph.D. New York: A Fawcett Columbine Book, Ballantine Books, 1989. Paperback. 301 pp.**

This book reveals positive new ways for women to transform their relationships with themselves and with men. At the core of Jeffers' thesis is reawakening the love that exists "within and around" us. Developing a more trusting and loving (less blaming) attitude will change a woman's outlook and draw men to her, she says. The book emphasizes the use of "affirmations" that can eliminate negative thinking, raise self-esteem, help women to be "at peace" with themselves and men, and build genuine intimacy. Jeffers teaches women how to put away the "Victim Mentality," understand men's real feelings, and take possession of their creative loving power. She also discusses how women can break the "four biggest barriers to love," and she describes the "five steps" for handling anger.

33. ***Passions: How to Manage Despair, Fear, Rage and Guilt and Heighten Your Capacity for Joy, Love, Hope and Awe.* Dr. Georgia Witkin. New York: Villard Books, 1992. Hardcover. 191 pp.**

Witkin describes passion as a "peak emotion" that takes hold of "both the mind and the body." In this book, she teaches the reader how to keep negative passions under control while allowing positive ones to surface, flourish, and enrich daily life. Based on a "Passions Survey" given to 400 men and women (ages 18-63), the book is designed for those who are afraid of feelings, have difficulty "feeling" their passions, deny the significance of passions, or lead lives of continual emotional upheaval. It traces the roots of "eight great passions" in order to teach how to relish, survive, control, or get help for emotions. Through the use of research, cases, and quizzes, Witkin helps the reader see how passion works and how to achieve a more balanced life.

34. ***Perfect Women: Hidden Fears of Inadequacy and the Drive to Perform.* Colette Dowling. New York: Summit Books, 1988. Hardcover. 269 pp.**

Perfect Women is a comprehensive examination of how women compulsively push themselves to attain perfection in their appearance, achievements, would-be exemplary families, and careers. Dowling suggests that insecurity inherited from their mothers, "fear of inadequacy" or personal failures, and low self-esteem drive women with destructive results in work, family, and social lives. She strongly emphasizes the necessity for women to rebuild a solid and genuine sense of self-worth. Her book profiles perfectionistic women as examples that can enlighten us. Topics also include: dieting and exercise, eating disorders, common needs for approval and recognition, self-respect, and self-hate.

35. ***The Pleasers... Women Who Can't Say No—And the Men Who Control Them.* Dr. Kevin Leman. Old Tappan, NJ: Fleming H. Revell Co., 1987. Hardcover. 320 pp.**

This author studies those women who live to please others, especially men, often without regard for themselves or their own wishes. Leman offers practical strategies for: understanding the fundamental causes of this self-defeating behavior; becoming less afraid of necessary conflict; breaking the cycle; and learning to live in a healthier manner. His book discusses mastering the art of "saying no" to domineering, "impassive," critical, or even abusive men. In addition, it examines the relationship of perfectionism and guilt to this dilemma and includes examples of physical, mental, and emotional control. Leman guides women toward improving their present relationships and toward learning how to identify controlling men in advance in the future.

36. *Recovery from Co-Dependency: It's Never Too Late to Reclaim Your Childhood.* **Laurie Weiss and Jonathan B. Weiss. Deerfield Beach, FL: Health Communications, Inc., 1989. Paperback. 221 pp.**

In its treatment of the complex issues of recovery from co-dependence, this book suggests that the crucial issue is "connecting with one's inner child." Learning how to understand our feelings, love ourselves, and use "corrective parenting" can heal us. Aimed at therapists and victims alike, the Weisses' underlying premise is that Adult Children may be unknowingly living lives that are still affected by the baggage of a less than ideal childhood. Readers will find suggestions for "remapping" their lives. Victims who deny or suppress "the pain of...unmet early needs" can identify dysfunctional behaviors and substitute healthy patterns for addictive and compulsive ones, the authors claim. The guide inventories such behaviors and provides lists and charts.

37. *The Seashell People: Growing Up in Adulthood.* **Martha Horton. New York: M. Evans & Co., 1990. Hardcover. 191 pp.**

Horton tells her own personal story and many others as a basis for this book about people whose emotional skills are clearly childlike rather than adult. Calling the problem "widespread," she draws a picture of the kind of person who lives inside a seashell "screening" out problematic issues. The book analyzes the childhood of such people. Its purpose is to show readers how to: "heal" and love themselves, grow up in every regard, accept risk-taking as a normal and healthy part of life, master self-control, learn appropriately balanced adult responses to crises, and develop more fulfilling life-plans and relationships. Horton sees this type of immaturity as needlessly preventing success in many arenas.

38. *The Sensuous Woman: The First How-To Book for the Female Who Yearns to Be All Woman.* **"J." New York: A Dell Book, Dell Publishing Co., Inc., 1969. Paperback. 192 pp.**

This best seller was written anonymously by a woman who, in her own words, miraculously changed herself from being unnoticed to being "ravishingly sexy." In explicit terms, the book provides a step-by-step program to help women achieve a greater feeling of sexual freedom, develop their senses to the ultimate, and use all the aspects of their femininity for "giving and receiving pleasure." J's underlying theory is that although most women have the capacity and right to be sensuous creatures, they never refine their abilities to the fullest. In these pages, she reveals her secrets. Topics included are: improving our appearances, meeting men, sexuality exercises, sexual ethics, masturbation, men's fantasies, party sex, and orgasm.

39. *Slay Your Own Dragons: How Women Can Overcome Self-Sabotage in Love and Work.* Nancy Good. New York: St. Martin's Press, 1990. Hardcover. 190 pp.

The author writes for women who are eager to identify the conscious or unconscious obstacles that keep them from realizing their full potential. She has discovered patterns of negative thinking ("dragons") in love and careers that stand in the way of success and happiness. Her book examines "five battlegrounds of self-sabotage" and provides a ten-point plan for developing skills critical to becoming more positive, self-nurturing, and self-assured. Good urges women to work on eliminating their own "negative tapes." She offers advice on understanding the sources of patterns of self-sabotage, which often cause women to lose their goals just when they've almost achieved them. Compulsions, anger, addictions, money problems, and illness are discussed.

40. *The Snow White Syndrome: All About Envy.* Betsy Cohen. New York: Macmillan Publishing Co., 1986. Hardcover. 313 pp.

Cohen interviewed hundreds of women (famous and not) for this study of the causes, signs, and remedies for envy. Calling it a natural emotion, she nevertheless laments its rampant growth. If unchecked, she says, envy can diminish potential, impair self-image, "sabotage" goals, and seriously hurt relationships. The book's purpose is to help women define envy, evaluate their own self-destructive levels, determine if they are being envied, communicate more honestly, and redirect "pain and shame" to healthier goals. Snow White is used as an example of someone who has "liberated herself" from the "fear of being envied." Readers will identify with case illustrations exploring envy in birth families, current families, love relationships, friendships, and work.

41. *The Superwoman Syndrome: For Women Trying to Do It All—How to Decide What's Important in Your Life and Do It Well.* Marjorie Hansen

Shaevitz with men's responses by Morton H. Shaevitz, Ph.D. New York: Warner Books Inc., 1984. Hardcover. 254 pp.

This detailed handbook was written for women who, in trying to be "everything to everybody," often find themselves overwhelmed and very unhappy. Shaevitz defines the characteristics and underlying causes of this syndrome and describes the differences in male and female attitudes toward the carrying out of obligations. She sees this drive for perfection at home and at work as extremely debilitating to women. Thus, the book provides guidelines and systems to help simplify life, identify what and who is really important, and create more free time for healthy self-renewal as well as the nurturing of intimacy. It includes a "Superwoman Quiz" to determine one's level of affliction along with checklists and directions for taking greater control of one's life.

42. *Sweet Suffering: Woman As Victim.* **Natalie Shainess, M.D. New York: The Bobbs-Merrill Co., Inc., 1984. Hardcover. 263 pp.**

Citing masochism as a source of serious problems in a woman's sexual and marital relationships and as widely prevalent among females, Shainess outlines the fundamental origins and signs of this disorder: lack of self-esteem (creating extreme needs for approval), fear of control and rejection (even abandonment) by others, and a sense of "humiliation and guilt." Submissive women, who constantly feel oppressed and badly treated by others, will benefit from this study of masochism's effects on health, family, and social life. Shainess includes a questionnaire to evaluate one's level of masochistic behavior along with encouraging advice on how to break the cycle, become more assertive and self-reliant, and thereby develop healthier relationships.

43. *Too Good for Her Own Good: Searching for Self and Intimacy in Important Relationships.* **Claudia Bepko and Jo-Ann Krestan. New York: Harper Perennial, a Div. of HarperCollins, 1990. Paperback. 256 pp.**

As family therapists, these authors analyze the instinctual but damaging "Code of Goodness" by which women have commonly run their lives. Bepko and Krestan claim that "good girl" behavior and unfair "gender rules" are so ingrained in women that they lose touch with their own inner feelings and self-nurturing desires. "To be good is to know that you're never good enough," the book concludes. It presents specific exercises to help women live by a healthier new "Code of Balance" that allows them to love others without neglecting themselves. New choices can replace nagging self-doubt and self-reproach, the authors suggest. Case histories illustrate how women have been programmed to maintain control, give continually, look their best, "love first," and never show frustration.

44. ***Too Smart for Her Own Good: The Impact of Success on the Intimate Lives of Women.*** **Dr. Conalee Levine-Shneidman and Karen Levine. Garden City, NY: Doubleday & Co. Inc., 1985. Hardcover. 222 pp.**

This book explores the reasons for the modern dilemma facing women whose growing success in the workplace brings with it a deterioration in the quality of their intimate relationships with men. The authors see the problem as increasingly prevalent and as a source of great unhappiness for women who yearn for a permanent and enduring closeness with a man. The book is designed for those, married or unmarried, who want practical help on how to: insure that their intimate behavior is as positive and adult as their work conduct, change their negative patterns, learn to "trust, care, and share feelings" more openly, revise their expectations of men, maintain their femininity, and balance their career success with more satisfying personal lives.

45. ***Total Loving: How to Love and Be Loved for the Rest of Your Life.*** **"J." New York: Simon & Schuster, 1977. Hardcover. 256 pp.**

This author, quite clearly "pro love," sees a loving relationship as a "woman's birthright." In an often provocative and sensuous book, she covers all the areas women can work at to love successfully. As a basis, "J" asked happy couples to share their secrets for success. The results: women can reach genuine happiness by making their man feel loved and best of all, women don't have to sacrifice themselves to do it. "J" gives advice on how to recognize the wrong man and pick the right one, "create a love environment," know and care for both their body and his, and sense trouble signs. Quizzes and checklists test a woman's readiness for marriage and the appropriateness of particular living styles. The book also covers finances, children, sex, parents, and menopause.

46. ***The Total Woman: How to Make Your Marriage Come Alive.*** **Marabel Morgan. New York: A Pocket Book by Simon & Schuster, 1973. Paperback. 256 pp.**

Writing from her own personal success with a marriage that had grown mediocre, Morgan has developed a quick acting daily revitalization program to restore life and creativity to a boring or failing marriage. Her claim is that women can single-handedly rekindle romantic longing, develop more open lines of communication, "break down barriers," and put "sizzle" back into marriages by accepting, adapting to, appreciating, genuinely admiring, and even adoring the men in their lives. With these techniques, Morgan assures women that they can change themselves into a man's best friend—something he desperately wants and needs—and by doing this, a woman can make him the "total man."

47. *The Type E Woman: How to Overcome the Stress of Being Everything to Everybody.* **Harriet B. Braiker, Ph.D. New York: A Signet Book, New American Library, 1987. Paperback. 288 pp.**

Braiker explores how women, who often strive too hard for excellence in managing their diverse roles, can learn to cope by living more effectively day-to-day. If women are able to gain better control of this destructive tendency, the author predicts they will have calmer lives and see an improvement in their relationships with others, especially men. The book analyzes in-depth the causes of this problematic drive for high achievement and it highlights the inevitable negative results such as overwhelming demands, exhaustion, and conflict. It includes a 21 day regimen of exercises for mastering more appropriate management skills.

48. *Type Talk*: *Or How to Determine Your Personality Type and Change Your Life. Based On the Myers-Briggs Type Indicator.*™ **Otto Kroeger and Janet M. Thuesen. New York: A Tilden Press Book, Delacorte Press, 1988. Hardcover. 293 pp.**

Written in layman's terms, *Type Talk** helps readers identify their own personality types as well as those of others. Based on the premise that no style is superior to any other, the book encourages us to develop greater harmony and productivity in all our everyday interactions by regarding individual differences as strengths. In the opinion of Kroeger and Thuesen, accepting the valid "uniqueness" of others can change the way we love, parent, work together, and resolve conflict. They closely examine 16 personality types and four temperaments. The book also includes a self test for easy evaluation of our own style. It states that this "scientifically validated approach" will encourage "interdependence" and thus help us build stronger relationships in all parts of our lives.

49. *Unfinished Business: Pressure Points in the Lives of Women.* **Maggie Scarf. Garden City, NY: Doubleday & Co., 1980. Hardcover. 581 pp.**

Scarf writes from years of research about the interrelationship of physiology and psychology on the major stages (teens through sixties) of a woman's life. Using case studies from each period, she examines how unresolved difficulties from one period can create "excess baggage" in each of the next. This creates problems that can cause illness, anxiety, confusion, and depression, a topic she analyzes in depth. Probing what it really means to be "female," Scarf investigates such areas as: pressure points, opportunities for personal growth, and "love, loss, hormones, self-image and aging." Menopause and its effects are also treated, all with the hope that increased understanding can resolve any accompanying problems.

50. *The Wendy Dilemma: When Women Stop Mothering Their Men.* **Dr. Dan Kiley. New York: Arbor House, 1984. Hardcover. 233 pp.**

Kiley names his book for the storybook character, Wendy, who subserviently mothers the famed Peter Pan. Wendy is the opposite of Tinkerbell who never "sacrifices herself for fear of rejection." The book explores problems that occur in women who are besieged by a lack of confidence as a result of low self-esteem. It contends that when women resort to mothering men in order to be accepted by them, they develop negative behaviors and encounter numerous frustrations. Society's role in ingraining feelings of inadequacy is also a topic. In order to develop healthier, interdependent, and more successful relationships where neither partner is totally reliant upon the other, Kiley suggests women look to the ideas he presents in this book.

51. *What Smart Women Know.* **Steven Carter and Julia Sokol. New York: M. Evans and Co., Inc., 1990. Hardcover. 204 pp.**

In a series of short, pithy maxims, these authors present rules for smart women to learn from and live by. They stress that women will find it far less painful to gain their experience from reading about the trials and errors of others than by undergoing their own. The book deals with numerous topics, both simple and profound, in an easy, direct fashion. Topics include self-esteem, self-image, obsessions, friendships, dating, "con jobs," jealousy, sex, disease and sex, falling in love, enabling, compromise, marriage, cooking, pregnancy, men and abuse, "elusive" men, men who disappear, sexually addicted men, the "controlling" man, affairs, terminating relationships, post-divorce, and aloneness.

52. *What Wives Wish Their Husbands Knew About Women.* **Dr. James Dobson. Wheaton, IL: Tyndale House Publishing Inc., 1975. Paperback. 189 pp.**

This practical guide offers insight into certain gender-related factors that may cause dissatisfaction in marriage. The book provides specific constructive advice for achieving greater harmony and for negotiating areas of conflict. Dobson intends to help men and women alike realize that there are "unique emotional needs and aspirations" present in females that their male partners frequently don't know about, consciously disregard, or interpret incorrectly. Topics include: difficulties with children, boredom stemming from isolation or loneliness, issues of poor self-image, causes of depression, feelings of exhaustion, time pressures, and emotional and physical problems related to the menstrual cycle.

53. *When Am I Going to Be Happy? How to Break the Emotional Bad Habits that Make You Miserable.* **Penelope Russianoff, Ph.D. New York: Bantam Books, 1988. Hardcover. 287 pp.**

Russianoff gives women practical remedies for identifying and curing "emotional bad habits," the most damaging of which is negative thinking. She describes the many faces of this self-defeating "inner demon," studies its causes in families and society, and then offers tested techniques to change the behaviors and the addiction to the cycle. "Guilt, hysteria, anxiety, low self-esteem, depression, (and) perfectionism" are all examined as roadblocks to happiness and peace of mind. Numerous examples show women how loneliness, inferiority, jealousy, and insecurity can destructively impact their lives. The book emphasizes that learned habits can be broken. It assures women that the choice to change is their own, as is the ability to become positive beings.

54. *Where's My Happy Ending? Women and the Myth of Having It All.* **Lee Morical. Reading, MA: Addison-Wesley Publ. Co., Inc., 1984. Hardcover. 176 pp.**

Morical talked with thousands of women about their often nagging dissatisfaction with "liberation." He discovered that they were still saddled with most of the housework even though they were working full-time, and that they somehow felt that nirvana had eluded them. Writing for housewives as well as career women (ages 21–65), the author gives practical advice on how to look for joy each day of the journey rather than for a reward at the end. Despite the popular feeling that the "housewife is demographically dead," the book suggests that she too can be happy. It exposes various myths, i.e., "getting a job" or "staying home" as miracle solutions. Morical believes freedom of choice exists and that the only power women need is to define their own needs and control their own lives.

55. *Why Do I Think I Am Nothing Without a Man? Solutions to Female Dependency Problems.* **Penelope Russianoff, Ph.D. New York: Bantam Books, 1981. Hardcover. 155 pp.**

Again Russianoff writes for women. Sadly, she sees a large number (even successful career types) as mistakenly believing that the only "complete" life revolves around a man. Her book gives special emphasis to the analysis of "desperate dependence" and its origins as well as to the importance of developing "emotional independence." It holds that a solid sense of identity, self-worth, and self-fulfillment is fundamental to happiness whether women have an ongoing relationship or not. Russianoff stresses the value of friendships with women and men and debates the need for sex in a healthy life.

She offers advice on developing careers and financial independence, the advantages of living alone, and decreasing dependence on men as "mirrors and mentors."

56. *Why Women Worry ...and How to Stop.* **Jane and Robert Handly with Pauline Neff. New York: Prentice Hall Press, 1990. Hardcover. 240 pp.**

These authors propose that women worry far more than men. The book's goal is to help women "step off the worry-go-round" in order to lead more fulfilling, anxiety-free, and happy lives. Based on personal experience, seminars the authors conduct, and the latest research, the book includes quizzes, goal sheets, illustrations, and techniques for breaking the self-defeating habits of destructive worrying. It encourages "pearl worry," the type that leads women to develop constructive alternatives. *Why Women Worry* analyzes four distinct kinds of worry and "five skill tools" to stop the cycle and help women master more productive "problem-solving skills." The intent is for readers to achieve greater personal and professional success. Handly and Neff view raising self-esteem levels as critical.

57. *A Woman's Worth.* **Marianne Williamson. New York: Random House, 1993. Hardcover. 143 pp.**

Williamson claims to have no real goal here but to let her own "guts" flow forth. Yet she does hope to "open a door" for women. An inspirational writer, she speaks about a woman's inner life, how good it is to be a woman, how that differs gloriously from being a man, and how being unafraid to champion our loving and nurturing feminine qualities can "empower" women and cure the ills of the world. Williamson sees women as crying out to be themselves, truly female. Her problem with society is that its male-dominated system restricts a woman's ability to be a "queen" and to wield the power she so rightly desires. In a frank yet spiritual way, she urges women to give up the "slave-girl" role and not wait for someone else to "restore our worth." Topics include: beauty, age, relationships, sex, children, and careers.

58. *Women & Love: The New Hite Report: A Cultural Revolution in Progress. Thousands of Women Speak Frankly About Love and Relationships Today.* **Shere Hite. New York: St. Martin's Press, 1987. Paperback. 729 pp.**

Hite has written a comprehensive, far-reaching, and what she hopes is an honest study of the "innermost feelings" of women. It is based on the responses of over 4500 participants to questions about love and intimate relationships. The author's sweeping examination brings new depth of insight and understanding to the analysis of this unique aspect of contemporary society and the issues affecting it. The book concentrates specifically on the heretofore private thoughts of American women. Especially pertinent to our topic are the sections defining the nature of love and discussions of problem areas in love relationships including difficulties in resolving conflicts.

59. *Women & Money: The Independent Woman's Guide to Financial Security for Life*. **Frances Leonard. Reading, MA: Addison-Wesley Publ. Co., Inc., 1991. Paperback. 262 pp.**

Drastically increased life expectancy, Leonard suggests, requires women to take control of their lives and arrange their priorities better to insure financial stability and independence. Directed primarily at mid-life women (ages 40+), the book graphically offers suggestions, strategies, and "quick tips," for marrieds and singles in areas such as pensions, social security, health insurance, and safeguarding marital property. This activist lawyer also includes checklists to help women evaluate their own personal condition and an appendix on doing their own legal research. Chapter 1 on divorce covers such topics as: problems with no-fault divorce, support, evaluating and protecting retirement benefits, property, attorneys, and selling one's home.

60. *Women & Self-Esteem: Understanding and Improving the Way We Think and Feel About Ourselves*. **Linda Tschirhart Sanford and Mary Ellen Donovan. New York: Penguin Books, Viking Penguin, Inc., 1984. Paperback. 454 pp.**

While numerous studies have revealed that women show alarming signs of low self-esteem and little ability to run their own lives, these authors found very little of substance written on the subject prior to their own work. They view low self-esteem as the result of "female oppression in male-dominated culture" and the cause of many harmful psychological problems affecting modern women. The book provides practical help through step-by-step exercises for those who want to feel better about themselves and to change. Women can thus eliminate feelings of not being "good enough" and can lead more productive and fulfilling lives, they say. Part II on Intimate Relationships is helpful for women experiencing marital problems.

61. *Women & the Blues: Passions that Hurt, Passions that Heal*. **Jennifer James, Ph.D. San Francisco, CA: Harper & Row, Publishers, 1990. Hardcover. 280 pp.**

James brings strength and specific solutions to those suffering from unhappy emotions such as "frustration, pain, despair, (and) depression" in dealings with friends, lovers, family, or even themselves. Citing the pressures of modern society as one possible culprit, she laments the female need to be "all to everyone." A "Quick Help" section for more immediate relief precedes the book's three main parts. Part I focuses on 37 problems with action-oriented advice for each; Part II explores the reasons for pain and lack of self-nurturing; and Part III provides ideas for a future life grounded in healthy "joy and passion." James outlines practical coping skills and stresses the importance of self-love and a sense of humor.

62. *Women and Their Fathers: The Sexual and Romantic Impact of the First Man in Your Life.* **Victoria Secunda. New York: Delacorte Press, Bantam Doubleday Dell Publ., 1992. Hardcover. 483 pp.**

Secunda sees the little studied father-daughter relationship as the foundation for a woman's later romantic and sexual unions. She believes that this connection, which acts as a "dress rehearsal" whether the father was present or not, can determine both the successes and difficulties women later encounter. The book studies good and bad fathering including the impact of men who were unable "to be counted on" or were "emotionally or physically unavailable." Based on research and interviews with experts, daughters, and fathers, the book helps women remove the mystery of this bond and develop the ability to handle romantic situations more successfully. It also discusses a father's interest in his daughter's life and his ability to communicate his feelings and friendship.

63. *Women Who Love Too Much*: *When You Keep Wishing and Hoping He'll Change.* **Robin Norwood. Los Angeles, CA: Jeremy P. Tarcher, Inc., 1985. Hardcover. 266 pp.**

This book is written for the kind of women for whom "being in love is being in pain." It identifies certain specific female response patterns that are rooted in problematic family backgrounds as the cause of serious relationship problems later on. Through case histories and interviews, Norwood studies women who are addicted to destructive relationships, are self-sacrificing, and who suffer from low self-esteem and dependency problems. She outlines characteristic fears and behavior patterns in these often obsessed individuals in the hope of helping women develop an understanding of the nature of genuinely healthy attachments.

64. *Women's Burnout*: *How to Reverse It, and How to Prevent It.* **Dr. Herbert J. Freudenberger and Gail North. Garden City, New York: Doubleday & Company, Inc., 1985. Hardcover. 244 pp.**

Causes, symptoms, resulting relationship problems, and solutions for female burnout are the subject here. Based on counseling and 100+ interviews, the book tackles a problem affecting all types of women, not only "high achievers." Freudenberger and North see denial as only magnifying stress. They believe that heightened self-awareness is critical for developing a healthier approach to multiple demands. Their guide explores why women are driven to cycles of "agitation and exhaustion" and it studies the dynamics of burnout at home, in love, and in careers. It lists warning signals along with a "12 point checklist for Burnout Prevention and Recovery" and gives a comparison of burnout and depression. The emphasis is on learning skills for "pacing oneself" and reducing overextension.

65. *Working It Out: The Domestic Double Standard. How Working Women Cope with Having (to Do) It All.* Judith K. Sprankle. New York: Walker and Company, 1986. Hardcover. 211 pp.

Sprankle examines the complex dilemmas working women encounter in fulfilling their obligations on the job and at home. Having interviewed dozens of diverse working wives and mothers, she concludes that duties are seldom shared equally with men, who persist in placing their jobs first. Females are "never off the hook" at home, she says. The book is quick to point out that women have trouble delegating and "compromising on standards" they expect which keeps the insidious problem alive. Sprankle looks at the underlying causes and suggests many practical management techniques to simplify and divide up responsibilities. Topics include: housework, problems in working at home, family goal setting, and innovative ways to handle "multiple roles."

66. *Your Erroneous Zones: Bold But Simple Techniques for Taking Charge of Your Unhealthy Behavior Patterns.* Dr. Wayne Dyer. New York: Funk & Wagnall's, 1976. Hardcover. 241 pp.

Dyer defines an erroneous zone as a "self-destructive behavior." He illustrates, often by case studies, numerous examples of behaviors that block a person's ability to be happy. His book also helps readers discover why they persist in perpetuating them. In a step-by-step "counseling session" style, Dyer teaches us how to identify and eliminate the negative behavior. At the end of each chapter, the author presents specific techniques. His emphasis is on being responsible for one's own choices and living in the present by learning to get rid of feelings such as guilt, anger, and worry. Topics include: "neurotic messages," "psychological support systems," anger, procrastination, and a description of the person free of all such behaviors.

For additional help in "Understanding Ourselves First," see also books numbered:

68: *Bad Guys*

70: *Beyond the Male Myth*

71: *The Casanova Complex: Compulsive Lovers and Their Women*
72: *The Classified Man*
77: *The Inner Male*
93: *Men Who Hate Women and the Women Who Love Them*
94: *The Myth of Male Power*
96: *Perfect Husbands (& Other Fairy Tales)*
99: *Secrets About Men Every Woman Should Know*
103: *Some Men Are More Perfect Than Others*
106: *What Every Woman Should Know About Men*
113: *Women Men Love, Women Men Leave*
114: *Workaholics*
124: *The 30 Secrets of Happily Married Couples*
126: *The Art and Practice of Loving*
128: *The Art of Staying Together*
130: *Born for Love*
138: *Courage My Love*
142: *The Dance Away Lover & Other Roles We Play in Love, Sex and Marriage*
143: *The Dance of Intimacy*
145: *Do I Have to Give Up Me to Be Loved by You?*
157: *Intimate Partners*
159: *Intimate Strangers*
160: *Husbands, Wives & Sex*
173: *Living, Loving & Learning*
174: *Love*
176: *Love Cycles: The Science of Intimacy*
177: *Love Is Letting Go of Fear*
193: *Men Are from Mars: Women Are from Venus*
194: *Men, Women and Relationships*
196: *The New Male-Female Relationship*
199: *Nobody's Perfect,* Weisinger & Lobsenz
200: *One Question That Can Save Your Marriage*
201: *One to One*
203: *Passages*
205: *Peer Marriage*

207: *The Power of Unconditional Love*
211: *Relationshift*
212: *A Return to Love*
214: *The Road to Intimacy: Beyond Co-Dependence*
215: *Second Honeymoon*
223: *That's Not What I Meant*
236: *The Dance of Anger*
249: *If This Is Love, Why Do I Feel So Insecure?*
250: *The Incompatibility of Men and Women*
252: *Jealousy*
256: *Love and Addiction*
261: *Money Demons*
269: *The Stranger in Your Bed*
279: *When Someone You Love Is Someone You Hate*
281: *You Just Don't Understand*
286: *Back from Betrayal*
289: *The Erotic Silence of the American Wife*
292: *Have a Love Affair With Your Husband (Before Someone Else Does)*
293: *His Needs Her Needs*
299: *Men Who Can't Be Faithful*
302: *The New Other Woman*
304: *A Passion for More*
306: *Secret Loves*
309: *Woman Versus Woman*
317: *Get Rid of Him*
323: *Life Changes: How Women Can Make Courageous Choices*
326: *Loving & Leaving*
327: *Nice Women Get Divorced*
329: *Our Turn*
330: *Overcoming Indecisiveness*
342: *Women in Transition*
413: *Head and Heart*
415: *Mothers and Divorce*
417: *Our Money Our Selves*
423: *The State-By-State Guide to Women's Legal Rights*

424: *Strassels' Tax Savers*

425: *The Survival Guide for Women*

446: *Guilt*

447: *Guilt Is the Teacher, Love Is the Lesson*

463: *Opening Up*

464: *Ordinary Women, Extraordinary Lives*

471: *Ten Days to Self Esteem*

475: *Why Me • Why This • Why Now*

480: *Alone—Not Lonely*

483: *Coping*

486: *Flying Solo*

516: *The Woman Alone*

519: *At Long Last Love*

527: *Getting to "I Do"*

537: *How to Marry the Man of Your Choice*

542: *Real Love*

547: *Smart Women: Foolish Choices*

550: *Were You Born for Each Other?*

551: *What Has She Got?*

2

Understanding the Men in Our Lives

The Secrets Men Keep

Modern men can be enigmas to the women in their lives. The Women's Movement and the Sexual Revolution have brought about visible and invisible changes that simultaneously tend to strengthen and sabotage male/female relationships. While men throughout the ages have been characterized as less openly communicative than women, especially in the area of emotions, today's men suffer from unique dilemmas.

Many of the authors in this chapter address the widely contrasting expectations women have of men. On the one hand, society has molded males to be unemotional, aggressive, competitive, protective, and the sole providers for their families. Today's women often reject all of this. What many want instead is a gentle, communicative man who is in touch with his emotions, is willing to share in household and child-rearing duties, accepts women as an equal partner financially, intellectually, and sexually, and moreover, is interested in love, romance, and intimacy. For men, to whom work and competency have been primary, this can mean a drastic change in roles. Further confusion results when, influenced by their own traditional upbringings, women send out mixed messages and still expect the man to be a "Prince Charming."

The books in this chapter can help both men and women understand better what it means to be male. Some authors categorize men into types; others analyze them in depth. Their inner secrets, needs, fears, and hopes are surveyed along with reasons why so many are unhappy, abusive, unfaithful, suffer from workaholism, or undergo cycles of crisis. Another frequent topic is also the increase in commitment-phobic men. Marriages can only benefit from a deepened knowledge of this side of the equation.

67. *The 40 to 60 Year Old Male*: *A Guide for Men —and the Women in Their Lives —to See Them Through the Crises of the Male Middle Years.* **Michael E. McGill, Ph.D. New York: Simon & Schuster, 1980. Hardcover. 289 pp.**

This book was based on 250 interviews selected from those men who responded to a questionnaire sent out to 1000. The question: what types of crises, if any, had they experienced in the middle years of their lives? The author studies these responses, the men themselves, and the many people involved closely with them, whether they be wives, family, co-workers, bosses, or mistresses. McGill strives to give psychological advice to all those affected in such vital areas as: the fear of not reaching goals, the loss of youth and good looks, dealing with the empty nest, confronting one's mortality, and searching for adventure. He also tries to identify precisely which men may have a tendency toward such crises.

68. *Bad Guys: Women's Tales from the Relationship Front.* **Brook Hersey. New York: Bishop Books, 1994. Paperback. 264 pp.**

The hope of this author, a journalist, is that women learn to judge their mistakes less harshly in their attempt to connect better with men. Hersey's book is an unscientific compilation of 47 "verbatim transcripts" from women about men who have had negative effects upon them. She empha- sizes that these men were not necessarily evil nor were the women completely blameless or outright "victims." In hindsight, the women inter- viewed reflect upon the character of these men who fall into three stereo- types: "aggressive men," "wounded men," and "hot/cold men." Reasons for becoming involved as well as reasons for splitting are analyzed. The book proposes that while it may not possible to change such men, women can learn how to take control of their lives and leave if necessary. Hersey focuses on both the men and women involved.

69. *Being a Man*: *The Paradox of Masculinity.* **Daniel H. Bell. Brattleboro, VT: The Lewis Publishing Co., 1982. Hardcover. 158 pp.**

This social historian lost his own marriage and job and consequently writes from a decidedly personal perspective. Bell has also talked with 100 white, middle-class men about their struggles with "new roles" and their attempts to find workable solutions with women. He examines how men have devel- oped their concepts of manhood and how the women's movement has altered traditional masculinity. His book analyzes the ways in which men react to new demands from women, children, parents, and the workplace and how they balance them with personal needs. Topics include: sharing two incomes, coping with duties, resentments, fears, rewards, the influence of "violent contact sports" on male character, the hidden "softer side" of men, fatherhood, and divorce and remarriage.

70. *Beyond the Male Myth: A Nationwide Survey. What Women Want to Know About Men's Sexuality.* **Anthony Pietropinto, M.D. and Jacqueline Simenauer. New York: Times Books, a Div. of Quadrangle, The New York Times Book Co., 1977. Hardcover. 430 pp.**

Believing that women wanted and needed to know more about the intimate feelings of men regarding sex and sexuality, these authors first surveyed females. With this input, they then created a detailed questionnaire to study a controlled "random cross section" of 4000+ American men. All races, ages, social and economic classes, and geographical locations were included. As the first such study since the much earlier Kinsey Report, the book reveals what a broad sampling of men really think and shows women how to enhance their intimate and other relationships with men. Topics include: how men perceive women, types of women desired by men and types rejected, worrisome female traits, what men look for in wives, major areas of conflict, reasons for cheating, and the "ideal sex life."

71. *The Casanova Complex: Compulsive Lovers and Their Women.* **Peter Trachtenberg. New York: Poseidon Press, a Div. of Simon & Schuster, 1988. Hardcover. 283 pp.**

Written by a reformed victim of this compulsive disorder, *The Casanova Complex* studies in depth the nature and life-styles of "chronic woman-izers." It also examines the predominant personality characteristics of women who are unhealthily attracted to such men. The author investigates societal forces that influence these dysfunctional lovers who frequently see women as "instruments of pleasure, ego gratification, and relief." In the book, Trachtenberg profiles six types of Casanovas with information based on his own personal experience and on in-depth interviews with men and women who have shared the often devastating secrets of unsatisfying lives.

72. *The Classified Man: Twenty-two Types of Men (and What to Do About Them).* **Susanna M. Hoffman, Ph.D. New York: Coward, McCann & Geoghegan, 1980. Hardcover. 309 pp.**

Hoffman has created a guide (frequently humorous) to the kinds of men women should search for or run away from. Her book, illustrated with a series of graphs and charts, portrays 22 categories of men (e.g., "The Instant Barricader, The Kid, The Sugar Pie Honey," etc.) and the ways they relate to themselves as well as to the women in their lives. She also forecasts a woman's chances for building a successful relationship with each of these men. The book analyzes such salient characteristics as: customs, hangouts and homes, attire, communication and love making styles, and "sex signals, money markers and family aspects." The authors, who very much like men even though they see humor in their flaws, also discuss what being drawn to each kind of man reveals about women.

73. *Crisis Time*: *Love, Marriage and the Male at Midlife.* **William A. Nolen, M.D. New York: Dodd, Mead & Co., 1984. Hardcover. 192 pp.**

Written by a doctor who survived his own mid-life crisis, this book makes the claim that all men go through an event like this between the ages of 45-55. Nolen says that symptoms vary but may include: eating, sleeping, sexual and work problems; depression and anxiety; health problems; tendencies toward excessive drinking or smoking; and difficulties in thinking and focusing. The situation can produce irrational behavior putting incredible stress on marriages, the book notes. Nolen explores the underlying causes, both psychological and physical, including the possible connection with "brain chemistry alterations." He gives advice to women about how to identify warning signs. Nolen encourages women to act promptly to help both their husbands and their marriages, both of which could be in danger.

74. *Fire in the Belly*: *On Being a Man.* **Sam Keen. New York: Bantam Books, 1991. Paperback. 277 pp.**

Though it is aimed chiefly at men, this book can be used by both sexes since Keen claims women also have a limited understanding of men. The author believes that more males than ever are searching for "new roles" and definitions of what it is to be a man. He claims that masculinity, as we have known it, is being criticized and questioned and that current models are outmoded. Keen studies men at leisure, in careers, in love relationships, and "at war." His book is a guide for males seeking new definitions and expressions of these conflicting forces in their lives. Topics included are: passages on the path to manhood, ways in which manhood is evaluated, the importance of power and strength, and male-female relationships.

75. *The Hearts of Men: American Dreams and the Flight from Commitment.* **Barbara Ehrenreich. Garden City, NY: Anchor Press/Doubleday, 1983. Hardcover. 206 pp.**

Ehrenreich, a feminist, offers new insight into the social and cultural upheaval of the last two decades. She proposes that male fear of commitment and rebellion against the "breadwinner ethic" actually preceded and, in fact, caused the women's movement—a movement many observers, she feels, falsely blame for the near-collapse of the American family. Women, who had traditionally been financially dependent upon men, were now confronted with a new male psychology unwilling to bear responsibility for them through marriage. This changed women's "economic prospects," making it necessary for them to stand on their own. The book studies the sociological forces leading to this phenomenon and their wide-ranging effects.

76. *How Men Feel: Their Response to Women's Demands for Equality and Power.* **Anthony Astrachan. Garden City, NY: Anchor Press, Doubleday, 1986. Hardcover. 444 pp.**

Researched for ten years through 400+ interviews, this book covers a wide range of issues regarding the impact of changes in male behavior after the sexual revolution. Astrachan analyzes the "dynamics of power" in marriage, sex, and parenting as reflected in literature, drama, and the media. He concludes that the evidence shows that men have negative, even hostile, reactions. These reactions, he says, often cause them to reject the achievements of women. Certain men also attempt, through fantasy, to demote women as peers; they prefer to visualize them instead in the usual roles of wives, mothers, sisters, lovers, or even "whores." While some hope exists, the author believes that the negative emotions of fear, anger, and anxiety have offset the positives.

77. *The Inner Male: Overcoming Roadblocks to Intimacy.* **Herb Goldberg, Ph.D. New York: A Signet Book, NAL Penguin, Inc., 1987. Paperback. 285 pp.**

Goldberg treats the uniquely modern dilemmas facing men in the decade that preceded the writing of his book. During that period, unusual societal changes occurred along with the growth of new rules from the women's movement. The book examines the sometimes overwhelming impact of these shifts in sex-roles and how men and women can learn to resolve the problems of "mixed signals and mixed feelings." In his guide, Goldberg teaches couples how to be more spontaneous, direct, and honest. Topics discussed are: women who continue to dream of "the knight in shining armor," why men and women have communication blocks, and ways in which we all can really begin to understand each other's inner desires and dreams.

78. *A Knight in Shining Armor: Understanding Men's Romantic Illusions.* **Harvey Hornstein, Ph.D. New York: Wm. Morrow, 1991. Hardcover. 175 pp.**

Hornstein, after interviewing 150 men and women, developed the theory of the "Man Servant Syndrome," a condition that he feels most men fall prey to at some point in their maturing. His book notes that men, driven by a forceful need to prove competency, also frequently suffer from a lack of confidence in their abilities. In relationships, Hornstein says, this causes men to believe that women will reward them with everything they want if men can only prove worthiness, perhaps like the "Frog Prince" who is recognized for his "service" by being changed into a perfect man. Hornstein claims that a destructive and oppressive cycle develops whereby neither sex is happy and the myth of women needing protection continues. The book gives advice on breaking free of the syndrome and its rigid role expectations so that both sexes can be happier.

79. *The Male Dilemma*: *How to Survive the Sexual Revolution.* **Anne Steinmann and David J. Fox. New York: Jason Aronson, 1974. Hardcover. 324 pp.**

These authors propose that the 60s and 70s generations witnessed far-reaching role changes with the result being that, in developing their own satisfying identities, men may conversely feel that women want them to be something else. Based on 20 years of research, this book examines the psychological and social forces behind the changes and the ways in which they have drastically impacted marriage and traditional sexual relationships. The confusing and pervasive effects, primarily on the average male but also on women, are the focus of the work which covers such areas as: women's liberation, an analysis of traditional behavior pattern changes and conflicts felt by men through them all, and proposals for alternative life-styles and child rearing methods.

80. *The Male Ego.* **Willard Gaylin. New York: Viking, The Penguin Group, 1992. Hardcover. 276 pp.**

Modern American men are experiencing a crisis because their previous roles of "Protector (Warrior), Provider (Hunter), and Procreator (Sire)" are obsolete, according to Gaylin. He concludes that the male-dominated society men themselves have created is somehow hurting them the most. His book laments the fact that men, unlike women, have not developed new ways or arenas in which to apply their traditional virtues and thus often consider themselves failures. Their "fear of impotence," paranoia about "being screwed," treatment of women as "male jewelry," and frequent disillusionment with career are the results of damaged egos, Gaylin says. The book proposes that men rework their concept of manhood, develop more realistic goals, eliminate aggression as the expression of their anger, and redirect their strengths toward achieving more fulfilling relationships with men as well as women.

81. *The Male Machine.* **Marc Feigen Fasteau. New York: McGraw Hill, 1972. Hardcover. 225 pp.**

Fasteau studies the negative impact on society of men who have been traditionally raised to be "tough, unemotional and dominant." He shows how this upbringing has caused men problems in understanding and expressing their feelings to each other and to women. The book explores male sexuality, intimate and family relationships, social life, war, sports, business and public conduct, and working with women. Topics covered also include: the place of violence, success, winning, and power in the male life-system; the importance of status and hierarchy; and the effects of the absence of friendship outside the world of work. Fasteau's optimistic outlook, however, sees a future world with fewer gender stereotypes and role restrictions and greater satisfaction for both men and women.

82. ***The Male Ordeal: Role Crisis in a Changing World.* Eric Skjei, Ph.D. and Richard Rabkin, M.D. New York: G.P. Putnam's Sons, 1981. Hardcover. 247 pp.**

Written by a psychologist and a psychiatrist, this book analyzes the complex inner dynamics of closeness and struggle in male-female relationships. The authors believe that the past 20 years of developments in the feminist movement have radically affected and changed men's roles and their views of the world. The book concentrates on "male backlash against the women's movement" and the confusion the 30 men studied feel in the face of "retaliatory feminism." It examines conflicts in men who yearn for secure, close relationships with women yet deeply fear rejection. Skjei discusses the contrast of exterior self-confidence and inner unmet emotional needs as well as a variety of other stresses that affect male confidence levels.

83. ***The Male Paradox: Why Men Feel Like the Weaker Sex and How the Struggle Between Sexuality and Aggression Shapes Their Identity.* John Munder Ross, Ph.D. New York: Simon & Schuster, 1992. Hardcover. 350 pp.**

Designed to be read by both sexes, this book studies the mysteriousness and conflicts of masculinity. Case histories explore maleness and underscore the male's unconscious battle with his own aggressiveness as well as his "resistance" to "need" or "be like" women. Ross studies forces in the upbringing of men as well as desires, fears, communication difficulties, and stresses. The book uncovers a "vulnerability" men possess under the usual strong front. It investigates commitment, love, children, infidelity, job loss, violence, and health and analyzes the interpersonal dynamics in each. Ross reveals why men are ever unknowingly "at war with themselves" and with women who challenge their masculinity. The goal is to offer answers about how to resolve these conflicts and find peace.

84. *The Male Stress Syndrome*: *How to Recognize and Live With It.* **Georgia Witkin-Lanoil, Ph.D. New York: Newmarket Press, 1986. Hardcover. 246 pp.**

Complementing *The Female Stress Syndrome*, this book is for men and the women in their lives. It is based on 50 interviews and many surveys answered by men as well as the women with whom they are involved. These women often detect symptoms that their male partners overlook. Witkin-Lanoil focuses on the physical, emotional, job, family, and personal aspects of stress, discussing "ten hidden stresses" as well. Her goal is to increase readers' awareness and thus help them take remedial action to avoid mental, psychological, or even physical harm. Exercises, suggested strategies, management techniques, relaxation ideas, and ways to turn off "Type A Behavior" are offered. Competitiveness, competency and achievement worries, "fear of failure," and control issues are topics discussed as potential causes of stress.

85. *Manhood: A New Definition.* **Stephen A. Shapiro. New York: G.P. Putnam's Sons, 1984. Hardcover. 266 pp.**

This book proposes to help men heal what Shapiro sees as a sense of "mistrust" in themselves and other men. Today's world, he says, exacerbates this growing problem by being a place that encourages "violation of trust." Men who fall into this kind of dishonorable deception in public and private life can become "detached," silent, and confused, the author maintains. His book suggests that society and family life will suffer unless men arrive at a new vision of "manhood" that emphasizes honesty, forgiveness, and open communication of feelings. Through numerous case studies, Shapiro encourages men to begin strengthening friendships, intimate relationships, and business associations by maturely recognizing the need for truth in all their dealings.

86. *The Masculine Dilemma.* **Gregory Rochlin. Boston, MA: Little, Brown, 1980. Hardcover. 310 pp.**

Based on many years of psychoanalytic practice, teaching, and scholarly research, Rochlin's book is for the educated layman as well as the professional counselor. It focuses on the importance men place on power, competency, and the need to prove themselves. The study sees the male condition as an "endless trial" causing stress and an excessive drive for high achievement. At the root of the majority of these male anxieties is the "fatal flaw," fear of failure. Rochlin asserts that this fear creates complex dilemmas especially when women and work are added to the equation. In the author's opinion, the destructive result can be a weakened and constantly threatened sense of self-esteem.

87. *Maybe He's Just a Jerk: Women's Jerkline Stories About the Men in Their Lives.* **Carol Rosen. New York: Wm. Morrow, 1992. Hardcover. 240 pp.**

Rosen's project began out of desperation with her own attempts to improve her personal love relationships. She discovered that, regardless of her efforts, some relationships were hopeless because the man involved was simply a "jerk." Since Rosen was curious about the feelings of other women, she solicited their "jerksperiences" and even instituted a "jerkline," which they could call to share stories. The huge success of this vehicle prompted the author to try to help an even wider circle. The book is full of real examples of "con men, sleazy lovers, married seducers, mama's boys," and more. It teaches women how to: avoid hopeless men, stop ignoring women's own inner needs, stop blaming themselves, and begin looking for the right man.

88. *The McGill Report on Male Intimacy.* **Michael E. McGill. New York: Holt, Rinehart and Winston, 1985. Hardcover. 300 pp.**

During a ten-year period, McGill studied the emotional lives of over 5000 diverse men and women (ages 18-73). Here he examines the quality of caring he found. His book reveals the essential differences between the sexes, especially in regard to openness where men seem to have greater difficulty. McGill's purpose is to act as a guide for the development of greater satisfaction in all relationships. Areas discussed include: the substitution of sexual closeness for intimacy in men, the problems with letting money instead of attentiveness express love, the threatening nature (generally non-sexual) of affairs, difficulties experienced in mid-life, father-son competitiveness, and the vulnerability and loss of control feared in true intimacy.

89. *Men and Marriage.* **George Gilder. Gretna, LA: Pelican Publishing Co., 1986. Hardcover. 219 pp.**

The chief concern here is the collapse of the traditional American family due to the loss of clearly-delineated sex roles. Gilder favors a return to society's previously held value system and offers help to restore healthy family relations. This will begin to solve problems that he suggests are largely the result of the new "competition" between the sexes stemming from the women's movement. The book maintains that men need the structure of marriage and the connection of the family unit. Yet, they are frequently confused by new trends. Gilder also discusses: the financial impact of one vs. two incomes in families, the phenomenon of wives being replaced by younger women, and the questions surrounding the delaying of marriage and childbearing.

90. *Men and Marriage: The Changing Role of Husbands.* **Elizabeth C. Mooney. New York: Franklin Watts, 1985. Hardcover. 212 pp.**

Mooney clearly admits that this is not a scholarly study. Her broad purpose is simply to hold a "mirror to the lives of people" in order to examine how couples live and why they marry. The special focus is husbands. The book covers such issues as: dual career marriages that begin later and often postpone childbearing, couples who choose to live together unmarried, second marriages, and the frequently lowered appreciation of women in mid-life. Mooney sees altered gender expectations and too many potential options as a source of confusion to men. She offers ideas for removing rigid role requirements and working toward fulfilling the needs of both individuals while adjusting to change as it occurs.

91. *Men Talk: How Men Really Feel About Women, Sex, Relationships and Themselves.* **Dr. Alvin Baraff. New York: A Dutton Book, The Penguin Group, 1991. Hardcover. 269 pp.**

Baraff claims that "no one understands men." Since society's gender expectations have encouraged control, independence, and competition in men while discouraging communication or the seeking of help, male problems remain largely private. With men comprising only 15 percent of those seeking counseling "for themselves," Baraff saw a need. He created a "MenCenter" in Washington, D.C. that not only thrived but allowed him to study closely what men really think about themselves, women, sex, family etc. The result is this book, the first, he says, to actually look in on six months of group therapy with six real men. Baraff records dialogue from the sessions and supplements it with commentary. His book encourages both men and women to "listen when men talk."

92. *Men Who Can't Love: When a Man's Fear Makes Him Run from Commitment (And What a Smart Woman Can Do About It).* **Steven Carter and Julia Sokol. New York: M. Evans & Co., Inc., 1987. Hardcover. 235 pp.**

Based on interviews with hundreds of men and women, this book investigates the confusing phenomenon of men who search for close relationships but then find themselves to be "commitmentphobic." Its topics include: how women can recognize the problem in a man before plunging into a futile situation, how women can evaluate if the fear is permanent, and what women can do to help a man overcome his anxiety before he tries to escape from relationships that may, in fact, be right for him. The authors suggest that these fears often cause men to be unfaithful in their marriages and frequently to disregard the feelings of the very women who care for them.

93. *Men Who Hate Women and the Women Who Love Them: When Loving Hurts and You Don't Know Why.* **Dr. Susan Forward and Joan Torres. New York: Bantam Books, 1986. Hardcover. 294 pp.**

This is a book about the phenomenon of insecure women suffering from "addiction" to emotionally abusive, hostile, domineering, and intimidating men. The authors define this particular "misogynist" as the kind of individual who both loves and hurts the women he loves by demeaning, finding fault with, and even imposing excessively narrow limitations on their careers and social lives. Forward and Torres propose clear guidelines for women on gaining an understanding of themselves and of this type of destructive partner. They say that such an understanding will be the first step in overcoming the addiction, healing the hurt, recovering self-esteem, and restructuring or moving on to a new and healthier relationship.

94. *The Myth of Male Power: Why Men Are the Disposable Sex.* **Warren Farrell, Ph.D. New York: Simon & Schuster, 1993. Hardcover. 446 pp.**

Farrell offers contrarian theories in this book that analyzes men throughout history in a variety of cultures. Basically, he sees women as the sex that has been empowered and men as the powerless gender. His book provides many examples of male "disposability:" higher male suicide rates, lower life expectancies, lower net worths, greater risk of dying in professions like firefighting, coal mining, etc., less choice in deciding to remain at home or to work, death in the military, and death from capital punishment. Farrell's goal is to "bring the sexes back together" with love through dialogue. The founder of 600+ men's and women's groups, he emphasizes that men must learn to speak up if they wish their feelings to be heard. Women can stop feeling "oppressed" and put away their anger, he says, if women realize that old gender roles are now dysfunctional.

95. *The Passions of Men: Work and Love in the Age of Stress.* **Mark Hunter. New York: G.P. Putnam's Sons, 1988. Hardcover. 320 pp.**

This is a book about the eternal problem of balancing work and love. On the one hand, Hunter sees the modern era as one that is preoccupied with the equality of the sexes. On the other hand, he sees us as a society plagued by the sad reality of subconsciously "repeating our parents' lives." The author, through several hundred interviews, has drawn a picture of men who still view themselves primarily as "breadwinners," are often reluctant to commit to women, and many times are unable to give women the kind of affectionate nurturing increasingly demanded. The work uncovers the inner desires, frustrations, and stresses these men suffer and reveals what they want from themselves and the women in their lives. It shows how men can achieve balance and what women can do to help.

96. *Perfect Husbands (& Other Fairy Tales)*: *Demystifying Marriage, Men, and Romance*. **Regina Barreca. New York: Harmony Books, 1993. Hardcover. 280 pp.**

Barreca writes about the "myths, images and roles of the husband" throughout our society in research, literature, song, and cinema. With humor, she recounts her own story and search for an answer to why a husband continues to be a "valuable commodity." Her book tries to improve couple relationships by helping women understand the importance of being realistic while also knowing their own "needs, desires and…expectations" before marrying. Barreca's thesis is that the ideology surrounding marriage has changed drastically and permanently in recent history. Notwithstanding this, she laments the fact that old romantic ideas about marriage, ingrained from childhood, linger on in contemporary women. Problems arise when modern notions of equality conflict with old pictures of the man as the center of the family's economic and emotional "infrastructure."

97. *The Peter Pan Syndrome*: *Men Who Have Never Grown Up*. **Dr. Dan Kiley. New York: Dodd, Mead & Co., 1983. Hardcover. 281 pp.**

Written for women, this book is an in-depth study of the behavior, under-lying causes, and six major symptoms of men who have refused to grow up. These men are seen as unwilling or unable to accept adult responsibilities or feelings and as a result, are frequently divorced from their own true emotions. Kiley notes that they are often narcissistic and egotistical takers rather than givers; while they may appear normal, they often feel desper-ately lonely inside. The author explores case histories and provides women with a test to judge if their man is a "Peter Pan Syndrome Victim." In addi-tion, there is practical, down-to-earth advice about what women can do for themselves and these men. Special chapters speak to parents, wives, lovers, and victims about remedies and when to give up.

98. *The Seasons of a Man's Life*. **Daniel J. Levinson. New York: Alfred A. Knopf, 1978. Hardcover. 363 pp.**

In this book, Levinson proposes a theory that is termed "radical" by some. He suggests that the changes adult males undergo are predictable, specifi-cally "age linked to a timetable," and often accompanied by crises in their personal, business, and emotional lives. Based on an in-depth study of 40 men, this report analyzes the "dangers and stress points" common to each stage and their interrelationship with goals, success, attitudes, and behavior.

Levinson analyzes the underlying causes for problems with marriage and work as well as why men leave either their wives or their jobs (or both) during certain of these periods. The author claims to have discovered the "pattern of the adult life cycle."

99. *Secrets About Men Every Woman Should Know.* **Barbara De Angelis. New York: A Dell Book, a Div. of Bantam Doubleday, 1990. Paperback. 367 pp.**

Complete with quizzes, exercises, check lists, and a multitude of do's and don'ts, this book is an instruction manual that the author says all women should have read before they ever dated a man. The goal of the book is to: help women become more aware of their own power, understand the inner desires, feelings, and fears of men, and, therefore, create stronger and more satisfactory relationships. Based on hundreds of interviews with men, the book: warns against mothering men or expecting them to change, gives tips on identifying problematic men, guides women toward improving communication levels and sex lives, and lists numerous mistakes women make to turn men off.

100. *The Secrets Men Keep*: *Find Out What They Really Think and How They Really Feel.* **Dr. Ken Druck with James C. Simmons. New York: Ballantine Books, 1985. Paperback. 237 pp.**

Druck and Simmons probe the characteristics of men's deepest secrets: what they dream about, fantasize about, are afraid of, and worried about. Their book's goal is to help modern women remove the "mask of masculinity" and identify what men really desire out of their lives, their female lovers, and their counterparts. The authors attempt to uncover the kinds of things men are concealing and the real reasons for their sometimes confusing behavior. They include over 50 informative quizzes and exercises for the use of both partners. The hope is to offer aid in resolving the problem of men being "held captive by their own secrets" and thus improve the overall quality of relationships.

101. *Sexual Static*: *How Men Are Confusing the Women They Love.* **Dr. Morton H. Shaevitz. Boston, MA: Little Brown & Co., 1987. Hardcover. 175 pp.**

Sexual Static is a guide to understanding and resolving issues underlying the conflict between modern men and women in the aftermath of the women's movement. In it, Shaevitz characterizes men as disoriented by female independence and often lonely and confused, especially with regard to the new behaviors and roles expected of them. He suggests that while men may speak the new language, underneath it all, their subconscious views may remain very traditional. This, Shaevitz says, can cause them to send out mixed messages that confuse their partners in turn. Citing this confusion as today's largest roadblock to harmonious relationships, the author offers advice on how to improve couple communication, caring, and problem solving.

102. *Some American Men*. Gloria Emerson. New York: Simon & Schuster, 1985. Hardcover. 315 pp.

Emerson, a former *New York Times* correspondent, covered the war in Viet Nam. She is therefore at ease talking with men about their deepest feelings. Over a seven year period, she interviewed all types of American men about their thoughts on work, duty, love, and "other great risks." Her book is a "collective biography" of experiences these men have endured, reasons they act as they do, "what they fear, and what they believe is required of them." The award winning work is of interest because these men speak honestly about issues they may have previously kept secret. Topics include: feelings about fathers, love for fellow soldiers, needs to be in control, views on limitations and failure, "love for women," and the "loss" of this love.

103. *Some Men Are More Perfect Than Others*. Merle Shain. New York: Bantam Books, 1973. Paperback. 128 pp.

Shain has written a sincere and rather poetic reflection about how women want to be loved. It is interwoven with stories about life and descriptions of "the best kinds of men." Confessing that there are no perfect men, the author nevertheless points out that some have far better qualities than others. Her book discusses characteristics such as generosity, the ability to feel and like, playfulness and humor, versatility, commitment, openness, honesty, respect for women, caring, and nurturing. Shain thinks that women who need men to "give definition to their lives" are just as wrong as men who consider women subjects of "conquest." She traverses every angle of a relationship from dating to sex, fear of loving, marriage, affairs, "passive warfare," losing love, and women being on their own.

104. *Straight Talk*: *What Men Need to Know/What Women Should Understand*. Dr. James C. Dobson. Dallas, TX: Word Publishing, 1991. Hardcover. 237 pp.

Dobson explores the definition of manhood in the generation of the 90s with the goal of trying to make sense out of the too often bewildering expectations of men's roles. The contradictory demands of being strong and manly yet psychologically sensitive and communicative, of making substantial amounts of money yet participating equally in household responsibilities, of being a "four-star lover" yet being a hands-on father are viewed as stretching men to the point of frustration. This book offers concrete assistance in making all the elements work, aids men in understanding themselves, and helps women gain essential knowledge about their partners.

105. *Straight Talk to Men and Their Wives.* **Dr. James C. Dobson. Waco, TX: Word Books, 1980. Hardcover. 222 pp.**

This book is mainly for men. Dobson claims it can also be of great use to women who wish to understand their husbands better and help them be the family leaders so sorely missing in today's world. Emphasizing that the work of strengthening home life is now done mostly by women, the author summons men to join the cause as the "key to the preservation of the family." His book explores the damage done by the woman's movement to the "Judeo-Christian concept of manliness" and contends that America must return to strong male leadership in homes. This, Dobson stresses, will necessitate a second look at masculinity and a realignment of priorities for men. Home and family must hold first place, he argues. A man's work, emotions, God, wife, and children are studied in depth.

106. *What Every Woman Should Know About Men.* **Dr. Joyce Brothers. New York: Simon & Schuster, 1981. Hardcover. 268 pp.**

Researched in depth and illustrated with numerous case studies, this candid book hopes to increase women's knowledge of the reasons behind male behavior. Its goal is to help females relate to their counterparts more understandingly, confidently, and successfully in the areas of friendship, business, and love. Brothers examines phases in the life cycles of male adults in relationship to their moods, behavior patterns, and needs. Some topics discussed include: male sexual capacity and problems encountered, developing increased sexual pleasure, men and work, the "kinship of men" in business situations, romance and marriage, and the physical, emotional and psychological differences between the genders.

107. *What Men Really Think About Women, Love, Sex, Themselves: Ways to Help Your Relationship by Knowing What Men Think.* **Mark Baker. New York: Simon & Schuster, 1992. Hardcover. 317 pp.**

Baker wrote this analysis about the innermost feelings of men after interviewing a variety of males nationwide. He treats issues related to sexuality, women, romance, and love. His findings showed that "men often live undercover lives" in which they conceal their feelings of fear, pain, and confusion. The males Baker studied were often discontented with the overall quality of their lives, felt betrayed by the major changes brought about by the sexual revolution, and were uncertain about what they should really be or how they should act. Threatened, they often hid behind "masks" as a result, he says.

The premise of the book is that a deeper understanding of these significant factors can help women strengthen their relationships with men.

108. *What Men Really Want: The Definitive Guide to Love and Intimacy in the 90's. It Will Change the Way You Feel About Men and Women in Love.* **Herb Goldberg, Ph.D. New York: Penguin Books, 1991. Paperback. 224 pp.**

This book is a comprehensive guide to building open communication and a realistic relationship with a man. It stands firmly against the use of "feminine ploys" stating that if women desire truly loving relationships, they need to be real. Women also need to know a man's perspective on his deepest fears, beliefs, and insecurities. Goldberg feels that men desire intimacy as much as women and that of greatest importance to them are not issues such as a woman's beauty, e.g., but her genuine desire for and admiration of him. Good relating is readily possible, he contends, once women accurately understand this factor. A major theme is that an honest, happy, and enduring relationship needs to combat problems created by mixed signals and also reduce conflict based on a lack of understanding.

109. *What Men Won't Tell You But Women Need to Know: Television's Top Expert on Men Brings You a Full Report from Behind the Locker Room Door.* **Bob Berkowitz. New York: Avon Books, The Hearst Corp., 1990. Paperback. 177 pp.**

Writing for women from the male point of view, Berkowitz presents an "insider's guide" to men: what their real lives are like, what they fantasize about and dream of, what inspires their hopes, and what desperately frightens them. He provides here a practical handbook for women who are searching to improve the quality of their present relationships or who wish to find new ones that give them what they need and want. Topics discussed include: men's fears and feelings regarding the complex issue of commitment, ten causes for men acting like "jerks," innovative strategies for flirting and attracting men, ideas for interesting dates and trips, and how losing a job and aging affects men.

110. *What Really Works With Men: Solve 95% of Your Relationship Problems (and Cope with the Rest).* **A. Justin Sterling. New York: Warner Books, 1992. Hardcover. 209 pp.**

Sterling offers women a controversial and dramatic approach to solving relationship problems. In this book, he interestingly proposes that the overall success of a relationship is one hundred percent the responsibility of the women involved. The author bases his work on the tested results of his "Sterling Women's Weekend Workshops" where he counsels women with all types of relationship problems. The theory espoused here is that by giving a man "what he wants when he wants it" and by feeding his ego, remarkably positive results will follow. Sterling suggests that women be careful about mate selection right from the beginning in order to lay the proper groundwork so necessary for future happiness.

111. *Why Men Are the Way They Are.* **Warren Farrell, Ph.D. New York: Berkley Books, 1986. Paperback. 411 pp.**

Farrell has directed workshops with men and women for 20 years. His best seller, the result of these experiences, examines the "secret feelings and desires" of men. The author's goal is to help couples develop sincere and honest communication and thereby improve the quality of their relationships. Written for men as well as women, the book includes such topics as: a man's most urgent needs in a woman, the place of power in a man's life, his real opinions on the achievements of his female partner, actual sentiments on the impact of the sexual revolution, sexism, confusing signals men perceive being sent by women, and views on "unrealistic female expectations."

112. *Why Men Can't Open Up: Overcoming Men's Fear of Intimacy.* **Steven Naifeh and Gregory White Smith. New York: Clarkson N. Potter, Inc., 1984. Hardcover. 193 pp.**

Why Men Can't Open Up is a study of problems men and women confront in love relationships because of a man's inability to express himself openly to women or, for that matter, to other men. The idea is that men who can't communicate their own vulnerability are men who rob themselves and their partners of genuine intimacy. Naifeh and Smith illustrate their views with actual case histories and discuss traditional social forces that have magnified the problem. They strongly feel that men need to understand the ramifications of this issue if they are to live more fully. Part I studies male fears of open communication and closeness while Part II explores ways in which women can help and men can modify their behavior.

113. *Women Men Love/Women Men Leave: Why Men Are Drawn to Women and What Makes Them Want to Stay.* **Dr. Connell Cowan & Dr. Melvyn Kinder. New York: Clarkson N. Potter, Inc., 1987. Hardcover. 295 pp.**

Written from the male point of view, this book attempts to present a picture of men's basic needs in a partner. The authors stress that men do want love and commitment but seek this intimacy in a different fashion from females. The book is full of case studies and detailed descriptive examples of the types of women men love and leave. It also includes an analysis of the way love works and how women can change negative behavior patterns. An appendix at the end of the book contains quizzes to assess various styles of loving. Some topics covered are: women who fear intimacy, women who have "secret contempt" for men, the need to control, viewing men realistically, and friendship as a way to deepen love.

114. *Workaholics*: *Living With Them and Working With Them.* **Marilyn Machlowitz. Reading, MA: Addison Wesley Publishing Co., 1976. Hardcover. 189 pp.**

Machlowitz explores the causes, characteristics, and behavior patterns of workaholics (male or female) and how the presence of one affects the dynamics of a relationship. Based on hundreds of interviews, her study identifies four types of workaholics. It discusses how to live with one and offers advice for evaluating whether we can expect any reformation to occur. The workaholic personality is not always seen as a negative one by this author. In fact, her book outlines a number of virtues found in this type of individual. While the workaholic per se may be "surprisingly happy," Machlowitz analyzes how his or her partner may feel quite the reverse.

115. *Wrestling With Love*: *How Men Struggle With Intimacy With Women, Children, Parents and Each Other.* **Samuel Osherson, Ph.D. New York: A Fawcett Columbine Book, Ballantine Books, 1992. Hardcover. 371 pp.**

This study of "contemporary masculinity" explores the dichotomy between a man's search for intimacy and his simultaneous fear or rejection of it. Osherson says that this "paradox" originates in part from excessive emphasis on stereotypical manliness and "separation" in early childhood development. Such training creates an inner struggle, he thinks. The author argues that a man's overt drive for "independence" and "competence" often overshadows a secret but real yearning for close connecting. The book uses case histories and practical strategies from successful workshops to help men know themselves better. These efforts, Osherson says, will facilitate the elimination of self-defeating behavior patterns, help men "draw on their positive energy," and improve all their relationships.

For additional help in "Understanding the Men in Our Lives," see also book numbers:

4: *Bradshaw On: The Family*

25: *Light His Fire*

35: *The Pleasers…Women Who Can't Say No —And the Men Who Control Them*

57: *A Woman's Worth*

62: *Women and Their Fathers*

151: *Husbands and Wives*

154: *How to Keep a Man in Love With You Forever*

160: *Husbands, Wives & Sex*

166: *Intimate Partners*, Sager and Hunt

168: *Intimate Strangers*

193: *Men Are from Mars, Women Are from Venus*

194: *Men, Women and Relationships*

196: *The New Male-Female Relationship*

203: *Passages*

205: *Peer Marriage*

215: *Second Honeymoon*

223: *That's Not What I Meant*

250: *The Incompatibility of Men and Women*

252: *Jealousy*

261: *Money Demons*

281: *You Just Don't Understand*

285: *All the Good Ones Are Married*

286: *Back from Betrayal*

288: *The Don Juan Dilemma*

290: *Every Other Man*

293: *His Needs Her Needs*

295: *How to Keep Your Man Monogamous*

299: *Men Who Can't Be Faithful*

303: *Not With My Husband You Don't*

308: *Why Men Stray and Why Men Stay*

309: *Woman Versus Woman*

317: *Get Rid of Him*

520: *Beating the Marriage Odds*

523: *Cold Feet*

527: *Getting to "I Do"*

528: *Good Guys/Bad Guys*

532: *How to Find Another Husband...by Someone Who Did*

533: *How to Find Romance After 40*

534: *How to Make A Man Fall in Love With You*

535: *How to Make Love to a Man*

537: *How to Marry the Man of Your Choice*
547: *Smart Women: Foolish Choices*
548: *Someone Right for You*
550: *Were You Born for Each Other?*

3

An Overview of Marriage, Love and Divorce
Husbands and wives

A select number of books in this guide are very broad in nature. They propose to help readers gain an overall perspective on the institution of marriage in general and an understanding of the social trends affecting it during the last several decades. Some books also provide historical analysis and an outlook on the future. In many instances, the authors have based their work on the results of extensive surveys. Some of their texts study marriage alone; others treat the related areas of sex and love as well.

I have included these books for those who wish to move beyond their own specific day-to-day problems and spend some time on larger sociological issues such as the history of divorce in America. There are moments when too narrow an outlook can exaggerate our difficulties while the broader perspective can provide us with unique and helpful insights.

116. *Husbands and Wives: A Nationwide Survey of Marriage.* **Anthony Pietropinto, M.D. and Jacqueline Simenauer. New York: Times Books, The New York Times Book Co., 1979. Hardcover. 408 pp.**

When it was completed in 1979, this was the first national survey ever undertaken to study the responses of a widely divergent group of married people. By analyzing replies from 3900 participants, the authors try to develop a clearer view of the actual realities of marriage on all age, social, and economic levels. The book examines new, more liberated life-styles as well as growing divorce rates. People, rather than statistics, are the core of the study, which helps readers draw comparisons with their own lives. Topics covered include: mate selection, reasons for marriage, the self in marriage, fighting, most prevalent crises, needs of both partners, control issues, infidelity, attitudes toward divorce, and the outlook for a fulfilling and enduring remarriage.

117. ***The Kinsey Institute New Report on Sex: What You Must Know to Be Sexually Literate*. June M. Reinisch, Ph.D., Director with Ruth Beasley, M.L.S. New York: St. Martin's Press, 1990. Hardcover. 540 pp.**

The work of Dr. Alfred Kinsey in 1950 is meant to be supplemented by this book, not replaced or simply updated by it. A need for accurate information on basic sexual knowledge became clear to the authors through the high failure rates on a national sex information questionnaire answered by 1974 respondents. The authors aim for scientific accuracy in their reference book, which compiles clear answers to the questions most commonly asked about sex. They leave value and moral judgements to their readers. Chapters are complete in themselves and readers can refer to each independently. Topics include: male and female anatomy, sexual development, sexual function and dysfunction, homosexuality, aging, disabilities, disease, reproduction, contraception, masturbation, health, affairs, and divorce.

118. ***Love, Sex, and Aging: A Consumers Union Report*. Edward M. Brecher and the Editors of *Consumer Reports* Books. Boston, MA: Little, Brown & Co., 1984. Hardcover. 441 pp.**

This work is a detailed investigation of the "sexual attitudes and activities of Americans over the age of fifty." Its authors arrived at their results by compiling statistics gleaned from 4246 men and women, the majority of whom were married longer than 30 years. Some of those surveyed had marriages that had ended and others had never married. The conclusions drawn are that the quality of life can be very high, that social and family relationships can flourish, and that an active and pleasurable sex life can be maintained all the way through the 80s. The book analyzes numerous areas of day-to-day life but especially pertinent topics include marital happiness and faithful and adulterous marriages.

119. ***Marriage Divorce Remarriage: Social Trends in the United States*. Andrew J. Cherlin. Cambridge, MA: Harvard University Press, 1981. Hardcover. 142 pp.**

Cherlin provides us with "demographic data" on the "formation and disso-lution of marriage" after World War II and discusses the impact of various trends on the American family. He traces the growing numbers of divorces and various alternative life-styles; he also offers reasons for the drastic differences between different periods. The 1950s, when divorce was infre-quent, are seen as an anomaly. Based on extensive research, the book inves-tigates the interactions of the family throughout these periods and discusses the ability of the family unit to meet and adapt to the challenges of rapid redefinition. Cherlin divides the book into four parts focusing on: looking at "trends," understanding causes, analyzing the results, and lastly, on contrasting "black and white differences."

120. *Marriage, Love, Sex and Divorce: What Brings Us Together, What Drives Us Apart.* **Jonathan Gathorne-Hardy. New York: Summit Books, A Simon & Schuster Book, 1981. Hardcover. 384 pp.**

As a social historian, Gathorne-Hardy presents a broad historical overview of significant periods of change and stress in marriage, divorce, and sexual mores in the West. With increasing numbers of marriages breaking down and a new emphasis on personal freedom and fulfillment, the author suggests that Western society may be approaching one of its "massive shifts." His book focuses on how these trends are impacting relationships and what the future of marriage is likely to be. Some solutions are suggested. Gathorne-Hardy sees a preoccupation with romantic love as harmful to marriage. In this book, he examines new reasons for marrying rather than the obsolete ones of "sanctioned sex, security, and conformity."

121. *The Marriage Premise.* **Nena O'Neill. New York: M. Evans & Co., 1977. Hardcover. 229 pp.**

Looking at the overall nature of the institution of marriage, this book attempts to highlight shared characteristics in various marital scenarios, whether they be traditional or open and more liberated. As an anthropologist, O'Neill says she is interested in the fundamental assumptions underlying an institution that is still popular despite rising divorce rates and increasingly available alternatives. She sees most couples as still preferring sexual exclusivity, even when faced with far more radical choices. O'Neill contends that present day marriage appears more realistic with its "balance of power" and with most couples working hard to improve the quality of their relationships. The book does advocate, however, delaying marriage until the mid or late 20s to ensure a better chance of success.

122. *A Natural History of Love.* **Diane Ackerman. New York: Random House, 1994. Hardcover. 358 pp.**

Ackerman's study was motivated by a desire to find answers to her own questions. In the process, she reports finding little "serious research" on the topic. Her book consequently evolved into a comprehensive study of all facets of love from its evolution across world cultures to its emotional, religious, erotic, physical, chemical, and biological aspects. Tracing this "intangible" thing called love back to the Egyptians, Greeks, Romans and then through modern times, the author alludes to numerous pieces of art, writers, philosophers, myths and customs. Men loving women, men loving men, men loving boys, love for children, fathers, mothers, animals, cars etc. are all topics along with such themes as chivalry, troubadours, courtly love, monogamy, adultery, aphrodisiacs, and "the battle of the sexes."

123. *The Psychology of Love.* Robert J. Sternberg and Michael L. Barnes, eds. New Haven, CT: Yale University Press, 1988. Hardcover. 383 pp.

This is an unusual examination of the subject, Sternberg and Barnes suggest, in that a serious and scientific study of love had only been recently researched by experts. The editors attempt to probe the true meaning and dynamics of love by including chapters written by the day's leading professionals. These experts attempt to differentiate between love as an "attitude, an emotion, or set of behaviors," and to explore the distinctions between love and infatuation or caring. Other topics include: the nature of romantic or passionate love, "love as attachment," different styles of love, and the ways in which all of this knowledge can assist couples in developing and sustaining intimate relationships more successfully.

For additional help in "An Overview of Marriage and Love," see also book numbers:

203: *Passages*

209: *The Psychology of Romantic Love*

401: *Divorce Help Sourcebook*

4

Trying to Save the Marriage First

I love you, let's work it out

Helping women salvage a troubled marriage is the first goal of this guide and is by far the most frequent aim of the authors surveyed. Hence, the list of resources available in this chapter is extensive. Every conceivable facet of improving our relationships is examined by one of the vast number of self-help books published every year. With careful study, women should be able to select many choices appropriate for their own unique problems. Some books contain suggestions that coordinate very well with psychological work being done with professional counselors. For those who are working on their own solutions, there are a large assortment of books that set forth specific exercises and action-oriented programs.

Many of these choices overlap in their emphasis on intimacy, development of communication skills, conflict resolution, surmounting crises, creating partnerships, enhancing passion, and allowing for personal growth within a union. Others look at the benefits of marriage and commitment suggesting strategies for staying together through the predictable cycles and stages all couples inevitably encounter. Some authors focus on more defined topics such as finances, career issues, sex, handling criticism, fighting fairly, or on problems encountered in interfaith or intercultural relationships. All, regardless of any overlap, have their own distinct approaches.

Each of the books included here encourages readers to look at their problems in new ways and to resist the impulse of giving up on their marriages too easily.

124. *The 30 Secrets of Happily Married Couples.* **Dr. Paul Coleman. Holbrook, MA: Bob Adams, Inc., Publishers, 1992. Paperback. 189 pp.**

Coleman studied hundreds of couples for this book designed to help develop or improve skills for enhancing marriages. Each chapter may be read independently and covers a specific trait that the author's research showed as common to happy couples. Simple exercises aim at producing "rapid change" within hours or weeks and spousal cooperation is not crucial. Coleman emphasizes that couples direct their efforts toward change at themselves and the relationship rather than at their partners. The will to change is the most essential factor, he believes. Topics include: listening and communication, "spiritual beliefs and shared values," supporting mates, hidden agendas, logic, forgiveness, sex, affection, problem solving, and enjoying our time together.

125. *The Age of Taboo: Older Women–Younger Men Relationships.* **Arlene Derenski and Sally B. Landsburg. Boston, MA: Little, Brown and Co., 1981. Hardcover. 262 pp.**

These family therapists, who are both personally involved with younger men, have analyzed 50 couples (ages 17-78) where the woman is at least six years older than her partner. Their study reveals very lively, successful, and often "conflict free" relationships despite the overwhelmingly negative reaction of a society that has widely tabooed the practice. The book examines the causes of this cultural response as well as how the successful couples treat issues of power (of prime concern to the men), sex, children, money, financial security (of prime concern to the women), and status. It views this option as very viable, perhaps even better than conventional age differentials. Derensky and Landsburg also propose that women may have more promise of finding suitable partners if younger men can be potential mates.

126. *The Art and Practice of Loving.* **Frank Andrews, Ph.D. Los Angeles, CA: Jeremy P. Tarcher, Inc., 1991. Hardcover. 228 pp.**

This guidebook assists readers in developing and maintaining the ability to love to the fullest regardless of the changes and passages one goes through in life. Complete with 144 "practices for cultivating a loving heart," it is composed of hundreds of quotations and texts as well as a description of nine "myths" about loving and a discussion of behaviors that stand in the way of love. Andrews treats intimate relationships as well as others. Topics include: keeping our relationships harmonious, loving during times of crisis, loving in the face of loss, learning to love ourselves, and loving as a "path to God." The book encourages deep self-examination.

127. *The Art of Loving: The World-Famous Psychoanalyst's Daring Prescription for Love.* **Erich Fromm. New York: Perennial Library, Harper & Row, 1956, 1989. Paperback. 118 pp.**

Fromm analyzes all types of loving and their benefits. He states that "love is an art, not a pleasant sensation" and that we must study and practice it for optimum results. The book sees loving as one of the most important and fulfilling aspects of life and mastering the art of love as at the heart of human existence. Fromm discusses the importance of love in rounding out our total personality by deepening our self-knowledge and developing our courage. The author candidly teaches how to: conquer the fear of love, overcome anxiety and shame, and reap the rewards of hidden potential. He believes that western society has witnessed the breakdown of love and that its true embodiment, sadly, is something few of us ever attain.

128. *The Art of Staying Together: A Couple's Guide to Intimacy and Respect.* **Michael S. Broder, Ph.D. New York: Hyperion, 1993. Hardcover. 249 pp.**

Written for people who want to improve their intimate relationships and solve their own problems, this book offers practical options for resolving difficult issues and achieving happiness. Broder, a psychologist, includes several extensive "inventories" to help us determine exactly where we stand. He studies troubled unions in three categories: (1) the "prebound," originating when one partner was already involved with someone else, (2) the "one-sided," where the giving and taking are unequal, and (3) the "indifferent." The book does not judge relationships but rather suggests that individuals try to negotiate what works best for them. Topics include: passion, intimacy, comfort, values, communication, sex, fighting, jealousy, abuse, rules, monogamy, affairs, infertility, parenting and stepparenting, alternatives to divorce, and leaving.

129. *A Book for Couples. Notes on How to Live in the World…and Still Be Happy.* **Hugh and Gail Prather. New York: Doubleday, Bantam Doubleday Dell Publ. Group, 1988. Paperback. 209 pp.**

In this book on developing happy and successful marriages, the authors explain principles learned from their own 22 years of marriage as well as from experiences with couples in counseling. Hugh Prather, a father, minister, educator, and professional therapist, has been called "An American Kahil Gibran" by the *New York Times*. The book is for those who would like to create an "unshakable friendship." It discusses all important areas of intimate relating including: mastering the art of resolving conflict and fighting fairly, balancing power in decision-making, sex, dealing with financial questions, handling feelings of jealousy, raising children together, and keeping the relationship vital through our later years.

130. *Born for Love: Reflections on Loving.* **Leo Buscaglia. New York: Slack Inc. Publ., Random House, 1992. Hardcover. 298 pp.**

This internationally famous author and speaker makes an enthusiastic case for the fact that the act of "loving" is a deliberate and free choice that each of us makes. Buscaglia suggests that this choice has the power to give us incredible strength and offer us new and different ways of coping with the trials, tribulations, anxieties, and fears of life. Love also has the ability to greatly diminish our feelings of loneliness, Buscaglia states. His book is composed of separate and individual inspirational thoughts, reflections, and ideas on loving and can be of benefit to the actual lovers themselves, their extended families, and to friends.

131. *Centering & the Art of Intimacy.* **Gay Hendricks, Ph.D. and Kathlyn Hendricks, Ph.D. New York: Prentice Hall, 1985. Paperback. 124 pp.**

The Hendricks have written a book about innovative modes of relating intimately with specific exercises for improving communication abilities and reaching levels of "greater self-acceptance and mind/body awareness." They propose that these qualities will help us be more open to love by enabling us to be "centered." The book's premise is that we all yearn for a deep, all-encompassing, long-term love relationship but that the ways in which we handle our interactions often eliminate that possibility. Fearing intimate connection, almost as much as loneliness, prevents us from being genuinely relaxed and at peace with our partners and ourselves, they suggest. The authors emphasize being truthful, practicing the art of touching, and giving each other freedom and room.

132. *The Challenge of Marriage.* **Rudolf Dreikurs, M.D. New York: Hawthorne Books, Inc., 1946, 1974. Paperback. 274 pp.**

This book claims that the evolution of sexual equality has confused couples raised in traditions where male superiority was the rule. Dreikurs views this issue as the cause of serious problems in the realms of marital sex and love. He says that modern democratic partnerships require new approaches; they must utilize special interpersonal skills to resolve conflicts in a "spirit of mutual respect." Although these skills may be foreign to us, Dreikurs feels they will help us to: find more appropriate mates, improve our sex and love lives, deal with "infidelity and jealousy" more successfully, raise our children with less turmoil, and create greater family harmony. Nurturing the happiness of others as well as our own happiness will bring us positive long-term results.

133. *Changing Him, Changing Her.* **Michael E. McGill, Ph.D. New York: Simon & Schuster, 1982. Hardcover. 319 pp.**

McGill underscores the necessity for change in successful relationships and is convinced of the appropriateness of desiring such change in others. He counters popular opinion by suggesting that our reluctance to engage in conflict prevents us from asking for changes (and vice versa) that would allow our unions to grow much stronger. Writing from extensive research and interviews, the author outlines the needs of partners in relationships and suggests constructive and loving ways of changing each other to accommodate these needs. The book discusses "money,...power, sex and sharing, time and togetherness" as possible sources of our discomfort with the status quo and reasons for our desire for change.

134. *Conscious Loving: The Journey to Co-Commitment: A Way to Be Fully Together Without Giving Up Yourself.* **Gay Hendricks, Ph.D. and Kathlyn Hendricks, Ph.D. New York: Bantam Books, 1990. Paperback. 287 pp.**

Having counseled 1000+ couples over a 20 year period, these authors provide a program of specific techniques to "clear away unconscious agreements and patterns." Such patterns, they contend, can undermine the success of a marriage. Their goal is to help readers learn how to commit wholeheartedly to a relationship on a long-term basis and learn how to construct a genuinely intimate partnership. The Hendricks offer suggestions for forgiving past hurts and allowing opportunities for energy and creativity to bring a new sense of fulfillment. The book covers such areas as: balancing power, compromising on needs for dependence and independence, enhancing communication skills, reducing conflict, and learning to negotiate agreements that both parties can follow.

135. *Couple Skills: Making Your Relationship Work.* **Matthew McKay, Ph.D., Patrick Fanning and Kim Paleg, Ph.D. Oakland, CA: New Harbinger Publishers, Inc., 1994. Paperback. 290 pp.**

This workbook teaches couples the skills necessary for solving specific problems. Probably only counselors will read it all; others will select a chapter and complete assessments, logs, exercises, journals, or problem charts. Action is the thrust rather than theory. The book has four parts: (1) "Basic Skills," (2) "Advanced Skills," (3) "Anger & Conflict," and (4) "Understanding and Changing What Goes Wrong." Concepts are repeated in several chapters. Having concluded that successful partnerships have common skill bases, the authors hope to help readers break destructive patterns and risk failure in order to try new ways of interacting. Some suggestions can be used unilaterally, others by the couple. Topics include: communication, listening, feelings, needs, negotiation, goals, defenses, and conflict.

136. *Couples: How to Confront Problems & Maintain Loving Relationships.* **Dr. Carlfred Broderick. New York: Simon & Schuster, 1979. Hardcover. 224 pp.**

Broderick is a therapist and director of a training center for marriage counselors. He has written an anecdotal and comprehensive book for those who wish to strengthen their relationships by approaching problems in innovative ways. Common and unusual issues are the subjects of candid discussions. The book provides exercises for acquiring new skills and behaviors to remediate problems. Topics examined include: preventing multiple roles from overwhelming us, increasing "emotional space," developing independence, creative communicating and listening, "ghosts" from previous marriages, anger, sex, infidelity, depression, mixed marriages, bisexuality, role reversal, dividing duties fairly, and financial crises.

137. *Couples: Exploring and Understanding the Cycles of Intimate Relationships.* **Barry Dym, Ph.D. and Michael L. Glenn, M.D. New York: HarperCollins, 1993. Hardcover. 267 pp.**

"Descriptive" is how these therapists define their book rather than science, research, or self-help. They try to understand normal couples with normal problems, not to fix those problems. With case studies, the authors map the three stages of all marriages: (1) "Early Expansiveness" characterized by intense romance and promise, (2) "Contraction" where individuals conflict, feel "betrayed" and pull apart, and (3) "Resolution" in which problems are solved and individual differences as well as couple goals are accepted. How couple identities and patterns are formed, the role gender plays, and the kinds of crises that occur are all topics. The thesis is that awareness of the cycle, from intimacy to separation to renewed and deepened intimacy, can comfort and guide us while we move through the pressures of life.

138. *Courage My Love: A Book to Light an Honest Path.* **Merle Shain. New York: Bantam Books, 1989. Hardcover. 113 pp.**

Shain has composed an often poetic "meditation on the very nature of love." Rather than a self-help book or a work that perpetuates "delusions" about idealistic relationships, she calls it a "celebration" of realistic love. The book states that contemporary culture has brainwashed us into feeling depressed and unfulfilled if we are not in a perfect, romantic, and dramatically ecstatic union. The author's underlying thesis is that we must look inward, developing our own loving, listening, and learning skills, rather than constantly bemoaning our partner's inability to give to us. Shain urges us to deepen our sense of commitment to working through the inevitably difficult moments and to have a "kinder, gentler" attitude to our partner's failings and our own.

139. *Courtship After Marriage: Romance Can Last a Lifetime.* **Zig Ziglar. New York: Ballantine Books, 1990. Paperback. 256 pp.**

This experienced motivational instructor, famous for his practical views, offers concrete techniques for keeping romance alive and even making it grow through years of marriage to the same partner. Based on a survey of couples married 25+ years and illustrated with real life anecdotes, it includes: quizzes to assess our marriage styles, "steps for starting over," ways to increase harmony and commitment, tips on preserving an exciting sex life, and secrets for finding happiness through giving love to our partner rather than demanding it of him. Ziglar's thesis is that soundly based genuine love is far more meaningful than "passion of the moment." He shows how enduring marriages grow deeper with time, fidelity, and thoughtful communication.

140. *Creating a Marriage.* **James Greteman. Mahwah, NJ: Paulist Press, 1993. Paperback. 106 pp.**

Greteman is concerned with the "processes and patterns" of life and love, which he feels must always be "gentle." He thinks that while individuals differ, we must all approach what comes step-by-step with our partner. The book offers advice to those already married or those contemplating marriage or remarriage. Composed of brief chapters with key elements and complete with case studies, it is divided in three parts: (1) the "first part of life," (2) "midlife," where we tend to become more "dissatisfied," and (3) the "latter part of life," where we grow more interested in our inner values. Greteman divides marriages into five parts: "romance, power, stability, commitment and co creation." Topics include: marriage ceremonies, spirituality, humor, sexuality, intimacy, children, conflict, forgiveness, and "synchronicity."

141. *Creative Marriage: Making Your Marriage Work in the 80's.* **Mel Krantzler. New York: McGraw Hill Book Co., 1981. Hardcover. 415 pp.**

As a psychologist, Krantzler writes about the "six natural passages" or "marriages-within-a-marriage" that are common to most unions. Different needs at different times will require that couples understand these stages in order to increase their mutual happiness and become productive problem-solvers as issues change. Krantzler offers a new outlook rather than a guide or handbook and he proposes that finding a new and fulfilling marriage is more possible with our current mates than with different ones. Topics include: the failings of open marriages, two-career family issues, the departure or return of children, caring for aging parents, alternative solutions to conflict, and finally, divorce as an opportunity for growth.

142. *The Dance Away Lover & Other Roles We Play in Love, Sex and Marriage.* **Daniel Goldstine, Katherine Larner, Shirley Zuckerman, and Hilary Goldstine. New York: Wm. Morrow & Co., Inc., 1977. Hardcover. 250 pp.**

The concept of "role theory" in this book suggests that most marriages pass through three stages with each partner playing one or more roles. Understanding the nature of the cycles and the inner dynamics of both the loving and the conflict can help us learn to vary our responses, weather dissatisfaction or turmoil, and make our marriages grow. The book describes the stages as: early romance and love; reality with the entry of problems, boredom, alienation, or infidelity; and finally a "mutual acceptance" and harmony. This very realistic approach expects problems to occur and be worked on as they do. Separate chapters examine the ten roles (e.g., "Prizewinner," "Victim" and "Provider") we play as partners to "get what we want" or defend ourselves.

143. *The Dance of Intimacy: A Woman's Guide to Courageous Acts of Change in Key Relationships.* **Harriet Goldhor Lerner, Ph.D. New York: Harper & Row, 1989. Paperback. 255 pp.**

Lerner, an internationally acclaimed authority on the "psychology of women," writes about how people can change in relationships in order to bring about greater levels of intimacy. Her book examines the problems we encounter and the "dances" we do with each other as we continually move from closeness back to distance. By understanding the patterns underlying our successes and troubles, we can learn how we might operate differently. Aimed primarily at relationships that are troubled, in "pain," or in need of healing, the book also seeks to make good relationships better. It suggests concrete steps to help strengthen both our partnerships and ourselves as individuals. Lerner's belief is that intimacy is "put to the test" more than ever when we commit to a relationship for the long-term.

144. *The Dirty Half Dozen: Six Radical Rules to Make Relationships Last. The Secrets Every Couple Needs to Know.* **William Nagler, M.D. and Anne Androff. New York: Warner Books, 1991. Hardcover. 120 pp.**

These authors believe that traditional counseling advice and conventional "rules" and myths governing love relationships are diametrically opposed to what really works. Their study, based on extensive research of successful and unsuccessful couples, reveals that "tension reduction" and being comfortable with each other are more critical to lasting relationships than are "love, passion, trust, romance, honesty or intimacy." Their simply formatted book contains chapters with brief axioms on the six "radical" rules. It discourages: always telling the truth, expecting passionate sex to last, talking everything over, and fighting (even fairly). Laced with humor, the book urges the reader to relax and view life "realistically instead of idealistically."

145. *Do I Have to Give Up Me to Be Loved by You?* **Drs. Jordan and Margaret Paul. Minneapolis, MN: CompCare Publishers, 1983. Paperback. 313 pp.**

This book is based on "Intention Therapy," a theory that our dominant behavioral ingredient is the "intent to protect ourselves against any pain." Insecurity is presented as one cause of this problem, which creates barriers to happiness. The Pauls believe that understanding this hidden motivation can help us look at negative behaviors more realistically, "take responsibility for our own fears," and conquer separateness. This will bring us closer, resolve conflict productively, and reduce the need for blame, they say. The authors include process exercises rather than specific solutions. Ideally, each party will encourage freedom and honest communication, which deepens intimacy, fun, caring, and sex. The book suggests that an evolution can occur for each person and the partnership by using these techniques.

146. *Equal Time: The New Way of Living, Loving and Working Together.* **Marcia Lasswell and Norman M. Lobsenz. Garden City, NY: Doubleday & Co., Inc., 1983. Hardcover. 231 pp.**

Lasswell and Lobsenz believe that changes in sex roles during the last ten years require the restructuring of our intimate living arrangements. Their new plan would accommodate greater flexibility and growth for both parties. Based on hundreds of interviews, the book discusses the effects of changed expectations, altered role patterns, increased responsibility and freedom for women, and the absence of rigid "rules" of the past. The purpose is not to analyze these things but to broaden our understanding in order to help us reduce the conflict and stress in relationships due to them. *Equal Time* illustrates ways (sometimes drastically changed) in which modern couples are handling these exciting new "partnerships." The book also takes a look at future possibilities.

147. *Family Politics: Love and Power on an Intimate Frontier.* **Letty Cottin Pogrebin. New York: McGraw Hill, 1983. Hardcover. 278 pp.**

Writing in favor of both the family and marriage, Pogrebin offers a new outlook on the way families and the individuals within them can become healthier. She stresses learning to be more democratic and less controlling than is the case in more traditional units. The book advocates a system allowing each partner to be autonomous, financially independent, expressive, and powerful in his or her own right without restricting the freedom of the other partner. There is a thorough analysis of positive and negative behavior patterns in different kinds of families including parent-child interactions. Certain bad influences in society, which undermine the strength of the unit, are exposed. The goal is to show the success of blending "individual freedom and group harmony."

148. *From Conflict to Caring: An In-Depth Program for Creating Loving Relationships.* **Doctors Jordan and Margaret Paul. Minneapolis, MN: CompCare Publishers, 1989. Paperback. 211 pp.**

This workbook concentrates on helping us enhance our capacity to be loving by clearing away "self-limiting" blocks. The therapist/authors include numerous checklists, "personal inventories," and exercises to assess the status of our current relating styles. They pay special attention to our common tendency to "protect" ourselves when conflict occurs instead of using problems to "learn from our reactions." Protection behaviors, other negative patterns, and "unloving responses" are all analyzed. The Pauls stress eliminating our desire to blame. They see the ability to be loving as a voluntary choice that is not dependent upon what someone else does. Topics also include: power struggles, forgiveness, healing, fear, listening, and support groups.

149. *From This Day Forward: Staying Married When No One Else Is and Other Reckless Acts.* **Louise DeGrave. Boston, MA: Little, Brown & Co., 1981. Hardcover. 213 pp.**

With a good deal of educated humor, DeGrave considers the lives and roles of modern women and outlines the unique and often contrasting problems faced in their marriages. She analyzes "rites and rituals" with a light touch but her overall conviction is that these areas can often be the cause of real conflict. Issues covered include: duties around the house, day-to-day living arrangements, problems in various phases of a marriage, children, infertility and adoption, relatives and in-laws, dilemmas revolving around sex, the handling of finances, the impact of religious beliefs, and issues centered on particular "personality styles."

150. *Getting the Love You Want: A Guide for Couples.* **Harville Hendrix, Ph.D. New York: Perennial Library, Harper & Row, 1988. Paperback. 296 pp.**

Hendrix writes as a counselor whose own marriage has failed. He has developed a ten-week course of therapy that couples can use at home without professional intervention. Emphasizing the need to be "passionate friends," the author outlines skills to end power struggles, improve communication, and increase our sensitivity to our "partner's needs." He feels that ongoing growth for couples can be facilitated by learning to deal with conflict in adult ways rather than resorting to "childhood tactics." The book is divided into three parts: "The Unconscious Marriage" characterized by romantic attraction, "The Conscious Marriage" describing methods of surviving when reality sets in, and "The Ten-Week Course" for improving our relationships.

151. *Going the Distance: Secrets to Life Long Love.* **Lonnie Barbach, Ph.D. Garden City, NY: Doubleday, 1991. Hardcover. 295 pp.**

Going the Distance contains commonsense advice for maintaining a vital and flourishing intimate relationship for the long haul. It advises us to recognize potential crisis points and to prepare in advance for problem solving. The author/therapist outlines six characteristics of healthy relationships with emphasis on a balance of power achieved through successful negotiation of conflict. Barbach includes a 50-point compatibility questionnaire along with techniques for eliminating stress, "relationship fatigue," and sexual boredom. The book's thesis is that good relating must be continually worked at and is very rewarding once achieved.

152. *Growing Together/Staying Together: Preserving Marriage & Family in the Face of Personal Change.* **Jurg Willi, M.D. Los Angeles, CA: Jeremy P. Tarcher, Inc., 1992. Hardcover. 333 pp.**

This Swiss psychiatrist studied his topic for over six years. He explores the dangers of modern society's inordinate focus on individualism and personal development. Willi sees this selfishness as harmful to the nurturing of a "stable family life." The result of such a one-sided emphasis, he says, can be destructive conflict impacting all relationships. Willi instead advocates an "ecological approach" that thinks about self-actualization in relationship to the "benefits and costs to others." His theories are based on both Christianity and Buddhism. They focus on enhancing love and marriages by encouraging couples to view life as a "joint venture" in which family concepts can foster growth for the individual as well as the extended unit.

153. *How to Have a Happy Marriage.* **David and Vera Mace. Nashville, TN: Abington Press, 1977. Paperback. 174 pp.**

The Maces have written a distinctive workbook which offers detailed, constructive guidance to couples who will agree to "commit themselves for 24 hours over six weeks" to working along with them in completing exercises and assignments in each chapter. Based on over 40 years of marriage counseling, the book speaks directly to couples and encourages them to develop new patterns of interaction by: examining their relationships honestly, setting goals that will allow both the individuals and the partner-ship to grow, improving communication skills, and trying to overcome conflict in new ways. The authors encourage self-help but emphasize finding professional support when necessary as well.

154. *How to Keep a Man in Love With You Forever.* **Tracy Cabot, Ph.D. New York: McGraw-Hill Book Co., 1986. Hardcover. 271 pp.**

This book follows Cabot's previous work, *How to Make a Man Fall in Love With You.* It observes that once they have found their man, women often worry about sustaining love for a lifetime. Cabot's research showed that learning a man's "inner love language" and defining him as either "auditory, visual or feeling" is the secret. She describes the characteristics and behaviors of these three types of men and discusses ways of interacting most successfully with each. Cabot's guide includes a self-test to analyze both the man and the woman. The book states that working on "powerful communication tech-niques" such as "anchoring" and "mirroring" can then cement a loving and intimate relationship. Topics include: infidelity, maintaining sex appeal, revi-talizing passion, "balancing power," and eliminating harmful conflict.

155. *How to Live With Another Person.* **David Viscott, M.D. New York: Arbor House, 1974. Hardcover. 156 pp.**

Written in easy language with concise short paragraphs, this book looks at problematic relationships in danger of dissolving. The goal is to salvage the unions and enrich them for the long term. Viscott's practical advice on guar-anteeing rights, satisfying needs, and granting freedom to each person can also be useful to those working on building a new relationship. Compromise is critical to allow each partner to achieve personal growth within the partner-ship, Viscott claims. In addition, the author states that "commitments need to be renewed." Other topics covered include: advice on day-to-day life, ways in which we can more clearly express and have our needs genuinely heard, the issue of fidelity, and what happens when breaking up seems unavoidable.

156. *How to Make Love All the Time: Make Love Last a Lifetime!* **Dr. Barbara De Angelis. New York: Dell Publishing, a Div. of Bantam Doubleday Dell Publ. Group, 1987. Paperback. 273 pp.**

De Angelis proposes that the "magic" of love can last forever if we consciously work at developing our skills. Her book is for married couples or singles who yearn to turn their "partnership into a union." As founder of the successful "Making Love Work Seminars," De Angelis presents a step-by-step guide with graphic charts, subdivisions, self-tests, quizzes, and lists. It progresses from learning how to define our ideal partner to determining compatibility and building a deeply honest and communicative relationship.

Topics include: four "big mistakes" in love, sex and five "sexual traps," using "love letters" and "duplication" during conflict, renewing passion, creative listening, preventing burnout, and knowing when to separate.

157. *How to Make Love to the Same Person for the Rest of Your Life * and Still Love It.* Dagmar O'Connor. Garden City, NY: Doubleday & Co. Inc., 1985. Hardcover. 224 pp.

The goal of O'Connor's book is to provide a strategy for the development and maintenance of an exciting, monogamous sex life. Its audience is couples who, tired of the singles scene, are ready for a lifelong total commitment to one person. This "second stage sex," in O'Connor's opinion, has the promise to surpass the rewards of any other. A sex therapist with 15 years of counseling experience, O'Connor outlines the problems we often encounter as couples such as monotony, the interference of family obligations, and the "temptations of infidelity." Coping mechanisms include: searching for varied sexual expression, rekindling spark, and trying to have our bodies "make friends" instead of requiring intimacy of our partner.

158. *How to Manage a Marriage.* Marie Kargman. Boston, MA: Foundation Books, 1985. Paperback. 185 pp.

This self-help book, written by a counselor with 25 years experience, is a practical guide for couples who wish to stay together by being their own (not their spouse's) marriage counselors. Kargman states that marriage is a "living relationship with cycles of dormancy and rebirth;" she uses actual case histories to address behavior problems that cause conflict. The book emphasizes the importance of communication and outlines a "listening contract" to insure that each of us hears our partner's feelings. Its focus is on how we can use individual personality traits in alternative ways rather than altering them completely. The author claims that we can revive our marriages to meet both partners' goals if we work at it with respect and nurturing.

159. *Husbands and Wives: Exploring Marital Myths/Deepening Love and Desire.* Dr. Melvyn Kinder and Dr. Connell Cowan. New York: Crown Publishers, Random House, 1989. Paperback. 304 pp.

Kinder and Cowan present modern strategies and ideas for what they call "Self-Directed Marriage." They explain how traditional cultural forces have converged to create "marital myths." Couples subscribe to these myths and later encounter numerous problems as a result. The book strongly encourages friendship in marriage as a way to deepen intimacy and love. It offers help in: establishing renewed sexual excitement, learning to be less demanding, understanding how our expectations of each other and of our marriage affect the relationship, dealing with finances and jobs, resolving conflict more successfully, and warding off the spectre of infidelity.

160. *Husbands Wives & Sex: How One Partner Alone Can Change the Dynamics to Renew Sex, Romance and Intimacy.* **Doris Wild Helmering. Holbrook, MA: Bob Adams, Inc. Publishers, 1990. Hardcover. 197 pp.**

Helmering claims that differences between male and female personalities can deeply influence the sex lives of couples. Based on interviews with real people, her book offers four tests to help us identify our own as well as our mate's personality type. The author notes that unsatisfactory sex is generally the result of poor relating in other parts of the marriage. She provides guidelines, effective even when one spouse works at them alone, for "changing the dynamics" and enhancing intimacy. Topics include: female aversion to "passive aggressives" and "passive takers," male aversion to "caretakers" and "correctors," control and power issues, creating a conducive atmosphere for sex, and dissimilar views on intimacy and marriage.

161. *In Defense of Marriage.* **Art Carey. New York: Walker & Co., 1984. Hardcover. 158 pp.**

A sincere and instructive personal narrative by a man who calls himself "a born again husband," this book extols the virtues of a good marriage and offers advice for those seeking to improve their relationships. Carey uses his own progress from a failed to a successful marriage to suggest certain characteristics and qualities that can provide the best chances of success. These are intimacy and commitment based on "buddy love" or "loving companionship linked to trust." The book differentiates between being "in love" and genuine loving and also exposes the fallacies regarding the pleasures of sexual freedom.

162. *Inter-Cultural Marriage: Promises & Pitfalls.* **Dugan Romano. Yarmouth, ME: Intercultural Press, 1988. Paperback. 162 pp.**

With ten years of experience as a cross-cultural trainer and counselor, Romano offers clear, practical guidelines for the special set of problems encountered by couples in inter-cultural marriages. In these unions, widely divergent sets of rules and values may have become ingrained in each spouse for generations. Filled with examples from the lives of actual couples, this handbook attempts to analyze the barriers that give rise to problems and then suggests concrete ways for coping and negotiating differences. Areas discussed include: food and drink, language, religion, social class, attitudes toward achievement, male-female gender expectations, reactions to illness, sex, and issues revolving around child-rearing.

163. *The Intermarriage Handbook: A Guide for Jews and Christians.* **Judy Petsonk and Jim Remsen. New York: Arbor House, William Morrow, 1988. Hardcover. 416 pp.**

This handbook explores solutions to complex challenges occurring throughout the life span of Jews and Christians in mixed marriages. With the trend increasing, the authors hope to provide alternative guidelines to thorny issues arising between these two quite different religious traditions. Based on interviews with families and professionals, the book includes: practical and psychological matters, exercises to open up communication, case studies, and recommendations for problem-solving. The pull of separate cultures is seen as a cause of tension with compromise clearly a crucial skill. Additional topics covered are: the decision to marry, parents, "choosing a family style," children, holidays, sex, negotiating differences, divorce, death, and burial.

164. *Intimacy: Strategies for Successful Relationships.* **C. Edward Crowther, Ph.D. New York: A Dell Book, 1986. Paperback. 207 pp.**

Crowther believes that no other trait insures the survival of love more than intimacy. He sees this quality, while not easy to achieve, as attainable by all human beings. His is a step-by-step workbook with case studies and established techniques for: using our natural ability to be intimate, evaluating the closeness of our relationships, avoiding "emotional sabotage," finding new communication methods to show our love, and recognizing "burnout." Self-tests and suggested assignments are included. The book emphasizes the positive role stress can play in the continuing growth of intimacy if we do not "abuse" it but rather use it as a catalyst toward conflict resolution. Additional topics are: fears, "game playing," sex, forgiving, and necessary skills.

165. *Intimacy: The Need to Be Close. How the Need for Intimacy Influences Our Relationships, Life Choices, and Sense of Identity.* **Dan P. McAdams, Ph.D. New York: Doubleday, a Div. of Bantam Doubleday, 1989. Hardcover. 252 pp.**

This book analyzes the nature of intimacy in depth and probes the issues surrounding it all the way from infancy through adulthood. The author sees the attainment of genuine intimate relations as much more difficult than finding actual love itself. McAdams gives special emphasis to the various types of challenges and blocks to closeness that today's world presents us and offers guidance on breaking through the barriers. He notes that the need for intimacy is by no means universal but his research does reveal that a tie-in clearly exists between our "desire for intimacy" and our physical well-being.

Once we master this special mode of intimate connecting, the author feels we will have the potential to change all of our relationships immensely.

166. *Intimate Partners: Hidden Patterns in Love Relationships.* **Clifford J. Sager, M.D. and Bernice Hunt. New York: McGraw Hill Book Co., 1979. Hardcover. 194 pp.**

Sager outlines seven different behavioral styles—"equal, romantic, parental, childlike, rational, companionate, and parallel"—as a springboard to a detailed analysis of how these styles relate successfully or unsuccessfully to each other. Readers learn how to define their own images and true emotional needs. They can then compare these portraits to the examples given. The book discusses at length how "unfulfilled expectations" and "unspoken contracts" can exist secretly in one partner's mind, acting later as repeated and confusing sources of anxiety and conflict. Sager offers techniques for: devising a "couple covenant" for more open dialogue; increasing the likelihood of compromise; achieving greater intimacy and happiness; and building a love that can last.

167. *Intimate Partners: Patterns in Love and Marriage.* **Maggie Scarf. New York: Random House, 1987. Hardcover. 428 pp.**

Scarf has carefully researched intimacy in marriage and other male-female relationships along with studying the underlying patterns that make it work or fail. Her book goes beyond superficial analysis to examine in depth the kinds of inherited emotional baggage that influence each party. It then studies the effects this baggage has on personality, self-image, and the successful negotiation of problem areas. Compatibility issues are discussed as are: ways in which relationships develop and change, how our birth family influences our relationships, "emotional triangles," sex, power, control, and autonomy. Scarf also provides self-help exercises for couples to improve their communication abilities and their relating styles.

168. *Intimate Strangers: Men and Women Together.* **Lillian B. Rubin. New York: Harper & Row, 1983. Paperback. 222 pp.**

Built on extensive psychological research and writing, this book draws on the author's career in counseling as well as on hundreds of interviews with couples. Rubin sees male character as largely defined by a "need for separation." When combined with the female desire for connection, this juxtaposition produces a dynamic that the author calls "Intimate Strangers." In an effort to examine these basic differences in male-female relating patterns, Rubin reveals how both sexes crave intimacy but are often thwarted in achieving it. She studies all aspects of relationships from attitudes toward careers, children, and communication to problems and expectations regarding sexuality.

169. *Journey of the Heart: Intimate Relationships and the Path of Love.* **John Welwood, Ph.D. New York: HarperCollins, 1990. Hardcover. 220 pp.**

In the area of love, Welwood states that American society is undertaking something unique: unions based on equality and "partnership" as well as "sexual passion" and romance. He notes that survival needs (physical or financial) and societal sanctions no longer insure the continuity of relationships; we connect voluntarily and stay only if we are happy. If our culture succeeds in making these types of new relationships workable, Welwood sees us as contributing to the human evolutionary process and the end of male-female conflict. The book focuses on what the path to this exciting intimacy requires: openness, honesty, and a willingness to see differences as positive "opportunities" to learn, change, and deepen both ourselves and the relationship.

170. *Keeping Your Family Together When the World Is Falling Apart.* **Dr. Kevin Leman. New York: Delacorte Press, Bantam Doubleday Publ. Group, Inc., 1992. Hardcover. 320 pp.**

Leman offers new answers for solving common problems in family living and making home life more sacred and fulfilling for all. He believes it is critical for spouses to place each other and their family (including the extended unit) above all else. Such unity and cohesiveness, in his opinion, will be strong deterrents to contemporary problems such as drug abuse, increasing high school drop out rates, and divorce. The book gives special emphasis to "Reality Discipline Principles." Leman incorporates these principles in a common sense program to help guide every facet of our lives in a more positive direction. He feels his advice will help us deal with our "marriages, children, and careers" more successfully. Topics include: living by solid values, nurturing our partnerships, integrating differences, and handling stress.

171. *Lasting Love: How to Give It, How to Get It, How to Keep It.* **Joel D. Block, Ph.D. New York: Macmillan Publishing Co., Inc., 1982. Hardcover. 252 pp.**

Block emphasizes strengthening unity in relationships rather than glorifying the ego, which has received too much selfish attention in recent years. He says that strong, committed partnerships can be one of life's joys if we devote ourselves to the hard work required. As a start, his book includes a "Relationship-Enhancement Inventory" that allows couples to test three different areas of their marriages: "mutual support, communication, and conflict resolution." He says that the answers will reveal weaknesses couples can then work on through studying 15 "Relationship Principles" and applying proven concrete solutions. Readers can attack specific problems in small steps, testing their progress semiannually with checkups.

172. *Life Mates: The Love Fitness Program for a Lasting Relationship. The Secrets of Opening Up Greater Intimacy and Communication.* **Harold Bloomfield, M.D. and Sirah Vettese, Ph.D. New York: Signet Books, Penguin, 1989. Paperback. 284 pp.**

While modern human beings seem to be increasingly involved in physical fitness programs that require ongoing commitments of time and effort, these authors see few of us working out as diligently on our love relationships. Hence they have created this system of "emotional workouts," a series of lifelong practical exercises with which we can continually refine the skills essential to happy relationships. The book presents fitness tests to evaluate our strengths and weaknesses. Topics covered include: eliminating jealousy, rekindling passion, mastering the "heart talk" technique to improve intimate communication, dealing with pain and anger, affairs, developing "emotional energy," and myths about personal growth.

173. *Living, Loving & Learning.* **Leo Buscaglia, Ph.D. New York: Ballantine Books, a Div. of Random House, 1982. Paperback. 264 pp.**

Buscaglia is a charismatic and lively "professor of love." His book is a compilation of amusing and touching lectures given by him around the world from 1970–1981. It is intended for those who want enrich their lives by knowing love. Buscaglia states that he is simply sharing his own ideas on growth and love and not necessarily attempting to instruct. The profound joys of living simply and spontaneously with large amounts of touching, smiling, caring, giving, loving, and especially being human are all topics of discussion. Buscaglia feels that love can solve many of the world's problems and that apathy is a very negative force. He encourages us to be open, positive, connecting, forgiving, and focused on today and now rather than on tomorrow.

174. *Love: A Warm and Wonderful Book About the Largest Experience in Life.* **Leo Buscaglia. New York: Fawcett Crest, a Div. of CBS Publications, 1972. Paperback. 207 pp.**

An "outgrowth" of Professor Buscaglia's "Love Class," this book is not designed to be a scholarly or scientific work on the subject. Instead, it is Buscaglia's chance to give us some of his deceptively simple ideas: how to become more fully human through opening ourselves up to "real love" and how to communicate our loving feelings to each other. The author sees love as the "largest experience in the life of a human being." The book discusses:

what love really is, the importance of loving ourselves first, our deep human need for love, and the responsibilities and requirements that love imposes upon each of us. There is also heavy emphasis on capturing the beauty of every moment of life rather than living for the future.

175. *Love and Money.* **Sylvia Porter. New York: Wm. Morrow and Co., Inc., 1983. Hardcover. 249 pp.**

For the married, divorced, and dating, this factual guide discusses the inner dynamics of money and love in intimate relationships. Its goal is to show how to untangle and manage the problems. The author, famous for her work in money matters, sees communication as "critical to maintaining a happy balance" between love and money. Especially pertinent to the subject of divorce is chapter nine in which she discusses: costs, making the divorce work, obtaining financial and legal knowledge, "the second wife," insuring support and alimony payments, taxes, pensions and social security. For couples, there are suggestions included for evaluating the compatibility of attitudes toward money. For singles, Porter offers advice on structuring a prenuptial agreement.

176. *Love Cycles: The Science of Intimacy. Enhance Your Health, Well-Being and Sexual Life by Taking Control of Your Hormonal Rhythms.* **Winnifred B. Cutler, Ph.D. New York: Villard Books, 1991. Hardcover. 331 pp.**

Cutler, a 22-year student of the "reproductive system of women and the men who love them," has developed controversial theories about the crucial importance of "love cycles" as governors of our relationships. She states that hormonal flow and biological patterns, determined by the menstrual cycle of women, create regular rhythms with ups and downs. Her hypothesis is that these physiological changes in women directly affect the men with whom they are intimate. If couples understand and act in accordance with (rather than against) these rhythms, Cutler predicts their sex and love lives, health, longevity, and happiness will be greatly enhanced. The book also explores the "mystery of sex," male-female attraction, and the connection to cosmic forces.

177. *Love Is Letting Go of Fear: How to Find Peace of Mind and Happiness from Within.* **Gerold G. Jampolsky, M.D. Millbrae, CA: Celestial Arts, 1979. Paperback. 131 pp.**

This unusual little book, written by a psychiatrist, is based on another work, *A Course in Miracles.* It is full of readings and daily exercises aimed at bringing about inner peace and healing. Illustrated with simple but profound, cartoon-like drawings, the book proposes the basic theory that happiness comes from within ourselves and need not be affected by actions or events from the past that we may see as hurtful. It views forgiveness as crucial to our ability both to receive and give love and to live in the present. Jampolsky believes that we have a "choice of experiencing peace or conflict" and that "letting go of fear" will allow us to choose correctly. Part III contains 12 daily lessons aimed at "constructively transforming" our lives.

178. *Love Is Never Enough: How Couples Can Overcome Misunderstandings, Resolve Conflicts, and Solve Relationship Problems through Cognitive Therapy.* **Aaron T. Beck, M.D. New York: Harper & Row Publishers, 1988. Paperback. 415 pp.**

Love is Never Enough is grounded in the theory that the mental process of making judgments and decisions and the ways in which people interpret or misinterpret their partners' actions or words have a direct bearing on relationships. The difficulties that intimate partners experience are often based on "cognitive distortions," it asserts. The aim of "Cognitive Therapy" is to help couples refine these mental procedures in order to eliminate the growth of misunderstandings. Beck analyzes communication between partners and provides practical techniques for working together to solve problems rather than to attribute blame. He includes numerous questionnaires to diagnose trouble spots such as negative thinking, inflexibility, or rigid expectations.

179. *Love Is the Answer: Creating Positive Relationships.* **Gerold G. Jampolsky, M.D. and Diane V. Cirincione. New York: Bantam Book, 1990. Paperback. 242 pp.**

Love Is the Answer is a realistic handbook on how one can achieve and sustain well-being and, as a result, harmonious personal relationships. In the process, Jampolsky sees compassion and constructive interaction as very important. He states that one can accomplish "inner healing" by letting go of fear, blame, and hostility. It is possible to facilitate the process of dealing with unresolved and damaging hurts of the past by learning the power of forgiveness and the capacity to love others unconditionally. The book outlines "Seven Stepping Stones" to inner happiness and health and includes "15 Daily Lessons" for use as inspiration in the process.

180. *Love Secrets for a Lasting Relationship.* **Harold H. Bloomfield, M.D. with poetry by Natasha Josefowitz, Ph.D. New York: Bantam Books, 1992. Hardcover. 152 pp.**

Dr. Bloomfield has written this book for those of us in new or long-standing romantic relationships. It is comprised of 72 individual one page "love secrets" followed by practical advice and relevant poetry. Designed to assist couples in enriching their relationships and accomplishing change, the book operates from the premise that "love grows stronger with practice." Topics included are: respect; developing an enthusiastic and positive attitude; communicating what we really need; the benefits of arguing; accepting criticism; self-forgiveness; fitness; placing "love first;" feeling sexier; the role of fantasy; relaxing; creating a loving attitude and a "love nest;" and dealing with crisis, jealousy, and fatigue.

181. *Loving Each Other: The Challenge of Human Relationships.* **Leo F. Buscaglia, Ph.D. New York: Fawcett Columbine, 1984. Paperback. 208 pp.**

Buscaglia is committed to the belief that deep and truly loving relationships are critical for individuals as well as for society at large. Without such connections, he sees the world as "perpetuating isolation" which causes severe problems. His book addresses the lack of information available for learning what it really takes to make good relationships work. According to Buscaglia, intuition is not sufficient; numerous skills are required, which his book discusses. Viewing divorce and detachment as pain avoiders, the author suggests we "give relationships a chance," and that we value the kind of loving that promotes growth over personal desires for freedom and individualism. *Loving Each Other* also treats issues such as honesty, communication, forgiveness, and jealousy.

182. *Lucky in Love: The Secrets of Happy Couples and How Their Marriages Thrive.* **Catherine Johnson, Ph.D. New York: Viking, Publ. by the Penguin Group, 1992. Hardcover. 343 pp.**

As the basis for her book, Johnson interviewed 100 American couples married for at least seven years, ranging in age from 20 to 80 and representing all income levels and geographic locations. At least 60 portrayed themselves as "very happily married." Johnson sees her findings as most hopeful and as running contrary to popular opinion that marital happiness is not a "realistic" goal. In this book, she shows us exactly what qualities and factors helped these individuals stay "romantically and physically in love." Johnson highlights their intense mutual "excitement" for each other as well as their "idealization" of one another. Her goal is to help us improve our own intimate relationships.

183. *The Magic of Conflict: Turning a Life of Work into a Work of Art.* **Thomas F. Crum. New York: Simon & Schuster, 1987. Hardcover. 254 pp.**

Crum's novel approach to conflict is based on "aikido," the Japanese martial art. In his opinion, society has long equated conflict with "contest" rather than "challenge," implying that one party must lose. The premise is that, since the world is an "extension" of ourselves, harmony and peace will thrive only if everyone wins. Failing to recognize this oneness, he maintains, creates our lack of fulfillment. The book provides principles and exercises that will teach one to no longer fear, avoid, or fight conflict. It says rather that everyone should welcome it as a chance to use their creative powers and see the world differently. Crum contends that these moments will be growth opportunities and will instead be considered "dances of energy." The key, the book emphasizes, is to redefine our problems as "stepping stones."

184. *Making It Together As a Two Career Couple.* **Marjorie Hansen Shaevitz and Morton H. Shaevitz. Boston, MA: Houghton Mifflin Co., 1979. Hardcover. 282 pp.**

The authors of this book are a two-career couple with four children and a nearly full-time professional emphasis on the topic. During seven years of research, the authors studied the complex problems encountered by middle class couples in balancing multiple demands without hurting their relationships. Their focus is on practical suggestions that can help couples constructively apply new approaches to difficult issues. Two-career families, the Shaevitzes claim, can have great rewards provided couples cooperate with a problem-solving mentality designed to address their specific concerns. This guidebook is meant to be a reference as each new problem arises. Topics include: communication, overload, household responsibilities, child care, finances, role changes, and career demands.

185. *Managing the Equity Factor: Or "After All I've Done for You."* **Richard C. Huseman, Ph.D. and John D. Hatfield, Ph.D. Boston, MA: Houghton Mifflin Co., 1989. Hardcover. 113 pp.**

Huseman and Hatfield's principal audience includes business people, couples in intimate relationships, or those individuals in general who are trying to improve their interactions with others. Their book is based on a simple but powerful premise: "the equity factor." In other words, we are pleased with our relationships if there is some basic equality between what we give and what we get. The authors call this mentality keeping an "equity score." Its extremes make us feel either "over-rewarded" or "under-rewarded," they say. Being "under-rewarded" can cause stress, negative behavior, or low productivity. The book offers guidelines for achieving and maintaining a successful balance by learning how to help everyone in the equation win. One motto to remember is that we all want to receive as well as give.

186. *Marital Choices: Forecasting, Assessing and Improving a Relationship.* **William J. Lederer. New York: W.W. Norton & Co., Inc., 1981. Hardcover. 262 pp.**

Marital Choices is a practical handbook with a holistic perspective. It is for readers who wish to improve the quality of their relationships. Lederer's book outlines a five-week program for acquiring the skills necessary to increase marital satisfaction without the use of outside counseling. The importance of being able to detect certain physical conditions, which can be sources of problems, is a distinctively unusual element. Part One concentrates on behavioral and psychological exercises for couples, some radical, and Part Two studies illnesses and physical conditions that can impact the dynamics of relationships. Equal rights for both partners are stressed.

187. *Marriage Is for Loving.* **Muriel James. Reading, MA: Addison-Wesley Publishing, 1979. Paperback. 254 pp.**

James has developed a realistic guide with exercises, case histories, and descriptions of her own experiences for couples interested in enhancing their "emotional, intellectual, and sexual intimacy." The book is divided into three parts and encourages us to look at the past, present, and future of our marriages. This kind of analysis enables us to study the strengths, weaknesses, and formative influences on our unions in order to "turn dreams into reality" today. Nurturing intimacy with large doses of tender, loving care is of prime consideration. James examines different views of marriage, new variations for the future, and ways in which each partner might satisfy fundamental needs for commitment while retaining independence and security.

188. *The Marriage Maintenance Manual: How to Get into It and How to Keep It Going.* **Clara G. Livsey, M.D. New York: Dial Press, 1977. Hardcover. 269 pp.**

This family therapist views marriage positively. She de-emphasizes negatives and constant ventilation of problems by concentrating on things that promote pleasure and enjoyment. Illustrated with guidelines, case studies, quizzes, and charts, her laid-back approach views individuals realistically rather than ideally. Married couples as well as singles who are seeking help in evaluating future mates, are the audience. Livsey calls marriage our most profoundly meaningful relationship, a "place to relax," and to let down our guard. She sees self-acceptance as indispensable to its success. Topics include: the advantages of marriage, handling boredom and stress, sex and infidelity, and relatives. Many healing strategies are offered.

189. *The Marriage Map: Understanding and Surviving the Stages of Marriage.* **Maxine Rock. Atlanta, GA: Peachtree Publications, Ltd., 1986. Paperback. 282 pp.**

Rock set out to analyze the characteristics of happy and successful couples for whom marriage was a "top priority." She therefore spent three years interviewing 100+ people (ages 19-78) representative of the entire nation and 12 marriage experts. The results of her study concluded that all marriages go through seven overlapping but distinct stages, which bring unique challenges. The author believes that if couples are aware of the "dynamics" of the stage they are in, they can work at resolving problems expected in that stage, take comfort in the fact that they are not abnormal, and resist the temptation to divorce. Two separate sections treat the reasons for marriage and its stages. Elaborate case studies illustrate successful behavior patterns.

190. *Marriage Without B.S.: It's All Here for You. Straight Talk from a Midwest Psychiatrist.* **John D. Baldwin, M.D. New York: Wyden Books, distrib. by Simon & Schuster, 1979. Hardcover. 200 pp.**

Baldwin writes as a psychiatrist with a failed marriage and a thriving remarriage. His straightforward book, illustrated with numerous case examples and dialogues, contains useful questionnaires: 20 questions on evaluating the feeling of our marriages, 29 on testing our "marriage quotient," and 30 on our marriage maintenance ability. The focus is on improving our relationships and getting rid of outmoded traditional views that Baldwin considers B.S. Topics covered include: preoccupation with sex, equality of the sexes, fair fighting, dealing with anger, dependency needs, security requirements, competition, intellectual compatibility, and evaluating the state of our own relationships.

191. *Married People: Staying Together in the Age of Divorce.* **Francine Klagsbrun. New York: Bantam Books, 1985. Hardcover. 320 pp.**

This book is based on interviews and extensive research with ordinary couples successfully married for more than 15 years. The approach is practical and pro-marriage. Klagsbrun is, however, deeply aware of the conflicts and struggles inherent in maintaining a fruitful union. Suggesting there are no "quick fixes," she sees "trust and compromise" as two qualities critically important for the development of mature intimacy and happiness. Topics include: the rising divorce rate, sex in and out of marriage, spousal competitiveness, the impact of friends and family, the pros and cons of having children, effects of infertility, career disappointments, and the potential for lasting good sex. A good marriage is by no means an impossibility according to this author.

192. *Masters and Johnson on Sex and Human Loving.* **William H. Masters, Virginia E. Johnson and Robert C. Kolodny. Boston, MA: Little, Brown and Co., 1982. Hardcover. 598 pp.**

Having conducted hundreds of interviews and studied the most recent scholarly research on the topic of love, these well-known authors have provided an extensive survey of the intricate issues surrounding the realm of human sexuality. They include psychological, social, and biological topics. The goal is to show that a deepened awareness of sexual issues will improve the overall character of our intimate relationships. Problems discussed include: "sexual burnout," "sexual victimization," diminished sexual interest, and difficulties in developing and sustaining intimacy. The book contains a variety of practical and useful guidelines for establishing communication regarding sexual issues and creating a more satisfying partnership.

193. *Men Are from Mars. Women Are from Venus: A Practical Guide for Improving Communication and Getting What You Want in Your Relationships.* **John Gray, Ph.D. New York: HarperCollins Publishers, 1992. Hardcover. 286 pp.**

This book provides a new perspective on male-female cooperation. It encourages partners to listen to each other as if they are from "different planets," speak different languages and require different kinds of emotional nourishment. According to Gray, "Martians" (men) find it hard to give and they respond best when they are "trusted, accepted, appreciated, and needed." "Venusians" (women) want to talk and feel happiest when they are cherished, understood, and respected. The book gives a detailed outline of gender differences, explicit examples, and tested solutions for effective listening and dialogue. Gray emphasizes that neither sex is superior and that through grasping our core differences, we can avoid conflict and reach a deeply rewarding love. Sharing our feelings in "love letters" is stressed.

194. *Men, Women and Relationships: Making Peace with the Opposite Sex.* **John Gray, Ph.D. Hillsboro, OR: Beyond Words Publishing, 1990. Paperback. 306 pp.**

Gray's thesis is that today's constantly changing expectations and sex roles demand fresh and creative approaches to male-female interactions. He believes that new innovative behaviors will help to establish mutually supportive love relationships. The book thus offers guidance on developing healthy self-esteem as a foundation, strengthening and polishing communication skills, and learning to let go of past hurts and resentments. It also studies the effects of stress in a relationship and how men cope with these factors very differently from women. Gray provides guidelines to help committed individuals find the love they want.

195. *The Mirages of Marriage: A Profoundly Original Look at the Marital Relationship with No-Nonsense Procedures to Help Solve Its Problems.* **William J. Lederer and Don D. Jackson, M.D. New York: W.W. Norton & Co., Inc., 1968. Hardcover. 473 pp.**

These authors favor marriage but believe that the institution in America is suffering. They propose that couples can keep their relationships in balance and healthy by themselves if they are willing to commit to the necessary rehabilitative work. The book first examines the state of marriage in 60s America, concentrating on "false assumptions" and unrealistic "anachronisms." It then progresses to a description of the techniques that couples can employ to heal discord and conflict, making the union more fulfilling to both. Topics include: evaluating our marriages and identifying problems, the family as an "interacting communications network," seeking help, and repairing the union or ending it gracefully if necessary.

196. *The New Male-Female Relationship.* **Herb Goldberg, Ph.D. New York: A Signet Book, Publ. by Penguin, 1983. Paperback. 289 pp.**

Goldberg writes about how men and women can rise above the conventional fixed "stereotypes" that make it difficult for them to really talk to each other and be themselves. His book praises the virtues of relationships where the struggles and disagreements that inevitably occur are vehicles for an ongoing development and strengthening of closeness. He sees these partnerships as unions of "best friends," which are satisfying as well as challenging. The book offers guidelines to facilitate the creation of such relationships. Goldberg covers such areas as: "mixed signals" given out by both sexes; characteristics of successful relationships; and working toward easier, less contrived, and more spontaneous ways of interrelating.

197. *No Fault Marriage: The New Technique of Self-Counseling and What It Can Do to Help You.* **Marcia Lasswell and Norman M. Lobsenz. Garden City, NY: Doubleday & Co., 1976. Hardcover. 252 pp.**

No Fault Marriage contends that marriages undergo many changes as they pass through inevitable cycles of conflict and stress. The authors claim that couples can pinpoint differences, resolve them, and achieve greater happiness if they master the skills of becoming their own therapists. Their book thus includes questions with which partners can evaluate their marriages and critique their individual decision-making and "love-styles." These checklists lay the groundwork for the all important need to compromise rather than to win. Lasswell and Lobsenz see "giving and receiving emotional satisfactions" as the foundation of healthy relationships today. Topics also covered are: failed promises, using differences as strengths, positive criticism, sex and intimacy, and communication.

198. *Nobody's Perfect: Advice for Blame-Free Living.* **Dr. Joy Browne. New York: Simon & Schuster, 1988. Hardcover. 334 pp.**

Browne has written a guide on how to enjoy a happier life with more relaxed and satisfying relationships. Her belief is that this can become possible through de-emphasizing excessively perfectionistic expectations of ourselves and others. As a media psychologist, she sees Americans as being bombarded by the pressure to improve themselves in every way and thus as basically insecure. Browne suggests that such need for perfection is frequently accompanied by faultfinding and blame assigning, which is extremely hurtful to personal relationships. Her book answers relevant questions in each of five sections relating to "family, friends-lovers, marriage, children and work." The tone is light and often humorous but serious when it comes to the goal of making us more tolerant and accepting of our own and others' human failings.

199. *Nobody's Perfect: How to Give Criticism and Get Results.* **Dr. Hendrie Weisinger and Norman M. Lobsenz. Los Angeles, CA: Stratford Press, 1981. Hardcover. 246 pp.**

These authors hope to redefine "criticism" by removing the automatic negative connotations of destructive attack. They have developed guidelines for using "positive criticism" to produce "positive results." In clear steps, the book reveals exactly how to express criticism so that one can facilitate a "beneficial two-person interaction" and thus enhance our relationships. Weisinger and Lobsenz encourage readers to criticize out of a desire to help the other party rather than to express anger. Topics covered include: how to criticize and be understood, appropriate timing, eliminating harmful techniques, rephrasing, "evaluating the cost/reward factor," sexual criticism, dealing with children, and avoiding excessive self-criticism.

200. *One Question That Can Save Your Marriage.* **Harry P. Dunne, Ph.D. New York: A Perigee Book, The Putnam Publishing Group, 1991. Paperback. 124 pp.**

Dunne's work with troubled couples helped him discover a powerful question that often led partners toward rewarding positive improvements when all else failed. That question, "What is it like to be married to me?," seemed to focus individuals on looking for change within themselves rather than in others. Part I offers concrete guidelines on how we can go deep within ourselves for answers to this question. Dunne contends that doing so will empower each of us to blame others less and analyze our own shortcomings and problematic character traits more. Part II looks at more specific issues such as fighting, communicating, negotiating, feelings, and intimacy. Case studies and numerous probe questions help us identify our hidden feelings and work with them constructively.

201. *One to One: Understanding Personal Relationships.* **Theodore Isaac Rubin, M.D. New York: Viking Press, 1983. Hardcover. 242 pp.**

"To be is to relate" is Rubin's central thesis in this book. He focuses on how to better interpret the dynamics of intimate relationships in order to recognize our strengths and weaknesses and correct them. Through case histories, the author illustrates three fundamental personality types. He then outlines the dangerous "locks" we can "force" our behavior into resulting in conflict or unhappiness. Constructive and honest interaction can also be improved through the use of a "therapeutic game," which Rubin discusses at the end. Other topics covered include: the need of individuals for approval, success, and stimulation, money and sex issues as sources of conflict, and preconceived ideas on sex-roles.

202. *Open Marriage: A New Life Style for Couples.* **Nena O'Neill and George O'Neill. New York: Avon Books, a Div. of the Hearst Corp., 1972. Paperback. 286 pp.**

The O'Neill's 1972 best seller offers a controversial, even startling, new marriage concept. The authors' extensive research found a pervasive discontent with tradition and a growing trend toward experimentation. They saw rising divorce rates with marriage becoming increasingly unpopular. The O'Neills thus pose alternatives through which partners can restructure outdated, "stifling, limited" and conventional relationships opening them up into "honest, undemanding and joyful" ones. While the sexual freedom suggested might not be workable for many today, the independence advocated could be useful. Concepts discussed include: "trust, liking, role flexibility, individual freedom and growth, and love and sex without jealousy."

203. *Passages: Predictable Crises of Adult Life.* **Gail Sheehy. New York: A Bantam Book, E.P. Dutton & Co. Inc., 1974. Paperback. 560 pp.**

Passages analyzes adult life cycles, something no one had done for adults (ages 18–50) as "Gesell and Spock did for children." Through 115 stories of middle class people, Sheehy studies predictable phases in life and their "critical turning points." In her opinion, the 20s, 30s, 40s and beyond are full of many changes in both personalities and sexual needs. The author maintains that if crises are understood, we can use them as catalysts for positive change rather than sources of conflict. Following life's stages chronologically, Sheehy notes that both sexes take the same "steps" but with distinctly different "developmental rhythms." The best seller's goal is to: study changes within individuals, compare men and women, and examine the "asynchronous patterns" of couples.

204. *Passages of Marriage: Five Growth Stages that Will Take Your Marriage to Greater Intimacy and Fulfillment.* **Dr. Frank and Mary Alice Minirth, Dr. Brian and Dr. Deborah Newman, Dr. Robert and Susan Hemfelt. Nashville, TN: Thomas Nelson Publishers, 1991. Hardcover. 335 pp.**

The basic premise of this work is that all relationships must go through five passages before they can achieve their true potential. The authors, doctors at the Minerth-Meier Clinic, are people whose individual marriages represent different stages in the process. They include a test so that couples may identify their own situations. The goal of the book is to act as a constant resource guide for couples who want to enrich their experience within the relationship. Critical to the process is understanding the potential of each phase and successfully solving inevitable problems that will arise. The book divides the stages at approximately the 3rd, 11th, 21st, and 31st years of the marriage and focuses on such areas as: idealism, "hidden agendas," identity issues, and losses.

205. *Peer Marriage: How Love Between Equals Really Works.* **Pepper Schwartz. New York: Free Press, 1994. Hardcover. 205 pp.**

An author, sociologist and researcher, Schwartz offers an analysis of the inner workings of partnerships where spouses are equals. Her book discusses both the benefits and the "costs" of these relationships that dramatically differ from traditional unions especially in the areas of mutual respect, finances, parenting, household duties, sex and power. Through in-depth interviews, Schwartz provides insight into the intense friendship, fairness and empathy these couples share in their "collaboration of love and labor." She reports that peer marriages eliminate the "provider role" which too often creates an imbalance of power. The couples who qualified were mostly middle class, contained one divorced partner about 50 percent of the time, and granted equal importance to the work of each member. The book hopes to show others the way.

206. *The Pleasure Bond: A New Look at Sexuality and Commitment.* **William H. Masters and Virginia E. Johnson. Boston, MA: Little Brown & Co., 1970. Hardcover. 268 pp.**

Masters and Johnson are experts in the study of sex. With their clinical and research expertise, they hope to bring readers to an improved understanding of sex and new ways of solving marital and sexual problems. Their book notes that false expectations, ignorance, and the inability to communicate openly about sex can make couples lose the excitement they once felt. They propose that sexual "knowledge, comfort, and choice" can strengthen unions and keep them loving, nurturing, and vital. Masters and Johnson also state that the emotional side of sex is crucial in creating the ultimate "pleasure bond." Based on five group discussions on the topic of sexual satisfaction, *The Pleasure Bond* also covers: the importance of sexual equality, the role of "loyalty and trust," and revising childhood definitions of sex roles.

207. *The Power of Unconditional Love: 21 Guidelines for Beginning, Improving, and Changing Your Most Meaningful Relationships.* **Ken Keyes, Jr. Coos Bay, OR: Love Line Books, 1990. Paperback. 228 pp.**

This author has written a book that is straightforward and full of illustrations and guidelines. Its premise is that all human beings are "made for loving" but much too frequently they gravitate toward inferior "substitutes" in the form of negative addictive behaviors. Keyes warns that these highly undesirable and dangerous behaviors tend to limit understanding, friendliness and openness. The book emphasizes the building of self-confidence and the development of self-nurturing skills in order to break down barriers and facilitate openness.

208. *Prescription for a Quality Relationship: Clear, Specific Strategies for Turning Relationship Stresses into Opportunities for More Love and Intimacy.* **Allen Fay, M.D. New York: A Fireside Book by Simon & Schuster, 1988. Paperback. 227 pp.**

Fay's goal is to help both single and married people learn useful skills to quickly improve the day-to-day functioning of their relationships. "Communication psychology" is the basis for his ideas. His book provides clear, constructive "prescriptions" to be implemented by the couple as a team or even by one spouse alone. It encourages couples to be aware and creative and to watch out for the "54 identifiable traps" that can undermine their happiness. Fay outlines these traps (e.g., "threatening," "dramatic behavior," "getting even") briefly in one or two pages in Part I. Questions then follow. Suggested "tools" in Part II include techniques like "collaborating," "whispering," "contracts," and exercises to increase our affection.

209. *The Psychology of Romantic Love: What Love Is, Why Love Is Born, Why It Sometimes Grows, Why It Sometimes Dies.* **Nathaniel Branden, Ph.D. Los Angeles, CA: J.P. Tarcher, Inc., 1980. Hardcover. 210 pp.**

Branden defines romantic love as a wonderful adventure in which one can become deeply attached to another person spiritually, emotionally, and sexually. His book delves into what romantic love really is and examines the topic historically, sociologically, philosophically, and psychologically. He reveals how, contrary to the opinion of many, romantic love can flourish and be a vehicle to uncommon happiness, heightened personal growth, and self-understanding. The book outlines the preconditions for this unique kind of connection and the process necessary to achieve and maintain it.

210. *Rediscovering Love.* **Willard Gaylin, M.D. New York: Viking Penguin, Inc., 1986. Hardcover. 288 pp.**

This author writes about romantic love and its vital importance in a world that seems to have succumbed to satisfying the selfish needs of "being loved" rather than giving love. He views love as a quintessential experience in life; it adds unequalled meaning and pleasure if allowed to flourish, something that modern existence has worked against. Gaylin traces the causes of the current lack of proper loving. He also offers thoughts on how to bring creative romance and pleasure back into our lives and develop our full capacity to love. Illustrated with ideas from some of our most outstanding writers, the book discusses the nature of healthy love and how the experience can be given more prominence.

211. *RelationShift: The Guide to Building Better Relationships.* **Kathryn Dale Perrett, M.A. Greensboro, NC: Tudor Publishers, 1989. Paperback. 187 pp.**

Perret focuses on exercises that will enable us to "shift our familiar ways of relating" and thus find deeper personal happiness and stronger interpersonal bonds. The premise is that any interaction includes pleasure and pain. Rather than shun the pain, we should see difficulties as challenges that us offer a chance to grow and develop our self-awareness. The author presents "observations" and recommended exercises in an unclinical manner. Her practical suggestions include: working on our relationship with ourselves and assuming responsibility for ourselves to improve success with others, ending the quest for the perfect mate, leaving bad relationships less painfully, improving communication, and getting the love we want with "honest commitment."

212. *A Return to Love: Reflections on the Principles of A Course in Miracles.* **Marianne Williamson. New York: Harper & Collins Publishing Co., 1992. Hardcover. 260 pp.**

Moved by the "self-study program of spiritual psychotherapy" in the book, *A Course in Miracles*, Williamson advocates a return to the kind of innocence, softness, and spirituality we all had as children. At that time, she observes, our self-concepts were not impaired nor were we taught to feel inferior, fearful, "separate from others," and competitive. The book sees the expression of a loving attitude as a way to solve the many problems human beings have in relating to one another both personally and professionally. Williamson proposes that we unburden ourselves of fear and ingrained negative mind sets. Her conclusion is that we should go back to a childlike openness in order to make "practical application" of our love and to enjoy improved health as a by-product.

213. *The Road Less Traveled: A New Psychology of Love, Traditional Values, and Spiritual Growth.* **M. Scott Peck, M.D. New York: A Touchstone Book, Simon & Schuster, 1978. Paperback. 316 pp.**

This best seller discusses the fundamental character of healthy loving relationships and their connection to mental and spiritual growth. Peck states that life is undeniably difficult. His position is that the way in which we confront and resolve our problems determines whether we will grow through self-understanding and thereby attain ultimate happiness. The author believes that attempts to avoid the suffering attached to problem-solving can create even greater stress and result in stagnation. Topics included are: the vital connection of mental and spiritual growth, the nature of romantic love, recognizing genuine compatibility, how dependency differs from love, achieving independence, developing sensitivity as a parent, and understanding our spirituality.

214. *The Road to Intimacy: Beyond Codependence. How to Form and Enjoy Healthy Relationships with Others—and with Yourself.* **Catherine Solange, Ph.D. New York: Warner Books, Inc., 1990. Paperback. 245 pp.**

Written primarily for those committed to recovering from codependence, this book offers practical suggestions for building healthy relationships. It shows that in sound relationships, partners possess self-sufficiency, inner peace, and "interdependence" rather than unhealthy dependence and attachment. Full of actual case illustrations, the book is a methodical guide with practical ideas, strategies, and examples of interactions upon which to measure our own relationships. Beginning with descriptions of functional and dysfunctional people and behaviors, it then moves into two sections: laying the groundwork for "interdependence" and a "roadmap" for learning how to develop more "functional" partnerships.

215. *Second Honeymoon: A Pioneering Guide for Reviving the Mid-Life Marriage.* **Dr. Sonya Rhodes with Susan Schneider. New York: Wm. Morrow and Co., Inc., 1992. Hardcover. 287 pp.**

This is a unique study of crises confronting marriages in mid-life when drastic changes can occur with the departure of children, financial instability, illness, job insecurity, infidelity etc. With previous roles removed, identity is now in question. Seen as especially significant is the tendency for men to become more "affiliative" in mid-life while women become more independent—a distinct reversal. The book describes "high risk" couples and behaviors so that we can learn how to preserve rather than end our relationships. It offers specific guidelines for dealing creatively with new problems and solving them positively. Rhodes and Schneider emphasize renewal through the "dynamic cycle" of conflict and healing, not withdrawal.

216. *The Secret of Staying in Love: How to Save Your Marriage through Building Self-Esteem and Opening Lines of Communication.* **John Powell, S.J. Niles, IL: Argus Communications, 1974. Paperback. 188 pp.**

Powell believes we are all capable of "celebrating life and love" and reaching our full human potential, though he laments that only ten percent of couples actually do. He sees the primary stumbling block as not loving ourselves enough to participate in the joy of loving others. His book thus stresses the critical need to build strong self-esteem as a foundation. Another theory is that the secret of loving and staying in love lies in developing true communication and honestly sharing one's innermost feelings. Good relationships, according to Powell, require an ongoing commitment to maintain that openness. The last section of his book offers 40 detailed questions designed to improve mutual understanding and intimacy.

217. *The Seven Marriages of Your Marriage: How Couples Can Make Love Last by Understanding and Managing the Many Marriages—and Divorces—in Every Committed Relationship.* **Mel Krantzler, Ph.D. and Patricia B. Krantzler. San Francisco, CA: Harper, a Div. of HarperCollins Publishers, 1992. Hardcover. 249 pp.**

This is a book for single, divorced, or married people who want to improve their relationship dynamics. It suggests that every marriage, rather than experiencing various stages, contains seven very different "mini marriages." Each, the authors say, has changed needs and requires new skills, compromises, and approaches to solve inevitable crises. The Krantzlers see couples who fail to identify these "marriages" as needlessly divorcing only to find similar problems with new mates. It is the book's belief that recreating our relationship each time and "divorcing (ourselves) of outmoded patterns" revitalizes our unions and prevents *actual* divorce. Some of the issues seen as key are: expectations, careers, mid-life, 50s uncertainty, post-retirement, and grief due to death.

218. *Sex Begins in the Kitchen: Because There's Company in the Living Room.* **Dr. Kevin Leman. New York: Dell Publishing, 1981. Paperback. 178 pp.**

As a well-known psychologist, Leman shows us how to have a richer, more rewarding emotional and physical relationship with our spouses. He sees good sex as a "natural culmination" of events that have occurred throughout the day. Such events are shows of affection, acts of thoughtfulness, and moments that show we truly care about each other. Leman believes that what we do rather than what we say is largely responsible for creating a high level of intimacy. Topics discussed include: hints and signs of impending problems, how birth order affects our partnerships, how to parent effectively while putting intimacy with our partner first, how to cope with conflict, and how to eliminate destructive "game-playing."

219. *Staying in Love: Reinventing Marriage and Other Love Relationships.* **Dr. Norton F. Kristy. New York: Jove Publications, Inc., 1980. Paperback. 247 pp.**

Kristy writes a guide for "reinventing" marriages and revitalizing our love lives. He advocates creating a "contract" with our lover in order to develop more appropriate relating patterns. This he believes will build intimacy rather than allowing neglect to kill the relationship. Using case histories, the book makes suggestions about how to: improve sex life and communication, understand marital games, and deal with jealousy, infidelity, and anger. Numerous solutions are offered for common problems such as repeating previous mistakes. A "State of Your Union Questionnaire" helps readers evaluate their own relationships. Kristy also examines radical alternatives such as swinging and swapping and the "roommate" concept for angry partners.

220. *Staying Together: Marriages That Work.* **Patricia O'Brien. New York: Random House, 1977. Hardcover. 240 pp.**

A Washington correspondent and interviewer of numerous couples, O'Brien focuses this study on the unique characteristics of six happy and successful marriages of 12+ years each. She believes that marriage is not for everyone. She does state, however, that singles are deprived of a sense of "continuity and a shared purpose" and that marriage, in no way, needs to signify the end of our special and individual selves. All the couples examined possess an ability to preserve their own space but also value the other's security as highly as their own. Qualities looked at include: the significance of honesty, flexibility, and shared interest in one other, the absence of boredom, and the importance of conflict resolution, sex, fidelity, and children.

221. *Struggle for Intimacy: Learning What Healthy Relationships Are and How to Achieve Them.* **Janet G. Woititz. Deerfield Beach, FL: Health Communications, 1985. Paperback. 101 pp.**

This national best seller looks at the unique challenges faced by adult children of alcoholics as well as others who have grown up with dysfunctional behavior patterns in their childhood homes. It attempts to describe the most important characteristics of stable and healthy relationships. The author's goal is to show how to develop sound unions by changing self-defeating habits and learning new, healthier ways to communicate and interact. Woititz discusses the reasons we choose certain mates as well as the role and impact of substance abuse and codependency in problematic relationships.

222. *Super Marriage: Overcoming the Predictable Crises of Married Life.* **Harvey L. Ruben, M.D. New York: Bantam Books, 1986. Hardcover. 261 pp.**

Ruben's goal is to help couples find the best kind of marriage, a loving bond grounded in "equality, mature intimacy, trust, communication, and romance." He estimates that only ten percent of all marriages attain this high quality. Since passages of intense crisis are inevitable between the various stages of every marriage, he shows couples how to employ "positive, problem-solving techniques" to settle difficulties. The resolved dilemma will then be a stimulus for even greater levels of happiness and stability. Citing numerous case histories, Ruben illustrates mistakes partners frequently make. Topics include: stress issues, money and work, interacting with friends and relatives, sex, raising children, and coping with illness and change.

223. *That's Not What I Meant: How Conversational Style Makes or Breaks Relationships.* **Deborah H. Tannen, Ph.D. New York: Ballantine, a Div. of Random House, 1986. Paperback. 214 pp.**

An internationally acclaimed expert on linguistics and communication, Tannen analyzes the dynamics of everyday language in relationships. Her premise is that communication, by its very nature, is "cross-cultural" because of differing genders, backgrounds, ages, and personalities. The book reveals how harmful misunderstandings, though unintentional, can occur and snowball "cumulatively" as time goes on. Recognizing the basic differences in our personal styles can help us examine how our use of language deeply impacts the success of our relationships. Tannen believes that learning how to "say what we mean" and changing how we interpret or speak to each other can often save marriages and put us in better control of a quality existence.

224. *The Triangle of Love: Intimacy, Passion, Commitment.* **Robert J. Sternberg. New York: Basic Books, Inc. Publishers, 1987. Hardcover. 319 pp.**

Sternberg's book embodies the latest scientific research on love as well as practical tools to use for "creating and sustaining" it. The author describes the dynamics of this pleasurable emotion as the triangular interplay of "intimacy, passion, and commitment." He contends that relationships differ based on how strong any one of these ingredients is and they thrive according to the similarities of our personal triangles. Intimacy is seen as particularly critical to happiness. The book examines: what love is made of, how it grows, how it differs from "liking," what role "attraction" plays, and how love can be misdirected in addiction. Case histories reveal the changes couples undergo as time passes. A "love scale" is included to permit readers to assess the extent of their love.

225. *Warm Hearts & Cold Cash: The Intimate Dynamics of Families and Money.* **Marcia Millman. New York: Free Press, a Div. of Macmillan, Inc., 1991. Hardcover. 191 pp.**

Warm Hearts & Cold Cash treats the complex question of how the general and specific handling of money issues affects a wide range of interactions within a family unit. The book examines money as an expression of love and approval and also as a vehicle used for punishment, threat, rebellion, or expressing anger. In addition, it studies money as a source of power, control, bonding, trust, freedom, and competition and thus as a factor in creating serious problems in each of these areas. Millman discusses the too often unpleasant facts about using money as substitutes for emotions. He encourages unselfishness and honesty to improve relationships.

226. *What Every Woman Ought to Know About Love & Marriage.* **Dr. Joyce Brothers. New York: Simon & Schuster, 1984. Hardcover. 335 pp.**

Brothers follows a relationship from courtship to marriage. Her book provides advice and numerous checklists for finding and keeping the right partner and overcoming life's challenges in order to remain happy for the long term. It analyzes the fundamental characteristics of successful marriages along with strategies for: determining compatibility, solving sexual and financial problems, preventing and dealing with infidelity (especially office romances), and enhancing intimate relating. Difficult turning points, earmarked as knotty issues, include: cohabitation, children, in-laws and relatives, and careers. Brothers sees women as the real caretakers of marriages and cautions them to "beware of comfortable familiarity."

227. *What Love Asks of Us: Solutions to the Challenge of Making Love Work.* **Nathaniel Branden with Devers Branden. New York: Bantam Books, 1983. Paperback. 298 pp.**

Branden has created a "guide to finding love, keeping love, and making love grow." His underlying belief is that we must understand what love consists of if we really expect it to endure. Unlike some other authors, this writer sees romantic love as attainable and one of the most exhilarating experiences in which human beings can participate. Providing positive answers and practical techniques for the most common problems faced by couples, Branden covers such topics as: the struggles of women, dealing with the demands of relatives, sexual values and compatibility, loving two people at once, jealousy, fidelity, communicating, "sabotaging love," work vs. love issues, and romance in the aging relationship.

228. *Why Men Don't Get Enough Sex and Women Don't Get Enough Love: With a Reassuring Ten Step Great Love, Great Sex Program to Transform Your Relationship— and Your Life.* **Jonathan Kramer, Ph.D. and Diane Dunaway. New York: Pocket Star Books, a Div. of Simon & Schuster, 1990. Paperback. 364 pp.**

Kramer and Dunaway examine male and female differences with regard to the underlying attitudes toward sex and love issues. The authors' hope is that by truly understanding and fulfilling each other's most intimate needs and desires, couples will find greater satisfaction and excitement in both of these vital areas. They see cultural conditioning as the cause of the widespread problem of men who can't openly express emotion and affection, especially to their female partners who desperately crave it. This step-by-step guide attempts to show individuals and couples the ways in which they can strengthen their intimate relationships, have more fun, and bring much needed romance into their lives.

229. *Work and Love.* **Jay B. Rohrlich, M.D. New York: Harmony Books, a Div. of Crown Publ., 1980. Paperback. 254 pp.**

Rohrlich writes as a Wall Street psychiatrist with a wide range of clients involved in legal and financial occupations. His book is based on the belief that success in either of the two important areas of work and love requires completely opposite strategies and approaches. He analyzes working and loving not as activities but rather as attitudes and "states of mind." In an attempt to guide the reader toward developing a healthy balance between career, family, and leisure activities, Rohrlich studies the fundamental characteristics of these uniquely different states of mind. The book is especially designed for those whose business lives are thriving but whose intimate relationships are far less than satisfactory.

For additional help on "Trying to Save the Marriage First," see also all books in chapters 5 & 6 as well as book numbers:

2: *Being a Woman*

4: *Bradshaw On: The Family*

5: *Career & Conflict*

9: *Don't Say Yes When You Want to Say No*

11: *Fascinating Womanhood*

14: *Golden Handcuffs*

16: *Growing Up Firstborn*

17: *Having It All*

19: *How to Be an Assertive (Not Aggressive) Woman in Life, Love and On the Job*

20: *I'm OK—You're OK*

22: *In Transition*

23: *The Late Show*

25: *Light His Fire*

26: *Looking Out for #1*

28: *Men Are Just Desserts*

38: *The Sensuous Woman*

45: *Total Loving*

46: *The Total Woman*

48: *Type Talk* *

51: *What Smart Women Know*

57: *A Woman's Worth*

58: *Women & Love*

62: *Women and Their Fathers*

68: *Bad Guys*

69: *Being a Man*

70: *Beyond the Male Myth: A Nationwide Survey*

72: *The Classified Man*

74: *Fire in the Belly*

76: *How Men Feel*

77: *Men and Marriage: The Changing Role of Husbands*

88: *The McGill Report on Male Intimacy*

91: *Men Talk*

94: *The Myth of Male Power*

96: *Perfect Husbands (& Other Fairy Tales)*

99: *Secrets About Men Every Woman Should Know*

102: *Some American Men*

103: *Some Men Are More Perfect Than Others*

105: *Straight Talk to Men and Their Wives*

106: *What Every Woman Should Know About Men*

107: *What Men Really Think About Women, Love, Sex, Themselves*

108: *What Men Really Want*

109: *What Men Won't Tell You But Women Need to Know*

110: *What Really Works With Men*

111: *Why Men Are the Way They Are*

113: *Women Men Love, Women Men Leave*

117: *Husbands and Wives*

118: *Love, Sex, and Aging*

123: *The Psychology of Love*

310: *12 Steps to Mastering the Winds of Change*

317: *Get Rid of Him*

344: *Adult Children of Divorce*

365: *A Hole in My Heart: Adult Children of Divorce Speak Out*

383: *What Should I Tell the Kids?*

426: *What Every Woman Should Know About Her Husband's Money*

452: *The Lessons of Love*

456: *Life's Parachutes*

463: *Opening Up*

471: *Ten Days to Self Esteem*

475: *Why Me • Why This • Why Now*

486: *Flying Solo*

518: *Are You the One for Me?*

519: *At Long Last Love*

522: *Choosing Lovers*

523: *Cold Feet*

524: *The Compatibility Quotient*

525: *Dare to Connect*

526: *Fit to Be Tied*

527: *Getting to "I Do"*

528: *Good Guys/Bad Guys*

530: *Haven't You Been Single Long Enough?*

531: *Hot and Bothered*

534: *How to Make a Man Fall in Love With You*

538: *Keeping the Love You Find*

539: *Learning to Love Again*

540: *Love the Way You Want It*

542: *Real Love*

547: *Smart Women: Foolish Choices*

550: *Were You Born for Each Other?*

552: *Why Love Is Not Enough*

5

Problem Areas in Marriages

When love goes wrong

All intimate relationships experience stumbling blocks. Most professionals warn that this is normal and should not come as a surprise. It is the way in which individuals and couples tackle these situations that determines the quality of their lives and their personal growth. Occasionally a clash becomes particularly threatening to a marriage and special help is required.

Anger, conflict resolution, fighting, communication difficulties, blocks to intimacy, and bad habits or destructive behavior patterns frequently lead individuals to contemplate divorce. Crises in daily living such as job loss, illness, or relocation may compound the problems. Relationships may be affected by incompatibility, anxiety, jealousy, or even depression. Some people are addicted to or obsessed with the wrong kinds of love. Others find it impossible to forgive partners when betrayal or wrongdoing has occurred. In the worst cases, abuse (physical, emotional, or verbal) can become destructive.

The authors in this chapter are encouraging. Even the most serious dilemmas and frustrations have hope of resolution, they claim, if their suggested techniques and strategies can be mastered. Divorce sometimes offers merely an easy escape. Issues that are left unsolved may return again later, even if partners are changed.

230. *Anger: The Misunderstood Emotion.* **Carol Tavris. New York: A Touchstone Book, Simon & Schuster, 1982, 1989. Paperback. 383 pp.**

Tavris writes from personal experience with anger, the "crucial emotion" she sees as unavoidable in human relations. Defining it as a "way of communicating" rather than as a "disease," she discusses situations where anger works effectively and others where it is dangerous. Her book counters many popular beliefs about the validity of expressing as well as suppressing anger. Based on research, workshops, and interviews, it analyzes the nature and effects of anger and offers innovative approaches to managing specific anger-provoking situations. Tavris believes the way this potentially volatile process is handled has serious implications for the family and society at large. As evidence, she cites increasing incidents in sports as well as highway violence.

231. *The Anger Workbook.* **Lorrainne Bilodeau, M.S. Minneapolis, MN: CompCare Publishers, 1992. Paperback. 114 pp.**

Complete with charts, quizzes, and checklists, this manual examines the nature of anger and the ways it is used in relationships. Bilodeau sees the emotion as a natural one and warns against repressing or denying it. She includes numerous exercises to guide individuals in understanding how their "attitudes" toward anger may be preventing them from dealing with it in a healthy and productive fashion. The book incorporates modern research into beneficial and destructive anger and helps the reader to see "how anger goes awry." Bilodeau stresses the importance of developing responses that are right for the individual. She labels her practical methods as a "new perspective" that, with work, will improve a relationship and restore peace of mind.

232. *The Angry Book.* **Theodore Isaac Rubin, M.D. New York: Collier Books, Macmillan, 1969. Paperback. 223 pp.**

Rubin believes that anger, a fundamental human emotion, is poorly understood and thus dealing with this feeling causes most people problems on some level. He warns that suppressing anger in a "slush fund" and not coping with it can create immense damage individually and in relationships. In clear, layman's language, using case histories, the book discusses the nature and causes of anger. It proposes that the development of healthier ways of handling it can lead to greater overall well-being and a more fulfilling life. Rubin says that this emotion can be used positively to promote growth and happiness, if a distinction is made between the constructive and destructive versions. His book includes exercises to assist the reader in developing skills for the expression of both love and anger.

233. *The Binds That Tie: Overcoming Standoffs & Stalemates in Love Relationships.* **Richard Driscoll. Lexington, MA: Lexington Books, 1991. Hardcover. 204 pp.**

Here Driscoll offers self-help for recognizing and overcoming the negative effects of destructive routines that have ingrained themselves in our relationships and threaten to destroy them. In this book, he outlines the dynamics of these slowly but insidiously developing negative patterns. He offers useful strategies for removing them from our lives and finding healthier and more mutually satisfying substitutes. The book analyzes ruts and bad habits in such areas as: communicating to our partners, showing appreciation, responding sexually, fighting, and accomplishing day-to-day routines. It also offers specific guidance for restructuring interactions and restoring the happiness that was once shared.

234. *The Case Against Divorce: Discover the Lures, the Lies, and the Emotional Traps of Divorce—Plus the Seven Vital Reasons to Stay Together.* **Diane Medved, Ph.D. New York: Ivy Books, Ballantine, 1989. Paperback. 258 pp.**

Medved advises readers to "just say no" to divorce in this practical handbook. She offers support in resolving marital crises rather than encouraging the reader to walk away from them. In a society that almost seems to promote divorce and even to glamorize the single life, the book proposes that we must become aware of the positive and rewarding aspects of remaining married to one person for the long haul. Suggesting that divorce should be the chosen route in only the most extreme cases, the author spends time debunking the myths about the benefits of divorce. She then exposes the weaknesses of pro-divorce theories.

235. *Come Here/Go Away: Stop Running from the Love You Want. The Ultimate Guide to Overcoming Fear of Intimacy and the Havoc It Can Wreak.* **Dr. Ralph Earle and Susan Meltsner. New York: Pocket Books, Simon & Schuster, 1991. Paperback. 257 pp.**

Earle and Meltsner concentrate on the internal struggle people feel when they yearn for a close relationship but fear the demands and "risks" that such deep bonding may entail. The authors define this conflict as the "Intimacy Paradox" and state that it is characterized by "mixed messages and self-destructive behavior," which can ultimately rule out intimacy. Their guide offers help in overcoming these types of blocks by understanding such topics as: the effects of previous relationships on the present, substitutes for closeness that may unknowingly cause individuals to shun intimacy, methods of breaking the cycle, and eight elements that are necessary for the development of genuine intimacy and positive growth.

236. *The Dance of Anger: A Woman's Guide to Changing Patterns of Intimate Relationships.* **Harriet Goldhor Lerner, Ph.D. New York: Harper & Row Publishers, 1985. Paperback. 239 pp.**

Written specifically for women and based on ten years of clinical study, this book is a thorough examination of the underlying causes of anger and the ways in which women display it. Lerner reveals the positive as well as negative effects of this emotion and discusses methods of turning it into a "constructive force for reshaping our lives." She sees anger, when used properly, as a force that can keep relationships together and also act as a catalyst for necessary change. The book examines: the difficulties women encounter in expressing their anger, how anger can be used to gain a stronger sense of self, and how women can cut down their use of angry outbursts while handling them judiciously when they do occur.

237. *Divorce Busting: A Revolutionary and Rapid Program for Staying Together.* **Michele Weiner-Davis. New York: Summit Books, 1992. Hardcover. 252 pp.**

In this book, the author promotes "Solution Oriented Brief Therapy" for solving conflicts within relationships, for increasing satisfaction, and for achieving positive results in as little time as one month. Weiner-Davis views impasses as breakable and she considers the average marriage well worth preserving. She is pro-marriage and thus Weiner-Davis attempts to break down widely held misconceptions about divorce as an acceptable solution to marital problems. *Divorce Busting* emphasizes moving forward rather than laboriously analyzing past difficulties. The simple theory is that one should do "more of what works and less of what doesn't." The techniques mentioned can be used alone or with a spouse.

238. *Don't Go Away Mad: How to Make Peace with Your Partner.* **James L. Creighton, Ph.D. New York: Doubleday, a Div. of Bantam Doubleday Dell, 1990. Hardcover. 272 pp.**

This is an easy-to-follow resource book for developing improved personal relationships. It encourages learning to understand five types of disagreements and ways to work them out in a fair and productive manner. The book explores: the "hidden structures" of fights, the rules of fair fighting, personality traits that may limit understanding, and skills that are needed to express personal views without being judgmental or critical of an opponent. It sees conflict resolution as a necessary and normal component of intimacy and as completely possible without major personality change. Creighton states that his problem solving techniques are tested and will be beneficial even if only one partner masters them, though it is ideal if both do.

239. *False Love: And Other Romantic Illusions. Why Love Goes Wrong and How to Make It Right.* **Dr. Stan J. Katz and Aimee E. Liu. New York: Ticknor & Fields, 1988. Hardcover. 344 pp.**

Based on counseling and case studies, this book examines the differences between false love and authentic, mature love. According to the authors, society often buys into the false love concept, one that promotes romanticism, illusions, and fantasies about the "fairy tale" and "happy forever after" nature of love. Katz and Liu show how people become addicted to the "seductive" power of these myths and subsequently have difficulty finding real love. They see real love as characterized by commitment, "choice," and an intimacy far deeper than surface emotion. They also maintain that such relating requires ongoing adaptation and work. The book discusses the practical skills necessary for "true loving" and describes numerous mistakes that can be made along the way.

240. *The Forgiving Marriage: Resolving Anger and Resentment and Rediscovering Each Other.* **Dr. Paul W. Coleman. Chicago, IL: Contemporary Books, 1989. Hardcover. 317 pp.**

Coleman sees forgiveness as not only possible but essential. A failure to forgive each other, he believes, is a roadblock to finding happiness within ourselves or with others. Harboring deep resentment keeps pain and anxiety alive, often hurting the recipient more than the perpetrator. This book helps couples learn to "recreate a loving relationship" by forgiving themselves and each other for anything—boredom, remoteness, selfishness, dishonesty, disillusionment, and even "unforgivable acts" such as infidelity. Coleman breaks the process down into phases and stresses the importance of admitting one's own weaknesses for the healing to work. Tested strategies and case studies methodically guide the reader to understanding what needs to be done.

241. *Forgiving the Unforgivable: Overcoming the Bitter Legacy of Intimate Wounds.* **Beverly Flanigan, M.S.S.W. New York: Macmillan Publ. Co., 1992. Hardcover. 270 pp.**

As a foundation for this work, Flanigan interviewed and studied dozens of individuals who had been profoundly injured in a love relationship but were somehow able to summon the ability to put the event behind them. This "letting go," he observes, enabled them to arrive at forgiveness and restored health. Without such forward movement, the author feels that the bitterness felt by many of us in similar situations can work to sabotage every aspect of our lives. Careers, intimacy, goal setting, and our future existences can be threatened. The book explains various types of "unforgivable injuries," analyzes their consequences, and outlines "six distinct phases" in the forgiveness process.

242. *Games People Play: The Psychology of Human Relationships.* **Eric Berne, M.D. New York: Ballantine Books, 1964, 1985. Paperback. 192 pp.**

This book is a classic analysis of the kinds of "games people play" in love, work, and families that affect all aspects of their human relationships. It is useful in identifying patterns and characteristics in the inner workings of a relationship and thus of assistance in remediating problems. Berne believes that a large proportion of the social interaction individuals have with others is woven into "game-playing," some of which can act as "substitutes for the real living of real intimacy." Part I delivers the theory of this approach; Part II includes descriptions of specific types of games; and Part III discusses how relating can be when it is "game-free."

243. *The Green-Eyed Marriage: Surviving Jealous Relationships.* **Robert L. Barker. New York: Free Press, a Div. of Macmillan, Inc., 1987. Hardcover. 256 pp.**

Having based her extensive research on couples suffering the effects of jealousy, Barker directs this study at the "victimized partner." The book provides concrete short- and long-term suggestions for understanding and dealing with the problem. It includes an in-depth questionnaire to evaluate the gravity of each partner's jealousy level. Complete with many case studies, Barker's book delves into: the underlying causes of jealousy, how it plays out in a relationship, its bad and sometimes good points, its relationship to stress, and the "emotional costs" encountered. Useful strategies are proposed to help reduce "jealous confrontations" and control them for the sake of developing a more satisfying partnership.

244. *How Not to Split Up*: *For Every Couple That Wants to Stay Together.* **Jane Appleton and William Appleton, M.D. New York: A Berkley Book, Berkley Publ. Corp., 1978. Paperback. 200 pp.**

The Appletons discuss the ways in which couples can improve their lives and change without having to "change partners." They see society as shifting dangerously and selfishly toward "growth and self-realization" through divorce. Here they present constructive advice about the rewards of staying together and avoiding divorce, which can bring unimaginable pain. Practical methods are given for handling what they label the seven toughest areas in a marriage: "boredom, leisure time, sex, fights, children, money, and careers." These challenges are the most common causes of divorce in their opinion. The book suggests that dealing with these areas successfully creates a deepened intimacy that can provide the critical glue for staying together.

245. *How to Keep Love Alive: Strategies for Using Conflict and Change to Make Love Grow.* **Ari Kiev, M.D. New York: Harper & Row, 1982. Hardcover. 207 pp.**

In this selection, Kiev concentrates on analyzing the "interpersonal dynamics of loving relationships." He examines various "predictable patterns" of conflict that commonly exist in most intimate partnerships. The book studies the roles individual partners play and specific methods they can use to handle this conflict most constructively. It claims that an enhanced understanding will enable committed couples to preserve and maintain the strength of their bond. Topics included in the wide spectrum of problems covered are: situations that create conflict, differing expectations, "fears of intimacy," communication problems, "separation anxiety," and reasons relationships do not succeed.

246. *How to Love a Difficult Man.* **Nancy Good. New York: St. Martin's Press, 1987. Hardcover. 244 pp.**

How To Love A Difficult Man presents strategic ideas for working through the thorny and often serious problems encountered in living with a difficult man—a man, who nevertheless is really loved. Good's difficult men range from those with only bothersome idiosyncracies to ones with menacing and even dangerous character traits. The book examines potential underlying causes for such negative behaviors as: commitmentphobia, critical fault-finding, displays of anger, and lack of affection and nurturing. Good's thesis is that harmony can be restored to these marriages. She advises women not to feel helpless or depressed but to take positive, constructive action, which should prove well worth the effort.

247. *How to Salvage Your Marriage or Survive Your Divorce: A Guide Book.* **Tanist Newton. Simi Valley, CA: New Vistas Publishing, 1988. Paperback. 198 pp.**

Newton has developed a decision-making tool both for people who are only considering divorce and for those already deeply involved in the process. The book analyzes: roles participants play; escapes; choices and dangers that need to be considered; and the frustrating challenges that ultimately lead to a fulfilling transformation. This guide presents strategies and options for dealing with change, releasing "emotional pressure," and accepting pain as a "teacher." Newton devotes attention to reconciliation potential, coping with frustrations, accepting change, and remaining optimistic about the future. Topics also include: sex and alcohol issues, co-parenting, dating, remarriage, and new careers.

248. *I Love You, Let's Work It Out.* **David Viscott, M.D. New York: Simon & Schuster, 1987. Hardcover. 287 pp.**

As a married psychiatrist, Viscott has been impressed by how those who love each other most can be the ones to hurt each other most as well. Thus he has designed a practical guide for making relationships work for those individuals who truly love each other. Using case histories and his own experience as an ABC Radio Talkhost, Viscott shows how the primary personality types interrelate, the obstacles they encounter, and what methods can heal hurts. He includes exercises to be done alone or together in order to improve understanding. Each chapter focuses on a specific area such as: making the most of time together, communication, finances, infidelity, constructive conflict, improved sex, rekindling romance, and separating if necessary.

249. *If This Is Love, Why Do I Feel So Insecure? Learn How to Deal with Anxiety, Jealousy and Depression in Romance —and Get the Love You Deserve.* **Carl G. Hindy, Ph.D., J. Conrad Schwarz, Ph.D. and Archie Brodsky. New York: A Fawcett Crest Book, 1989. Paperback. 403 pp.**

These authors closely examine the "causes, effects, and cures for obsessive romantic attachments." A combination of case histories and scholarly research, the book is a resource designed to help readers understand themselves better and improve their chances of finding healthier, less anxiety provoking, and more lasting love. Subjects include: learning to identify warning signals of obsessive love, dealing with the insecurity of loving a "fickle" man, conquering this kind of compulsive attraction, tracing the effects of the parents' marriage on the problem, and developing the skills for selecting more appropriate and supportive partners.

250. *The Incompatibility of Men and Women: And How to Overcome It.* **Julius East. New York: Avon Books, A Div. of Hearst Corp., 1971. Paperback. 187 pp.**

After interviewing hundreds of men and women, East concludes that "the two sexes just do not understand each other" and that they may be basically incompatible. In this book, he explores various differences and similarities between the sexes in an attempt to expose traditional myths about femininity and masculinity. These stereotyped roles, he contends, often "suffocate" the individuals involved and lead to sexual conflict and frustration. East explains the origins and inner dynamics of gender roles and how couples can "free themselves" to act in more fulfilling ways. The book studies how men and women look at themselves and then how they look at each other. It encourages them both to "stop using their differences as weapons."

251. *The Intimate Enemy: How to Fight Fair in Love and Marriage.* **Dr. George R. Bach and Peter Wyden. New York: Avon Books, a Div. of Hearst Corp., 1968. Paperback. 384 pp.**

Based on 122 revealing and forthright case histories of actual fights, this self-training handbook provides a variety of practical suggestions for mastering "above-the-belt fighting." It proposes that "constructive aggression" uses conflict to further the growth and happiness of the couple. In addition, the authors say it can prevent partners from insulting and hurting each other irreparably. The underlying theory is that fighting is critical to reducing tension and can be healthy and constructive if one follows fair and flexible rules. Bach and Wyden boast that 85 percent of those counseled improved their relationships using these tested and clear guidelines. They claim that real intimacy cannot be achieved without fighting; avoiders of conflict risk detachment, lack of interest, unfaithfulness, and even divorce.

252. *Jealousy.* **Nancy Friday. New York: A Perigord Press Book, Wm. Morrow and Co., Inc., 1985. Hardcover. 538 pp.**

Friday thoroughly examines the subject of jealousy in her intensely personal narrative. She frankly details relevant events in her own life and often converses with a psychoanalyst friend. The goal is not necessarily to "eliminate jealousy but to understand it" and to realize its sizable impact on a person's intimate relationships. The book's style enables readers to reflect on their own lives and the place that jealousy plays. Subjects discussed include: underlying causes, distinctions between jealousy and envy, male/female differences in the acting out of each, how jealousy is often disguised, positive and negative aspects, the link to genes or the original family unit, and the potential for curing jealousy successfully.

253. *Let's Have It Out: The Bare-Bones Manual of Fair Fighting.* **Arthur S. Hough, Ph.D. Minneapolis, MN: CompCare Publications, 1991. Paperback. 109 pp.**

This book's theory is that most people have traditionally learned only how to fight dirty. Thus, it notes, in order to avoid pain and conflict, many mistakenly steer clear of fighting altogether. Hough believes that fair fighting can help strengthen relationships and make everyone a winner. He gives three options to every couple: fighting dirty (which has destructive results); not fighting (which often prevents the resolution of conflict and therefore is not constructive); and learning how to fight fairly (which enables the relationship to grow and intimacy to deepen). The inner dynamics of fighting are discussed in depth with respect to stages a fair fight follows, taboos to be avoided, and what to do if a partner doesn't obey the rules.

254. *Living Together: Feeling Alone. Healing Your Hidden Loneliness.* **Dr. Dan Kiley. New York: Prentice Hall Press, 1989. Hardcover. 205 pp.**

Writing for women through the use of actual case studies and stories, Dr. Kiley rejects the "myth" that loneliness is a phenomenon occurring only when women are alone. He introduces ten practical ways that will help give women the self-esteem they need to overcome this increasingly common problem. In addition, his book identifies five steps ("surrender, withdrawal, reevaluation, reemergence, and discovery") for eliminating the tendency to find fault with one's partner and for removing the "vague…yearnings" that so many women feel. Kiley says that happiness and loneliness both originate within the individual. Once this fact is accepted, women can gain personal strength and dramatically improve their relationships as well. Positive self-affirmation is stressed.

255. *Looking for Love in All the Wrong Places: Overcoming Romantic and Sexual Addictions.* **Jed Diamond, L.C.S.W. New York: G.P. Putnam's Sons, 1988. Hardcover. 224 pp.**

This book offers readers practical advice for recovery from destructive addictions to things like attraction, romance, sex, and intrigue. Diamond outlines the causes (primarily insecurity and need for control) for this unhealthy kind of obsession. In addition, he describes the incredible havoc it can wreak on individuals and their families. His book includes a quiz for assessing a person's tendency toward this particular brand of self-destructive compulsion. It also discusses in depth a "Twelve Step Recovery Program" that is designed to overcome addiction and find workable, appropriate, and more fulfilling relationships.

256. *Love and Addiction.* **Stanton Peele with Archie Brodsky. New York: Taplinger Publishing Co., 1975. Hardcover. 284 pp.**

These authors see the ideal expression of love as a sharing of our fully-developed "best" selves with another person who is also committed to growth and positive self-fulfillment. They say that too frequently, insecurity and dependency needs lead individuals to be "addicted to love" just as insidiously as they might be addicted to drugs. These types of destructive bonding patterns, according to the authors, usually lead to "retreating from the world" and result in individuals or couples failing to reach their full potential. The book analyzes influences in society that perpetuate feelings of inadequacy and then it studies addiction to love as a solution. Peele and Brodsky give advice about how to identify positive and negative patterns in our relationships and strengthen our sense of self.

257. *Love Blocks: Breaking the Patterns That Undermine Relationships. Breaking Free from the Destructive Patterns in Relationships.* **Mary Ellen Donovan and William P. Ryan, Ph.D. New York: Penguin Books, Viking, 1991. Paperback. 404 pp.**

Donovan and Ryan feel that society is experiencing an "intimacy crisis" resulting in pervasive feelings of pain, loneliness, and dissatisfaction. Their prescription for a cure lies in helping men and women break their own personal "love blocks" and become more receptive to "taking in love." Focusing on trying to become more loving is not the optimal strategy, they contend. Their book, based on case histories and interviews, defines 15 "love blocks" or "inner obstacles" that are barriers to love and loving. It examines the origins of these blocks. The authors then give practical advice and exercises to help individuals let go of their barriers, change, and find greater fulfillment in all their relationships, not just the romantic ones.

258. *Love Busters: Overcoming the Habits that Destroy Romantic Love.* **Willard F. Harley, Jr. (Companion volume to *His Needs Her Needs*). Tarrytown, NY: Fleming H. Revell Co., 1992. Hardcover. 224 pp.**

Having studied the five basic needs of men and women in his previous book, Harley now focuses on the five most common behavior problems that cause unhappiness in marriages. He defines these bad habits, such as "angry outbursts," "selfish demands" and "dishonesty," or even the more serious challenges of substance abuse or infidelity, as "love busters." His book stresses that, if these destructive patterns are allowed to develop and snow-ball, they will destroy romantic love and endanger the marriage. Thus Harley has created an action-oriented plan for couples to revive romance by returning to the kind of mutual nurturing they shared in the early days of their relationship. He emphasizes "consideration" and "thoughtfulness."

259. *Love Knots: How to Untangle Those Everyday Frustrations and Arguments That Keep You from Being Happy With the One You Love.* **Lori Heyman Gordon. New York: A Dell Trade Paperback, Dell, 1990. Paperback. 111 pp.**

Heyman examines love relationships. Her particular focus is on the causes of problems stemming from "hidden expectations, beliefs, and assumptions" that partners have been raised with, and then, unconsciously carry with them. The book shows how trouble can arise if couples don't understand the power of these secret, faulty, or unrealistic factors. Ignoring the "validity of our differences" can undermine our ability to relate in an open, honest, and healthy way. *Love Knots* offers help in getting to the root of these underlying problems and thereby developing better partnerships. The book analyzes the complex protective mechanisms spouses develop for defense only to discover these same unconscious habits create conflict with their partners.

260. *Love Must Be Tough: New Hope for Families.* **Dr. James C. Dobson. Waco, TX: Word Books Publishers, 1983. Hardcover. 212 pp.**

Dobson addresses endangered marriages where one partner has grown detached and is treating the other with disrespect. He contends that this kind of destructive behavior may result in affairs, addictions, abuse, or indiffer-ence. His book is intended for the partner who wishes unilaterally to save the dying relationship. With strong Christian advice often flaunting conven-tional theories, Dobson urges "tough" actions, e.g., being strong rather than whining-pleading-physical wrecks, standing up for oneself, and "opening the cage door" allowing the "trapped partner out." He proposes that courageous permission can often jolt the disenchanted mate into reconsidering a marriage he or she may not really want to end. The book sees accountability not "appeasement" as vital to relationships.

261. *Money Demons: Keep Them from Sabotaging Your Relationships and Your Life.* **Dr. Susan Forward and Craig Buck. New York: Bantam Books, 1994. Hardcover. 277 pp.**

From a personal and professional perspective, this therapist writes for women about the emotional impact of money conflicts in their personal and love lives. The book devotes individual chapters to a specific "money pattern" that can wreak havoc. Questions, exercises, "self-help strategies" and case studies show what lies at the bottom of arguments about money. Topics include: spending too much or too little, fears of success or failure, coping with debt or gambling, choosing men with money problems, "enabling" a partner's habits, couple patterns, using money as a "weapon" in divorce, and problems arising from salary inequities. Forward sees money as intimately connected to personalities and also as something that can be used to escape from intimacy.

262. *Now That I'm Married, Why Isn't Everything Perfect? The 8 Essential Traits of Couples Who Thrive.* **Susan Page. Boston, MA: Little, Brown and Company, 1994. Hardcover. 240 pp.**

After unscientifically studying 32 "extremely happy" couples, Page concludes that mind-set, i.e., intending to have a great marriage, is key. She believes that society has painted a highly negative picture of marriage. This often causes couples to give up too soon. Unrealistic expectations and romantic myths, Page adds, can also be problems. Aimed at unhappy or happy couples, the book focuses on traits that work in the nineties, a new era for relationships. Topics include: commitment and desire to be together, spending time with each other, "goodwill," healthy communication, balancing separation and togetherness, "simple day-to-day pleasures," intimacy, sex, passion, and energy. Page offers numerous stories as examples and constructive exercises to help couples *be* the kind of people who create "perfect" marriages.

263. *Obsessive Love: When Passion Holds You Prisoner.* **Dr. Susan Forward and Craig Buck. New York: Bantam Books, 1991. Hardcover. 304 pp.**

This book is for the "obsessor and the target of obsession" as well. It is based on case histories and 20 years of counseling with people plagued by a destructive, uncontrollable, and extreme passion for someone who has no mutual interest in them. Forward describes the phases of obsessive love from "romance to rejection and from pursuit to revenge" in both married and single relationships. She then offers both these troubled individuals guidelines for resolving the problem. For the targets—ways to defend and protect themselves, including learning how to get their message across forcefully and clearly enough; for the obsessors—ways of decreasing their overwhelming need for the other and developing self-control.

264. *One-Way Relationships: When You Love Them More Than They Love You.* **Alfred Ells. Nashville, TN: Thomas Nelson Publishers, 1990. Paperback. 222 pp.**

Ells says that those whose style of loving is characterized by excessive self-sacrifice at their own expense are acting out codependent behaviors. As victims, he states, they are not offering the healthy, unconditional love they may think; instead, they are embroiled in a version of "imperfect love" that may have detrimental effects both on themselves and the relationship they are so devoted to nurturing. This kind of negative behavior usually traces its origins to previous "traumatic events" in an individual's birth-family life. The book provides long-term solutions for recovery by closely examining the underlying causes for such unbalanced behavior.

265. *The Passion Paradox: When One Loves More Than the Other.* **Dean C. Delis, Ph.D. New York: Bantam Books, 1990. Paperback. 310 pp.**

This book addresses the negative impact of problems that occur when unequal feelings (or unequal expression of feelings) exist in love relationships. Delis notes that when one partner's style is too intensely romantic, the other may react with precisely the unwanted response: withdrawal. *The Passion Paradox* reveals how such a dynamic can create unhappiness in the giver and guilt in the receiver. Delis sees this prevalent phenomenon as curable and offers "proven techniques" developed from years of client counseling. Interesting strategies include "Trial Closeness" and "Healthy Distance." The author analyzes the complexities of these troubled relationships and tries to help individuals revive romance. Singles who scare prospects away with too much attention may also benefit.

266. *Resolving Family and Other Conflicts: Everybody Wins.* **Mendel Lieberman and Marion Hardie. Santa Cruz, CA: Unity Press, 1981. Hardcover. 222 pp.**

These authors promote the theory that family members who interact in a secure and nurturing home environment, where differences are tolerated, can all win and be happy. They suggest that problems will inevitably occur but unfair criticism, negative undercurrents, sabotage, and dirty fighting will notably decrease. The book stresses the importance of process in resolving conflicts through a discussion of: family meetings, "active listening" to acknowledge what members have heard, and fair fighting rules. The notion is that when individuals take responsibility for their own feelings and are listened to, self-esteem rises and "defensiveness and frustration" lessen. Lieberman and Hardie encourage "six-step problem solving," which they outline in detail.

267. *Romantic Jealousy: Understanding and Conquering the Shadow of Love.* Ayala M. Pines, Ph.D. New York: St. Martin's Press, 1992. Hardcover. 300 pp.

Pines researched this topic for 12 years, ran workshops, and collected surveys from a thousand people. Her book is for those having romantic jealousy difficulties or those anxious to learn more. It analyzes the emotion of jealousy so that readers might: evaluate their own levels, check if their jealousy is normal, and spot "warning signs" to keep excessive jealousy from damaging relationships. Positive aspects, which even "strengthen love," are also discussed. Pines defines the feeling, contrasts it with envy, and explores it from both a male and female point of view. A questionnaire and many probing suggestions are included. *Romantic Jealousy* studies the causes from five approaches: childhood events, relationship-oriented causes, male-female "evolutionary forces," cultural determinants, and learned behavior.

268. *The Seven Basic Quarrels of Marriage: Recognize, Defuse, Negotiate and Resolve Your Conflicts.* William Betcher, M.D. and Robie MaCauley. New York: Villard Books, a Div. of Random House, 1990. Hardcover. 291 pp.

All couples quarrel. The theory here, however, is that surface issues may not be the real ones. Often lying hidden beneath the words, the book proposes, are deeper struggles that must be addressed if the goal is healthy conflict resolution and greater happiness. Betcher and MaCauley hope to help in "identifying, understanding, and working through" these quarrels. They believe that seven fundamental areas give birth to all arguments: "gender, loyalties, money, power, sex, privacy, and children." Betcher and MaCauley include a questionnaire to diagnose specific kinds of disagreements more readily. In this book, committed couples can learn what quarrels really are and how they can solve them without hurting each other or endangering the relationship.

269. *The Stranger in Your Bed: How to Break Down the Barriers to Relationships—and Achieve True Intimacy.* **Dr. Rosalie Reichman. New York: John Wiley & Sons, 1989. Hardcover. 226 pp.**

Reichman presents a practical guide for removing the conscious and unconscious barriers that block us from forming close relationships. She includes a questionnaire to help evaluate the "Intimacy Quotient" of single or married men and women who seek new or improved relationships. Her book analyzes specific types of people who shun intimacy: "Distancers," "Pseudo-Intimates," and "Intimacy Saboteurs." Readers can identify their own (or their partner's) traits in the examples given and then follow specific steps to remedy negative behaviors and better develop their abilities to be close. Reichman studies the causes and effects of this problem along with reasons for these tendencies to fear intimacy and keep others at arm's length.

270. *Surviving Family Life: The Seven Crises of Living Together.* **Sonya Rhodes, D.S.W. with Josleen Wilson. New York: G.P. Putnam's Sons, 1981. Hardcover. 299 pp.**

These authors have structured a guide for achieving fulfilling relationships through the working out of specific crises in seven different stages. Their claim is that every relationship passes through such stages, which are classified primarily by the presence or absence of children. The phases range from the newlywed stage to bearing children, school years, suffering through the conflicted adolescent period, readjusting as the nest is emptied, coping with the potential of children returning, and finally the arrival of aging parents. The authors identify "dangerous family patterns" in each stage and cover such topics as: game playing, power, money, sex, affairs, and ways to reinvigorate the marriage.

271. *Together on a Tightrope: How to Maintain Balance in Your Relationships When Life Has You Off Balance.* **Dr. Richard Fowler and Rita Schweitz. Nashville, TN: Thomas Nelson Publ., 1991. Paperback. 220 pp.**

The topic of this book is learning to handle the stresses and pain of life's traumas so that relationships and individuals can grow positively rather than crumble under the pressure. Fowler and Schweitz observe that life in the 90s often brings with it overwhelming tension stemming from job loss, financial problems, frequent family moves, and divorce. They believe that real or perceived disapproval by society can compound the crises. Their book addresses itself to: identifying constructive solutions to such discouraging problems, the need to cope positively with "emotional overload," avoiding excessive tendencies toward independence or dependence, and creating a support network to provide assistance in problem-solving.

272. *Tough Marriage: How to Make a Difficult Relationship Work.* **Paul A. Mickey, B.D., Ph.D. with William Proctor. New York: Wm. Morrow, 1986. Hardcover. 224 pp.**

Reverend Mickey proposes what he calls a "revolutionary kind of unity" in this book, which outlines 12 "commandments for a tough marriage." He concludes that couples must be committed to the marriage for the long haul, must make it their *top priority*, and must adhere to the commandments without fail if they are to be really happy. The book urges readers to eliminate modern narcissism by placing the needs of the marriage and spouse first. It says such commitment will help them survive life's inevitable crises and will strengthen love. Based on Scripture, the commandments encourage: "honoring" our partners, freeing ourselves from parents, eating and worshipping together, telling the truth, finding more time for each other, avoiding "romanticism," and working on building character.

273. *The Transition to Parenthood: How a First Child Changes a Marriage.* **Jay Belsky, Ph.D. and John Kelly. New York: Delacorte Press, 1994. Hardcover. 288 pp.**

In 50 percent of marriages, the advent of a child can cause serious problems, say these authors. Their book, not a self-help book per se, hopes to enlighten reader's about the period from the "third trimester of pregnancy to the child's third birthday." Following the stories of three "prototypical couples" drawn from a study of 250 in all, Belsky and Kelly show what happens in marriages where there is: no change, deterioration, or improvement. The biggest problems come, they note, from differences in background, emotions or even "biology." Knowledge of this possibility can prevent couples from being surprised by disillusionment, they think. The book examines six "capacities" crucial to success. Topics include: how happiness in a marriage affects parenting, why women become dissatisfied first, and why parenthood is so challenging.

274. *The Verbally Abusive Relationship: How to Recognize It and How to Respond.* **Patricia Evans. Holbrook, MA: Bob Adams, Inc., 1992. Paperback. 179 pp.**

This work is grounded in 40 interviews with women (ages 21-66) who have been victims of verbal abuse. Evans' goal is to train the reader to recognize this subtle but deadly behavior, which rarely has any witnesses beyond the victim. This victim may sometimes even question her own sanity. Designed for both men and women, the book studies the dynamics of controlling and destructive partners and suggests strategies for responding, breaking the cycle, and building a healthier partnership. Part I offers a questionnaire for self-evaluation and talks about common abusive patterns. Part II treats types of verbal abuse such as "withholding, countering, discounting, and trivializing." Evans states that both parties must change if the "manipulation and coercion" are to stop.

275. *We Can Work It Out: Making Sense of Marital Conflict.* **Clifford Notarius, Ph.D. and Howard Markman, Ph.D. New York: G.P. Putnam's Sons, 1993. Hardcover. 286 pp.**

These two psychology professors devoted 20 years to analyzing happy and unhappy couples to learn what determines success. Their book contains the results. It proposes that the way couples deal with differences is the key factor. The authors' "communication program" provides "clinically proven methods." It guides husbands and wives in understanding the critical issues, helps them examine the dynamics of communication and conflict resolution, and offers positive step-by-step strategies for handling problems. Exercises show couples how to grow more intimate and have more fun. Questionnaires, examples, and anecdotes are frequent. Topics include: prevalent myths, identifying "trouble spots" and pitfalls, six "truths of marriage," four "patterns of conflict," getting rid of harmful thoughts, and skills for "constructive" relating.

276. *What to Do When He Won't Change: Getting What You Need from the Man You Love.* **Dr. Dan Kiley. New York: A Fawcett Crest Book, Ballantine, 1987. Paperback. 227 pp.**

Kiley writes for the female who genuinely loves the man in her life, but who wants to work on resolving relationship dilemmas even if he will not join her in the effort. He cites numerous case studies and offers women various solution-oriented techniques including: methods for "loving confrontation," quizzes to determine their honest desires, a ten-step guide to reinvigorate their sex lives, five ways to remedy relationship difficulties, short personal practices to raise their self-confidence levels, suggestions for relaxation in times of extreme trouble, and even unusual ways to encourage their partners to be more involved in household responsibilities.

277. *When a Mate Wants Out: Secrets for Saving a Marriage.* **Sally Conway and Jim Conway. Grand Rapids, MI: Zondervan Publishing House, 1992. Hardcover. 217 pp.**

The Conways have developed a "step-by-step process" (with which their counseling center has had a 50%+ success rate) for saving troubled marriages. They believe that working to restore a marriage helps those who succeed as well as those who ultimately divorce. The theory is that knowing every effort has been made to save the union helps separating couples move forward in more healthy and guilt-free ways. The book's practical and biblical approach urges readers to: stay calm and hopeful in crises, try to uncover the real causes, communicate "carefully," recognize their own part in the problem, acknowledge the other's needs while meeting their own, view things with the other's eyes, analyze "baggage" each of them carries, and commit to change and growth by setting new goals.

278. *When Love Goes Wrong: What to Do When You Can't Do Anything Right.* **Ann Jones and Susan Schechter. New York: HarperCollins Publishers, 1992. Hardcover. 358 pp.**

This is a book for those suffering in unhappy relationships with controlling or abusive partners. It contains workable and comprehensive advice to: recognize abusers; define the problem; break destructive behavior patterns; and begin the process of change. The authors help readers determine if their relationships have "crossed the line" and what options are available for leaving without harm to themselves or their children. They stress gaining self-confidence and control of their choices. Case histories, charts, and questions assist in working to "reclaim (their) lives." Topics include: causes; resource agencies; finding support and safe refuges; and specific counsel for black, poor, or lesbian women.

279. *When Someone You Love Is Someone You Hate.* **Stephen F. Asterburn, M.Ed. and David A. Stoop, Ph.D. Dallas, TX: Word Publishing, 1988. Paperback. 141 pp.**

These authors provide constructive techniques for people involved in destructive "love-hate relationships." The goal is to aid the victims in making sense of their confused range of feelings. Based on actual case histories, the book strives to help readers: understand what is happening, stand up for their own rights, defend themselves against the cycle of abusiveness, "work through bitterness," and arrive at a place where forgiveness may be a possibility. Asterburn and Stoop conclude that those suffering from this dysfunctional way of relating can frequently direct negative emotions inward toward themselves. The result, they predict, can be our ultimate divorce from feelings in general. The book offers help for overcoming the victim's sense of powerlessness.

280. *Why Did I Marry You Anyway? Good Sense and Good Humor in the First Year...and After.* **Arlene Modica Matthews. Boston, MA: Houghton Mifflin Co., 1988. Hardcover. 242 pp.**

Matthews talks to the recently married or those considering the step. Her book analyzes early frustrations that can threaten or strengthen the future depending on how well they are handled. "Playing it by ear," the customary way of dealing with marriage, is not advised. The author suggests that "romantic myths" of fairy tale marriages delude people into taking the Polyanna approach of *expecting* rather that *working* at happiness. Instead of a scientific study, Matthews offers concrete help for learning how to coexist on a day-to-day basis without endangering love. Her book's last chapter offers tips from couples happily married for more than 15 years. Topics include: habits, the past, in-laws, attitudes toward sex, stepchildren, and handling two careers.

281. *You Just Don't Understand: Women and Men in Conversation.* **Deborah Tannen, Ph.D. New York: Ballantine Books, a Div. of Random House, 1990. Paperback. 330 pp.**

A best seller, this work is a by-product of the author's career in "analyzing everyday conversations." Tannen studies the complexities of male-female language styles and how spouses often speak "across two cultures." She believes that their "genderlect" leads to unintentional problems and misunderstandings. The concepts and examples set forth are designed to help men and women communicate with each other more effectively. Tannen argues that the characteristics of each gender's style are markedly different but "equally valid" and that both parties must understand them to preserve the health of the marriage. Especially pertinent is her discussion of male "report talk" and female "rapport talk." Topics also include: power problems, argument, interruption, and conflict.

For additional help on "Problem Areas in Marriages," see all books in Chapters 4 & 6 as well as book numbers:

1: *The Agony of It All*
3: *Bitches and Abdicators*
4: *Bradshaw On: The Family*
6: *The Cinderella Complex*
7: *Codependent No More*
8: *The Crisis of the Working Mother*
10: *The Emotionally Abused Woman*
12: *The Female Stress Syndrome*
13: *Getting Unstuck*
14: *Golden Handcuffs*
15: *The Good Girl Syndrome*
18: *Homecoming*
20: *I'm OK—You're OK*

24: *Letters from Women Who Love Too Much*

27: *Lovesick:The Marilyn Syndrome*

29: *My Enemy, My Love*

30: *My Mother, My Self*

31: *The New Suburban Woman*

32: *Opening Our Hearts to Men*

33: *Passions*

34: *Perfect Women*

36: *Recovery from Co-Dependency*

35: *The Pleasers…Women Who Can't Say No —And the Men Who Control Them*

37: *The Seashell People*

39: *Slay Your Own Dragons*

40: *The Snow White Syndrome*

41: *The Superwoman Syndrome*

42: *Sweet Suffering: Woman As Victim*

43: *Too Good for Her Own Good*

44: *Too Smart for Her Own Good*

47: *The Type E Woman*

49: *Unfinished Business: Pressure Points in the Lives of Women*

50: *The Wendy Dilemma*

51: *What Smart Women Know*

52: *What Wives Wish Their Husbands Knew About Women*

53: *When Am I Going to Be Happy?*

54: *Where's My Happy Ending?*

55: *Why Do I Think I'm Nothing Without A Man?*

56: *Why Women Worry*

57: *A Woman's Worth*

58: *Women & Love*

60: *Women & Self-Esteem*

61: *Women & The Blues*

63: *Women Who Love Too Much*

64: *Women's Burnout*

65: *Working It Out: The Domestic Double Standard*

66: *Your Erroneous Zones*

67: *The 40 to 60 Year Old Male*

68: *Bad Guys*

73: *Crisis Time*

76: *How Men Feel*

78: *A Knight in Shining Armor*

85: *Manhood: A New Definition*

87: *Maybe He's Just a Jerk*

89: *Men and Marriage*

71: *The Casanova Complex: Compulsive Lovers and Their Women*

75: *The Hearts of Men*

77: *The Inner Male*

79: *The Male Dilemma*

80: *The Male Ego*

81: *The Male Machine*

82: *The Male Ordeal*

83: *The Male Paradox*

84: *The Male Stress Syndrome*

86: *The Masculine Dilemma*

88: *The McGill Report on Male Intimacy*

92: *Men Who Can't Love*

93: *Men Who Hate Women and the Women Who Love Them*

94: *The Myth of Male Power*

95: *The Passions of Men*

96: *Perfect Husbands (& Other Fairy Tales)*

97: *The Peter Pan Syndrome*

98: *The Season's of a Man's Life*

100: *The Secrets Men Keep*

101: *Sexual Static*

104: *Straight Talk*

106: *What Every Woman Should Know About Men*

107: *What Men Really Think About Women, Love, Sex, Themselves*

109: *What Men Won't Tell You But Women Need to Know*

110: *What Really Works With Men*

111: *Why Men Are the Way They Are*

112: *Why Men Can't Open Up*

114: *Workaholics*

115: *Wrestling With Love*

116: *Husbands and Wives*

117: *The Kinsey Institute New Report on Sex*

118: *Love, Sex, and Aging*

119: *Marriage Divorce Remarriage*

120: *Marriage, Love, Sex and Divorce*

310: *12 Steps to Mastering the Winds of Change*

317: *Get Rid of Him*

328: *One Door Closes, Another Door Opens*

362: *Healthy Divorce*

365: *A Hole in My Heart: Adult Children of Divorce Speak Out*

383: *What Should I Tell the Kids?*

451: *If Love Is the Answer, What Is the Question?*

452: *The Lessons of Love*

456: *Life's Parachutes*

462: *Necessary Losses*

464: *Ordinary Women, Extraordinary Lives*

467: *Resilience*

469: *The Sorrow and the Fury*

470: *Staying On Top When Your World Turns Upside Down*

471: *Ten Days to Self-Esteem*

472: *When Bad Things Happen to Good People*

473: *When the Worst That Can Happen Already Has*

474: *Whoever Said Life Is Fair?*

475: *Why Me • Why This • Why Now*

477: *Winning Life's Toughest Battles*

486: *Flying Solo*

518: *Are You the One for Me?*

522: *Choosing Lovers*

523: *Cold Feet*

524: *The Compatibility Quotient*

526: *Fit to Be Tied*

527: *Getting to "I Do"*

528: *Good Guys/Bad Guys*

530: *Haven't You Been Single Long Enough?*

531: *Hot and Bothered*

534: *How to Make a Man Fall in Love With You*

540: *Love the Way You Want It*

547: *Smart Women:Foolish Choices*

550: *Were You Born for Each Other?*

552: *Why Love Is Not Enough*

6

Preventing and Surviving Affairs

Sex, lies and forgiveness

Infidelity is probably the most formidable crisis that a marriage can face. Judging from overwhelming statistics provided by surveys and studies, however, it may now be the norm not the exception for male and female partners to stray at some time during the marriage.

Most partners find sexual betrayal especially difficult to forgive. Not too long ago, adultery would almost certainly have been considered cause for divorce. Today, however, with greater knowledge and understanding (and the additional threat of AIDS if the single life is resumed), growing numbers of couples are attempting to treat affairs as the symptom of mutual underlying problems instead of one spouse's sin.

These authors, who write about affairs and affair prevention, often speak candidly from personal experience. Their successful recoveries provide inspiration as well as advice to others. They stress the benefits of monogamy with open and honest communication seen as the vehicle by which a new beginning is possible.

Many books covered in this chapter explore the secret inner lives of unfaithful men and women while offering insight into the precipitating causes for such alliances. Sex, perhaps surprisingly, seldom emerges as the primary factor. Some guides help women fight to get their husbands back; others discuss specific strategies for preventing affairs or analyze the chronically sex-addicted male. All suggest that the issue is not cut-and-dry and that infidelity rarely needs to signal an automatic divorce.

282. *Adultery: An Analysis of Love and Betrayal.* **Annette Lawson. New York: Basic Books, Inc., 1988. Hardcover. 440 pp.**

Lawson's book relies on extensive research with hundreds of males and females actually involved in affairs. It analyzes the confusing lives and inner feelings of adulterers as well as possible causes and results of the problem. The book sees adultery as a frequent reason for the failure of marriages and thus a critical area for examination. Lawson believes individual freedom and the development of the "me" is often in competition with the traditional romantic concept that includes sexual fidelity. She examines the full range of painfully perplexing emotions and competing demands as well as changes in male-female roles. According to the book, adultery can be a rebellious reaction intertwined with the notions of "conquest and self-affirmation."

283. *The Affair: A Portrait of Extramarital Love in Contemporary America.* **Morton Hunt. Cleveland, OH: The World Publishing Co., 1969. Hardcover. 317 pp.**

Though shockingly high percentages of mates were reportedly involved in affairs, Hunt found little research exploring this phenomenon and its effects. Through 80 interviews and the use of questionnaires, the author delves into all elements of the participants' secret lives including emotions ranging from elation to pain and suffering. He looks closely at what happens before and during as well as after. The study covers all types of affairs from one night stands to the serious varieties that threaten marriages. Topics include: the precipitating causes, "secret fantasies," misgivings before acting, committing to adultery, guilt feelings and incredible mood changes, the varying degrees of involvement, and the positive or negative aftereffects on everyone including society.

284. *Affair Prevention: Specific Techniques That Can Strengthen and Protect Your Marriage.* **Peter Kreitler with Bill Bruns. New York: Macmillan, Inc., 1981. Hardcover. 212 pp.**

Writing from personal experience, this Episcopalian minister warns that not even happy marriages are immune to the threat of an affair. His realistic and positive book is preventative in nature and claims that we can learn techniques to safeguard ourselves and our spouses. Kreitler and Bruns say that readers can also find ways to avoid divorce and restore loving harmony within a marriage damaged by the destructive effects of infidelity. Topics include: "types of affairs," underlying reasons, positive and negative effects, how society encourages affairs, detecting "danger signs," warding off boredom, understanding attraction and temptation, dealing with unfaithful spouses, "the role of religion," improving our sex lives, and learning from our mistakes.

285. *All the Good Ones Are Married: Married Men and the Women Who Love Them.* **Marion Zola. New York: Times Books, 1981. Hardcover. 257 pp.**

This book focuses on men, their mistresses, and their wives. Based on extensive research and interviews with all three parties, it exposes the inner realities, secrets, challenges, rewards, and heartbreaks of affairs. Zola provides case histories of primarily urban, white, and middle class subjects. Her analysis uncovers common patterns including: destructive female competition, women interested in married men at work, men in need of both a wife and a mistress, and men finding their only safe harbor in the affair. A scarcity of eligible males comes forth as one possible cause. The plight of the powerless mistress and the complete control of the man who "calls the shots" in the relationship are also topics.

286. *Back from Betrayal: A Ground-Breaking Guide to Recovery for Women Involved with Sex-Addicted Men.* **Jennifer P. Schneider, M.D. New York: A Hazelden Recovery Book, Ballantine Books, 1988. Paperback. 330 pp.**

Schneider focuses on male sex-addiction as a "compulsive disorder" that often afflicts the female partner with feelings of shame, betrayal, and helplessness. The author does not view any "inadequacy" in the female as a cause. Writing from a professional counseling background and personal experience with a sex-addicted husband, Schneider offers support and guidance to the wives in question. She stresses the importance of making mates accountable for their actions and aware of consequences. "Enabling behavior" simply perpetuates the disorder in the addict, she claims. The book gives advice on: breaking destructive patterns, the negative impact of keeping the problem secret, the importance of open communication, finding professional help, and using the "12-Step Recovery Program."

287. *Beyond Affairs.* **James and Peggy Vaughn. Hilton Head Island, SC: Dialog Press, 1980. Paperback. 212 pp.**

Written by two counselors who have remained married for 25 years despite the husband's infidelity, this book delves candidly and deeply into the inner dynamics of extramarital affairs. Alternating from the male to the female point of view, the book discusses the often overwhelming emotions and deep soul-searching that results on both sides when an affair is discovered or revealed. It also talks about the "silent, creeping cancer" of uncertainty when a spouse suspects infidelity but is not sure (which happens 80 percent of the time, they claim). The blows to egos and pride and the ensuing pain are described in detail. The authors show how the relationship can recover with large amounts of honesty and understanding, which could ultimately lead to growth for both parties.

288. *The Don Juan Dilemma: Should Women Stay with Men Who Stray?* **Jane Carpineto. New York: Wm. Morrow, 1989. Hardcover. 228 pp.**

Carpineto has created an in-depth analysis of compulsive "womanizers." She hopes that women will be able to understand the causes, characteristics, and symptoms of such behavior and take action to solve the destructive problem. Blaming both the men and the women who "consent to participate," the book gives women specific solutions for: recognizing the "dances" that are done in these relationships, confronting the issue with their mate, helping men come to grips with the problem, finding the strength to "empower" themselves to act, making the decision to end the relationship or not, and identifying traits to avoid in the future. The author feels that women will not find happiness until the addiction is broken and she is convinced it *can* be with her help.

289. *The Erotic Silence of the American Wife.* **Dalma Heyn. New York: Turtle Bay Books, a Div. of Random House, 1992. Hardcover. 304 pp.**

The subject of this book is the sexual nature of American women and the changes they bring about in their lives by their own infidelities. The author sees female affairs as a growing trend (equaling the number for men) and one that surprisingly often brings great pleasure to the women involved. The book is a subjective rather than scientific look at a matter previously considered "taboo." It discusses some women's underlying feeling of loss of self in marriage and a replenishment of self in the affair. Heyn says that women enter affairs younger in age and in years of marriage than previously thought and that their chief predicament is being able to continue the affair *and* the marriage, which they often feel the affair helps.

290. *Every Other Man: How to Cope with Infidelity and Keep Your Relationship Whole.* **Mary Ann Bartussis, M.D. New York: Thomas Congdon Books, E.P. Dutton, 1978. Hardcover. 207 pp.**

Bartussis cites infidelity as the most prevalent problem in modern marriage with surveys showing that 50 percent of respondents cheat on their mates. As an experienced psychiatrist, she has written a practical guide for: understanding the underlying causes, recognizing potential susceptibility, surviving infidelity, and preventing it before it even begins. Her book provides a "step-by-step crisis guide" that women can use in "desperate moments." Topics covered include: when to suspect infidelity, the different types of cheating, how to move foward to action, dealing with hurt, betrayal and indignation, deciding whether to end the relationship, and reinforcing the marriage if the decision is to stay.

291. *Faithful Attraction: Discovering Intimacy, Love & Fidelity in American Marriage.* **Andrew M. Greeley. New York: TOR, Tom Doherty Assoc., Inc., 1991. Paperback. 343 pp.**

Greeley, a priest, rejects the popularly held myths about marriage and its decline in a book that addresses the day-to-day existence of husbands and wives. He strongly believes the institution is not collapsing and that new intimate behavior patterns are the result of economic and technological changes. These trends, his book notes, have created an atmosphere that allows greater freedom, sometimes causing problems. Greeley analyzes happy and unhappy marriages in order to identify the qualities that make the good ones work. Topics included, to show people how to modify unsatisfactory aspects of their lives, are: money, sex and fidelity, children, working mothers, romance, social class, religious issues, cohabitation, and divorce.

292. *Have a Love Affair With Your Husband (Before Someone Else Does).* **Susan Kohl and Alice Miller Bregman. New York: St. Martin's Press, 1987. Paperback. 177 pp.**

This book speaks to the need for improving marriages that may have been happy and exhilarating in the past but have since deteriorated into just comfortable companionship, often even boredom. The authors stress the importance of: women working at revitalizing their sexuality, rediscovering sources of energy, trying to "put passion back into the relationship," getting rid of long-standing grudges and hostility, and making effective use of the pleasant memories of earlier days. Kohl and Bregman also give women tips on developing their physical bodies into more sensual instruments and benefitting from the stimulating effects of massage and fantasy.

293. *His Needs Her Needs: Building an Affair Proof Marriage.* **Willard F. Harley, Jr. (Companion volume to *Love Busters*) Grand Rapids, MI: Fleming H. Revell, A Div. of Baker Book House, 1986. Hardcover. 224 pp.**

Harley proposes that two areas cause discord in marriages: mates neglect to "care for" and to "protect" each other. In this volume, he examines the first area, how spouses "fail to make each other happy." As a prerequisite, his guide stresses the importance of identifying the five most fundamental "needs" of both men and women. Once partners have learned what their spouses genuinely desire, they are prepared to follow a series of exercises provided in the book. These activities are designed to help partners communicate and answer each other's needs, thereby enhancing intimacy and love.

Husbands and wives whose needs are met will not resort to affairs, he says simply. Among the prime requirements of women, according to Harley, are "affection" and "conversation." Most important for men, he believes, are "sexual fulfillment" and "admiration."

294. *How to Get Him Back from the Other Woman If You Still Want Him: A Step-by-Step Plan That Works.* **Diane Baroni and Betty Kelly. New York: St. Martin's Press, 1992. Hardcover. 232 pp.**

These *Cosmo* editors interviewed hundreds of men, women, and professionals about infidelity. Saying that 70 percent+ of American men are guilty, they warn against immediate divorce if a woman still loves and wants the man. Resolution of this problem can bring a couple to new levels of intimate trust if handled well, the book proposes. Statistics cited reveal that most men stay with their wives after affairs. With the "odds on our side," Baroni and Kelly think women can win their husbands back by careful planning. Key concepts include: avoiding the "victim" role and self-blame, understanding his ego problem, coping with feelings of shock, humiliation, and rage, and using a "Nine-Step Formula" to get him back. The book also discusses the ten biggest reasons for affairs and the six "Stages of Healing."

295. *How to Keep Your Man Monogamous.* **Alexandra Penney. New York: Bantam Books, 1989. Hardcover. 192 pp.**

Having interviewed 200+ men about their reasons for "staying or straying," Penney believes that monogamy is still possible even if 50-65 percent of males cheat. She attributes infidelity to unmet male ego needs, which she analyzes in depth. Her book suggests techniques for understanding and satisfying "male ego-structure" without compromising a woman's commitment to her own personal self-respect and goals. Through case histories, Penney delineates three types of cheaters and reveals the basic causes, styles, and results of their infidelities. Male and female attitudes toward monogamy, situations that promote problems, and correlations to age and life-style are probed. The author also presents concrete advice to counter the trend and conclusions on what the "other woman" offers.

296. *How to Win Back the One You Love: Surefire Strategies From a Best-Selling Author and a Psychiatrist.* **Eric Weber and Steven S. Simring, M.D. New York: Macmillan, 1983. Hardcover. 177 pp.**

This book offers concrete strategies for salvaging any relationship from the throes of separation or divorce even if the process has already begun. The authors see divorce as virtually "glamorized" by modern society. In their opinion, however, women should reject it as an all but desperate alternative. The book's position is that partners should accept conflict as an inevitable part of intimacy and should master techniques to make handling it more constructive and fair. With honest dialogue, they believe even problems like infidelity can be resolved. Illustrated with case histories, the guide covers such areas as: problems with sex, finance, and hostility, preventing trial separations, understanding a woman's strengths in influencing her partner positively, and getting our partners to move back in.

297. *Love & Betrayal: Broken Trust in Intimate Relationships.* **John Amodeo, Ph.D. New York: Ballantine Books, 1994. Paperback. 290 pp.**

Carrying around the unresolved baggage of betrayal can seriously affect the ongoing quality of one's life and intimate relationships, says this author. His book looks at all types of "broken trust" from gossip and small lies to infidelity. Amodeo understands the heavy emotional toll such betrayal can take, but encourages readers to look at it objectively, understand their own role, and try to move past the pain toward a healing forgiveness of everyone involved. Rebuilding self-esteem and regaining an ability to trust and love others again is critical, Amodeo emphasizes. Topics include: "common reactions to betrayal," dealing with ambivalence, accepting "lack of control," and "letting go" of the hurt. The book concludes with a guide to local resource and recovery programs, audiotapes, periodicals and books.

298. *Love Me Love Me Not: How to Survive Infidelity.* **Daniel J. Dolesh and Sherelynn Lehmann. New York: McGraw Hill Book Company, 1985. Hardcover. 192 pp.**

Written for spouses with unfaithful mates, this book provides practical, concrete, and sympathetic advice about how to: recognize the warning signs of trouble, cope with the emotional chaos, get in touch with one's feelings and actions, and react constructively. The authors use fictional case studies of seven "betrayed individuals" who embody the characteristics of the hundreds of couples examined. Topics include: precipitating causes of affairs, "when and how to act on our suspicions," obtaining professional or legal counseling, strategies for handling the children, decision-making with regard to ending or rebuilding the damaged relationship, ways to reconstruct the marriage, and the challenges of living alone if necessary.

299. *Men Who Can't Be Faithful: How to Pick Up the Pieces When He's Breaking Your Heart.* **Carol Botwin. New York: Warner Books, 1988. Hardcover. 291 pp.**

Citing a 70 percent rate for male infidelity, Botwin writes for the large number of women who suspect (or know) their partners are (or have been) unfaithful. The book is based on case histories, interviews with 76 affected men and women, and relevant scholarly work. A questionnaire is included to determine the likelihood of infidelity as is an appendix with "Thirteen Ways to Affair-Proof Your Marriage." Botwin categorizes the kind of men who cheat, outlines causes, discusses ways to attack the problem, and probes whether change can occur to save the relationship. She also offers potential solutions and ways to recognize hopeless cases. The book studies how men and women differ in their attitudes about infidelity as well how societal and age related influences contribute to the problem.

300. *The Monogamy Myth: A New Understanding of Affairs and How to Survive Them.* **Peggy Vaughn. New York: Newmarket Press, 1989. Hardcover. 208 pp.**

This book is grounded in ten years of research by a husband and wife counseling team who survived his painful multiple affairs. Its premise is that "monogamy is not the norm" today. Vaughn urges readers to face the statistics and embark on a new approach: open, honest, and trusting communication developed through her six step program. The author treats the underlying causes and actual experiences of adulterers as well as the painful discovery process and later recovery or dissolution. Her book analyzes society's part in promoting affairs and outlines high risk situations common today. Steps are suggested for: overcoming normal temptations, diffusing desire through communication, and creating greater intimacy and depth in the relationship.

301. *More Than Just a Friend: The Joys and Disappointments of Extramarital Affairs.* **Dr. Tom McGinnis. Englewood Cliffs, NJ: Prentice Hall, 1981. Hardcover. 203 pp.**

McGinnis realistically examines the essence of affairs from a non-judgmental viewpoint. Having worked with hundreds of people in what he calls a lonely "subculture," the author concludes that positive and negative effects as well as "joys and heartaches" occur. His book is intended for those who are contemplating an affair or are involved in one already as well as for those attempting to recover from the effects of a spouse's or a friend's infidelity. Participants discuss their experiences and the author offers his own "Prescriptions for Living," which are suggestions on how one can use an affair as a growth and learning experience. Rather than "condemnation," McGinnis pleads for compassion and suggests that divorce is not the only answer.

302. *The New Other Woman: Contemporary Single Women in Affairs With Married Men.* **Laurel Richardson. New York: Free Press, a Div. of Macmillan, Inc., 1985. Hardcover. 192 pp.**

Richardson explores the unique subculture of single women who participate in affairs with married men, a growing phenomenon resulting in part at least from men being in "short supply." Based on eight years of research, statistics, and interviews with 55 such women (white, ages 24-65), the book analyzes: reasons these affairs start, what qualities characterize them, why they are less "stigmatized" today, and how they end. Since 20 percent of all women lack "potential mates," and over 50 percent of all men are likely to stray before 40, this trend may increase, affecting all male-female relationships in some way, she says. The book profiles the positive and negatives aspects of the life of this "normal, everyday woman" who actually has much in common with females in general. Actual women tell their real stories.

303. *Not With My Husband You Don't: How to Fight for Your Marriage, Your Man and Your Future.* **Margaret Kent. New York: Warner Books, Time Warner Inc., 1990. Paperback. 193 pp.**

Kent's research showed that every woman worries about her husband's faithfulness. Having spoken to many survivors, she guides the reader through sensible steps for winning a man back if he does stray. Quizzes and self-tests help analyze her temperament and assist in determining whether her husband is cheating. The book offers tough techniques for women who know an affair has occurred. In such traumatic crises, Kent urges women to stay calm and to "think before [they] act." She shows that the odds favor wives if they can gain control, assess the damage and define the options, avoid embarrassment, and take positive action. Topics include: "25 reasons men cheat;" lessening the chances; "manipulating the mistress;" telling the man that his infidelity is known; and using "sex, friendship, reason, and confrontation" to fight back.

304. *A Passion for More: Wives Reveal the Affairs That Make or Break Their Marriage.* **Susan Ripps. New York: St. Martin's Press, 1993. Paperback. 293 pp.**

Ripps reveals a surprising fact: the nineties have bred many women who are not satisfied simply being wives and mothers. Instead they thrive on the sense of control they get from having affairs. She reports her interviews with all kinds of ordinary women (25–55 years old) who are having four types of affairs: "empowering," "sex-driven," "self-esteem," and "love." Some of these liaisons cause the marriage to end in divorce, Ripps says, but others help keep it alive. The book proposes to be nonjudgmental as it exposes how these unions begin, how the women manage to "juggle" both husband and lover, and what the rewards (from great sex to real fulfillment) and disadvantages (including guilt) are. Education, jobs, money, mobility, and increased freedom, according to the book, have allowed women to venture into this new life more frequently today.

305. *Private Lies: Infidelity and the Betrayal of Intimacy.* **Frank Pittman. New York: W.W. Norton & Co., 1989. Hardcover. 309 pp.**

Pittman believes the frequency of infidelity today may make it the norm rather than the exception. His book looks at the problem objectively and offers advice on how to save the marriage and learn to make fidelity work. He incorporates cases and relevant pieces of "music, literature, and film." The dangers of AIDS, secrecy, and quick decisions to divorce are topics of discussion as are guilt, jealousy, and the impact upon children. Pittman's goal is to "stop people from risking so much for so little." Infidelity and the "myths" surrounding it are defined with attention given to passages in a marriage when the danger may be greater. This work also examines four types of affairs: "accidental," "habitual," accommodating, and romantic.

306. *Secret Loves: Women With Two Lives.* **Sonya Friedman, Ph.D. New York: Crown Publishers, Inc., 1994. Hardcover. 208 pp.**

The "tandem life-style" is what Friedman writes about in this book that gives women and men insight into why and how wives go outside their marriages for fulfillment. The author, a psychologist and TV talk-show host, interviewed 113 such women (mostly in mid-life) about their reasons for having lovers and husbands at the same time. The affairs revealed are long-term and meaningful rather than fleeting encounters and the women in them come from every type of background. They are "ordinary" females, who may suffer from emotional emptiness or look for an escape from "subjugation." Guilt as well as societal pressure against such liaisons are discussed. Friedman is candid in her sympathetic portrayal. Her bottom line is that while women put great emphasis on children and family, personal happiness is equally important.

307. *Sex, Lies and Forgiveness: Couples Speaking Out on Healing from Sex Addiction.* **Jennifer P. Schneider, M.D. and Burt Schneider. New York: A Hazelden Book, HarperCollins Publishers, 1990. Paperback. 284 pp.**

Having survived the problem of the husband's sex addiction in their own marriage, this counseling team runs workshops for other recovering couples. Their research into the varieties and manifestations of this disorder has shown it can be rooted in dysfunctional childhoods lacking in proper nurturing. They conclude that addicts yearn to "fill the void" but find nothing is enough. Their book claims that healing is possible through a special "12 Step Program" concentrating on: honesty, acknowledgment of the need to change, determination to succeed, and goal-oriented action. Based on 142 completed questionnaires, it analyzes 85 recovering couples and how they achieved their progress. Actual addicts and co-addicts talk about the trials and rewards of their ongoing struggle.

308. *Why Men Stray and Why Men Stay: How to Keep Your Man Monogamous.* **Alexandra Penney. New York: Bantam Books, 1989. Paperback. 208 pp.**

This guide provides solutions to understanding the fundamental intimate needs of men. It shows how, by filling these needs, women in turn will get precisely what they want and also prevent rampant infidelity and its aftermath from destroying intimate relationships. Penney identifies those periods in relationships most prone to crisis and defines six common but serious mistakes individuals make with respect to love and sex. The book includes a discussion of conflicting male and female views of monogamy and the impact of these factors on the partnership. It also explores some reasons behind the man's attraction to the "other woman."

309. *Woman Versus Woman: The Extramarital Affair.* **Shirley Eskapa. New York: Franklin Watts, 1984. Hardcover. 210 pp.**

Calling it the "first analysis of the battle" that can occur between two women over one man, Eskapa based this book on 500+ interviews of which 150 were with "the other woman." She paints the battle as often damaging and ugly, with the identity of each woman at stake rather than the particular man who may be merely a symbol. *Woman Versus Woman* analyzes the "solitary secret life" of the "other woman" and her prospects for happiness if she wins. Losers and survivors are seen along with the inner lives of the straying men. The result of such infidelity need not be divorce, Eskapa suggests, if a wife keeps her senses and avoids "hysterical reactions." With the proper perspective, she feels the event can even strengthen some marriages. Readers also learn why men gravitate toward another woman in the first place.

For additional help in "Preventing or Surviving Affairs," see also book numbers:

  1: *The Agony of It All*
 22: *In Transition*
 51: *What Smart Women Know*
 67: *The 40 to 60 Year Old Male*
 70: *Beyond the Male Myth: A Nationwide Survey*
 71: *The Casanova Complex: Compulsive Lovers and Their Women*
 73: *Crisis Time*

76: *Men and Marriage*

77: *Men and Marriage: The Changing Role of Husbands*

79: *Men Who Can't Love*

83: *The Male Paradox*

87: *Maybe He's Just a Jerk*

88: *The McGill Report on Male Intimacy*

98: *The Seasons of a Man's Life*

103: *Some Men Are More Perfect Than Others*

116: *Husbands and Wives*

117: *The Kinsey Institute New Report on Sex*

118: *Love, Sex, and Aging*

121: *The Marriage Premise*

128: *The Art of Staying Together*

132: *The Challenge of Marriage*

136: *Couples* (Broderick)

137: *Couples* (Dym)

142: *The Dance Away Lover & Other Roles We Play in Love, Sex and Marriage*

151: *Husbands and Wives*

154: *How to Keep a Man in Love With You Forever*

155: *How to Live With Another Person*

157: *How to Make Love to the Same Person for the Rest of Your Life—and Still Love It*

172: *Life Mates: The Love Fitness Program for the Lasting Relationship*

188: *The Marriage Maintenance Manual*

191: *Married People*

205: *Peer Marriage*

215: *Second Honeymoon*

219: *Staying in Love*

226: *What Every Woman Ought to Know About Love and Marriage*

227: *What Love Asks of Us*

240: *The Forgiving Marriage*

248: *I Love You, Let's Work It Out*

255: *Looking for Love in All the Wrong Places*

258: *Love Busters*
270: *Surviving Family Life*
383: *What Should I Tell the Kids?*
441: *Forgive & Forget*
442: *Forgiveness*
448: *How to Fall Out of Love*
452: *The Lessons of Love*
456: *Life's Parachutes*

7

Breaking Up

Between marriage and divorce

To divorce or not? That is the question. Even the actual initiator passing through this painful transition worries about the chaotic aftermath. Everything the family unit has grown accustomed to appears to be in turmoil. The future, an unknown, is deeply frightening. Emotions are on overload and rational thought is difficult if not impossible. The notion that an individual might grow through this experience is laughable at first, yet women frequently meet others who have divorced and have mysteriously gone on to lead even more fulfilling lives.

Many of this chapter's selections are excellent resources to consult during this troubled time. Readers can learn how a variety of individuals handle their own personal traumas, which provides them assurance that their experience is not abnormal or unique. Several authors address themselves to making choices and to the complex area of effective decision-making, while others explore the rewards of taking risks. Advice is offered on ending relationships properly and understanding the leavetaking process. Most books acknowledge the pain but view the breakup as a turning point, even an opportunity for a new beginning for all of the parties.

Surviving this period requires strength and, sometimes, a willingness to seek help. Fortunately such assistance is increasingly available through counseling and by reading the kinds of books listed below.

310. *12 Steps to Mastering the Winds of Change: Peak Performers Reveal How to Stay on Top in Times of Turmoil.* **Erik Olesen. New York: Rawson Associates, 1993. Hardcover. 251 pp.**

Olesen, a therapist and motivator, interviewed high achievers like Walter Cronkite, Julia Child and Steve Allen to study how they coped with setbacks and change. The result is a guidebook combining these models with

Olesen's professional expertise. It offers strategies for managing tough times and turning them into growth opportunities. The book identifies 12 steps including such techniques as: committing to goals, learning when to "let go," being optimistic, maintaining a sense of humor, paying attention to our bodies, and developing self-confidence. A "First Aid Primer" lists problems and refers readers to specific chapters and support phone numbers. Olesen urges readers to convert negatives into positives, especially fear into energy and mistakes into knowledge, in order to emerge stronger from the crisis.

311. *Bailing Out: The Healthy Way to Get Out of a Bad Relationship and Survive.* **Barry Lubetkin, Ph.D. and Elena Oumano, Ph.D. New York: Prentice Hall Press, 1991. Hardcover. 226 pp.**

Bailing Out is a book for those contemplating, engaged in, or even finished with a relationship. The authors acknowledge that breaking with the status quo generates fear, guilt, and anxiety, yet they emphasize the sizable negative consequences of stagnating in unhappy unions. In a step-by-step manner, the book guides readers in: assessing the promise of the relationship, learning how to make the right decision and manage the process, choosing the best time, acquiring strength to handle the early days, and developing "survival skills" either to thrive alone or find a more fruitful partnership. Leaving, if necessary, can be an "affirmative act" that provides the freedom to achieve one's full potential. Case studies, charts, checklists, and log suggestions are included.

312. *Between Marriage and Divorce: A Woman's Diary.* **Susan Braudy. New York: Wm. Morrow, 1965. Hardcover. 252 pp.**

Written by a woman who was raised to believe the perfect marriage would surely be hers and who later found her own wonderful "Prince Charming," this book explains what happens when the myth is shattered and life falls apart. It is a piece of nonfiction that is based on the author's diaries and her memories of the breakdown of a six-year marriage. Braudy explores the emotions she faced as she passed through this transition and emerged as a new and different person. The author writes with the purpose of helping other women find consolation and "not feel alone" in this traumatic passage.

313. *Choices: Making the Right Decision in a Complex World.* **Lewis B Smedes. New York: Harper & Row, 1986. Hardcover. 121 pp.**

This text is a resource for enhancing the ability to perform the decision-making process more effectively, especially when tough choices are at hand. Smedes stresses long-range planning rather than acting impetuously and emphasizes the necessity of developing a "consistent pattern of moral values" that are grounded in ethical thinking. Such a value system will free the conscience, allow an individual to feel good about making the right decisions, and further personal growth. The book suggests methods for: arriving at the decision, judging its validity, knowing how to identify wrong versus right choices, and applying the elected decision to a particular "real life" situation.

314. *Coming Apart: Why Relationships End and How to Live Through the Ending of Yours.* **Daphne Rose Kingma. New York: Fawcett Crest, Ballantine Books, 1987. Paperback. 189 pp.**

Coming Apart is a detailed "first aid kit" for surviving all stages of the end of a relationship. Kingma's thesis is that an emphasis on falling in love has overshadowed learning about endings. She analyzes symptoms of incompatibility and reasons for parting. The book also offers guidance on minimizing pain and guilt with "parting rituals" and suggests steps for promoting healing and growth. Citing this loss as one of life's most traumatic, Kingma still sees the event as a learning experience, which can bring new hope, creativity, confidence, and independence. Individuals should experience all the necessary emotions on the way to creating a different but richer existence, she says, but they should resist the sense of failure that could leave them feeling out of control and fearful.

315. *Creative Divorce: A New Opportunity for Personal Growth.* **Mel Krantzler. New York: M. Evans & Co., Inc., 1974. Hardcover. 268 pp.**

As a divorce therapist, Krantzler accompanies his readers through the entire process. While his book emphasizes acknowledging the pain and mourning, it promotes a positive outlook that concentrates on the potential growth opportunities change can initiate. Krantzler offers advice on: seeing the failed marriage realistically, accepting responsibility for changing our own negative behavior patterns, welcoming the chance to be our own person and live alone successfully, and developing improved capabilities for relating to our children, ex-spouses, and new mates. *Creative Divorce* analyzes emotions like anger, feelings of failure, and uncertainty about the future in order to bring about the healing needed to proceed with life's challenges.

316. *The Divorce Experience.* **Morton Hunt and Berenice Hunt. New York: McGraw Hill Book Company, 1977. Hardcover. 306 pp.**

This text, based on 200 in-depth interviews and a national survey of 984 separated and divorced individuals, is not a how-to book but a picture of the actual "world of the divorced and divorcing" in 1977. It covers the gradual and often traumatic passage from separation through actual divorce and reemergence as a new individual. The Hunts discuss the impact of divorce on life as well as the common habits and life-styles of the divorced, their struggles and challenges, and their shared experiences. Readers may feel less alone as they identify with: swings of emotion from depression to euphoria, problems surrounding connections to their children, the development of new social environments, and meeting prospective new partners.

317. *Get Rid of Him.* **Joyce L. Vedrai, Ph.D. New York: Warner Books, 1993. Paperback. 318 pp.**

Vedrai writes for women about summoning the courage to analyze their relationships and then to improve them or "move on." Divorced herself, she also researched the stories of many other women. She describes the excuses women have for remaining in the wrong situations. Her book is full of easy-to-read, practical advice about assessing one's unions. It also lists reasons for a woman to leave the man in her life. These include "begging for love" to being blocked in careers, not being able to spend money, jealousy, cruelty, infidelity, lack of sexual interest, boredom, his continual unemployment or his inability to be alone. Vedrai warns against remaining in the relationship "only for the money, the security or the children." While change can be frightening, Vedrai says winning the freedom to find the right man is "life-enhancing."

318. *The Greatest Risk of All: Why Some People Take Chances That Change Their Lives —and Why You Can Too.* **Walter Anderson. Boston, MA: A Marc Jaffe Book, Houghton Mifflin Co., 1988. Hardcover. 242 pp.**

"To know oneself and to act on that knowledge" is the greatest risk to Anderson. His book recounts personal stories as well as interviews with others, some famous, who have grown and flowered by taking risks. People like Carol Burnett and Gloria Steinem talk about the impact difficult decisions have had on their lives. The work stresses the necessity of taking chances as well as the associated fears and dangers. It states that acting upon our inner convictions has a fundamental tie to happiness and self-actualization. Anderson assists readers in determining: if a change is necessary; evaluating options; and being comfortable with the dynamics of the process. He defines what people stand to lose when they risk as well as what they gain especially in the area of confidence.

319. *Growing Through Divorce: With Working Guide.* **Jim Smoke. Eugene, OR: Harvest Publishers, 1985, 1986. Paperback. 256 pp.**

Complete with a "Working Guide," discussion questions, and exercises, this action-oriented book walks readers through all the phases of the painful divorce process. It gives them practical advice on letting go, forgiveness, taking charge of themselves and their family, and potential remarriage. Smoke outlines the inevitable stages of shock, adjustment, and growth as individuals learn from the experience and make the transition positive rather than negative. He says the choice is theirs and they should allow God to help. Topics include: seven causes of divorce, having the patience to grow day by day, reexamining life issues, putting the ex "in focus," making the separation clear, avoiding childish reactions, and dealing with mourning and other emotions.

320. *How to Get Out of an Unhappy Marriage or an Unhappy Relationship: The Intelligent Woman's and Man's Guide to the Marriage Break by a Noted Clinical Psychologist.* **Dr. Eugene Walder. New York: G.P. Putnam's Sons, 1978. Hardcover. 269 pp.**

This is a handbook for individuals who suspect they may have reached the end of a relationship. Walder includes numerous evaluative exercises and checklists to aid in the decision-making process and to minimize the chances of making a mistake. He guides the reader through the entire process, starting from the point of detecting initial warning signs. The book emphasizes a positive approach to divorce and a new life in order to achieve good results. Advice is offered about: communicating the situation to the children, coping with the physical and emotional issues of separation, being on one's own, and facing the challenges of developing new romantic relationships.

321. *Learning to Leave: A Woman's Guide.* **Lynette Triere with Richard Peacock. New York: Warner Books, 1982. Paperback. 392 pp.**

Learning to Leave comprehensively studies the entire leave-taking process in a step-by-step fashion. The guide covers such topics as: how to know when it's right to leave, overcoming the wide range of emotions that often accompany the uncoupling such as panic, guilt, hostility, and grieving, selecting an appropriate time for an exit, structuring a nurturing support system to help sustain a woman in the process, problems with cash flow and work, legal matters and mediation, helping the children through the transition, dealing with ex-partners, and making new lives as single people.

322. *Leavetaking: When and How to Say Good-bye. How to Successfully Handle Life's Most Difficult Crises: Getting Fired/Retirement, Divorce/ Leaving Home, Dealing with Loneliness, Death of Loved Ones, the Corporate Move, the Empty Nest.* **Dr. Mortimer R. Feinberg, Gloria Feinberg and John J. Tarrant. New York: Simon & Schuster, 1978. Hardcover. 286 pp.**

These psychologists give step-by-step strategies for dealing with situations requiring "leavetaking," a phenomenon that will always be unavoidable in life. Admitting that trauma is likely to accompany the process, they stress, nevertheless, how important negotiating these passages well is to our happiness and continued growth. Since fear and pain often accompany parting or being left/rejected, individuals may postpone necessary departures too long. The book makes a distinction between "role loss and object loss." It exposes "neurotic patterns" begun in childhood and offers advice for changing them. An in-depth discussion proposes techniques for managing divorce and other leavetaking crises so that they might occur less disruptively.

323. *Life Changes: How Women Can Make Courageous Choices.* **Jason Hatch Lennox and Judith Hatch Shapiro. New York: Crown Publishers, Inc., 1990. Hardcover. 217 pp.**

Lennox and Shapiro focus on women and the ten major life transitions (including divorce) that affect family life, careers, and financial stability. As women redefine themselves, the authors encourage a positive, goal-oriented attitude toward the risks change brings. They examine the various ways shifting gears can be accomplished to achieve personal growth. The practical guide breaks down what can sometimes be imposing tasks into logical and workable segments. It offers concrete "minitasks" at the conclusion of each chapter to assist readers in taking action. The underlying theory is that change is a powerful motivator for self-development, not something to be feared or merely survived.

324. *Life Choices: How to Make the Critical Decisions—About Your Education, Career, Marriage, Family, Life Style.* **Gordon Porter Miller. New York: Thomas Y. Crowell, 1978. Hardcover. 166 pp.**

Experienced in running decision-making seminars for widely divergent audiences, Miller proposes to teach the reader the skills necessary to master decision-making theory. He suggests these skills be applied regularly to life, especially in moments that require hard personal choices. Methodically guiding readers through all the necessary steps, the author stresses being in control of their own lives and focusing on the direction of a life plan. The book uses case histories and exercises liberally. Topics include: determining options, zeroing in on needs, goals, and values, ways to select the most appropriate choice, understanding the obligations and personal costs of the decision chosen, and knowing how to set the wheels in motion.

325. *Living Through Your Divorce.* **Earl A. Grollman and Marjorie L. Sams. Boston, MA: Beacon Press, 1978. Paperback. 164 pp.**

This book falls into five sections that follow the divorce process chronologically: 1) Separation, 2) Grief, 3) Decisions, 4) Rebuilding and 5) Becoming Whole Again. The intent of the authors is to "offer comfort" by helping readers to: understand the legitimacy of their own emotions, realize that disorientation, sadness, and pain are normal expressions of loss, and gain confidence in the knowledge that moving beyond this moment to a fulfilling new life is possible. The style is conversational with quasi-poetic reflections and counseling. Topics include: guilt, panic, fatigue, anger, ambivalence, numbness, denial, grief, depression, friends, relatives, money, the legal process, and reorganization.

326. *Loving & Leaving: Why Women are Walking Out on Marriage.* **Brenda Rabkin. Buffalo, NY: McClelland and Stewart, Firefly Books Ltd., 1985. Paperback. 230 pp.**

Rabkin studied 80 women who walked out on "perfectly good marriages" that seemed intact and included no abuse. Numerous case studies probe the causes of this growing trend. While the husbands she examines were hard working and committed, they often seemed bogged down in traditional role expectations and were resistant to the independent growth their wives craved. The book analyzes the risks this "agonizing decision" presents to women who no longer want simply to be "taken care of by men." Love and security are important, Rabkin says, but self-respect, intimacy, and an "equal partnership" are more significant. She finds the culprit to be the institution of marriage itself, which traps women into focusing on the demands of others rather than on their own needs.

327. *Nice Women Get Divorced: The Conflicts and Challenges for Traditional Women.* **Geneva Sugarbaker, M.S. Minneapolis, MN: Deaconess Press, 1992. Paperback. 193 pp.**

Sugarbaker writes from personal experience and from information gathered during many interviews with "nice women" facing divorce. She defines these shaken females as women: for whom divorce was never an option, whose parents had enduring marriages, whose husbands and children were often more important than themselves, who took great pains to save their marriages, and who now must cope with feelings of failure, shame, and guilt. The book comforts "nice women" but also assures them they can overcome their sense of victimization. Sugarbaker agrees that the romantic dream of a fantasy marriage and emotional/financial protection has been shattered. But she says that women can let go of their ingrained cultural conditioning and rely on their own competence to build new self-esteem and an independent future.

328. *One Door Closes, Another Door Opens: Turning Your Setbacks into Comebacks.* **Arthur Pine with Julie Houston. New York: Delacorte Press, 1993. Hardcover. 172 pp.**

Inspirational remarks from more than 50 well-known figures fill this graphic little handbook designed to show the kind of attitudes that are needed to turn "negatives into positives" in life. Boxes with memorable mottoes inside are used to help keep readers on track when problems threaten. Pine and Houston stress that each roadblock is a new opportunity to refine ourselves. People like Margaret Thatcher, Wayne Dyer, and Wally Amos each tell how they handled a particular adversity. Topics include: coping with change, firings, believing in oneself, seeing everything as possible, persistence, communication, personal appearance, illness, avoiding inertia, the benefits of action, developing an interest in others, ego, support networks, the importance of analyzing and thinking, and learning to take control of the moment.

329. *Our Turn: The Good News About Women and Divorce.* **Christopher L. Hayes, Ph.D., Deborah Anderson and Melinda Blau. New York: Pocket Books, 1993. Hardcover. 311 pp.**

While this book reports on divorced women in mid-life, it can benefit the unmarried as well if they wish to see how women can successfully live alone. It is based on the "Divorce After 40 Study" conducted by the National Center for Women and Retirement. The research surveyed six pivotal areas: "employment, finances, legal matters, emotional health, building a new life, and perspectives on retirement." Respondents were 40-60 years old, white, middle class and married 23 years on average. The authors see their findings as both surprising and encouraging: the 352 women were thriving, having rediscovered themselves and having found new purpose in life. Section I covers the "growing pains" of breaking up and Section II deals with "moving on." The book dispels the "7 Myths" about divorced women.

330. *Overcoming Indecisiveness: The Eight Stages of Effective Decision-Making.* **Theodore Isaac Rubin, M.D. New York: Harper & Row Publishers, 1985. Hardcover. 208 pp.**

No human being can escape decision-making, Rubin contends. Moreover, he says that the basic quality and success of our lives is directly related to the effectiveness of our abilities in this area. In a step-by-step fashion, his book guides us through the process: identifying particular personality styles in decision-making, pointing out blocks that hinder progress, stressing the need for prioritizing goals, and finally encouraging wholehearted commitment to the decision when it is made. Rubin believes that the ability to make good decisions puts us in control of our lives and helps us grow toward happiness, self-understanding, and fulfillment.

331. *Overwhelmed: Coping With Life's Ups & Downs.* **Nancy K. Schlossberg. Lexington, MA: Lexington Books, D.C. Heath & Co., 1989. Hardcover. 152 pp.**

Schlossberg proposes that one can develop mental skills to embrace change and transitions rather than fear them. Just as bodies can be trained to endure exercise, so can we condition our minds to understand what is confronting us, she says. We can then evaluate our "resources for coping" and take positive action to manage each situation successfully. This action-oriented handbook assists readers in building useful lifelong skills by introducing case studies and a systematized group of activities. Its techniques will help: clarify our situation, work out alternatives, develop strategies, progress to appropriate solutions, and grow personally in the process. Schlossberg also urges readers to seek support wherever possible and professional help when necessary.

332. *Pathfinders: Overcoming the Crises of Adult Life and Finding Your Own Path to Well-Being.* **Gail Sheehy. New York: Wm. Morrow, 1981. Hardcover. 494 pp.**

Sheehy describes "pathfinders" as the kind of people who somehow successfully survive life's inevitable traumas. She bases her book on over four years of interviews and research. In addition, she relied on the results of 60,000 "Life History Questionnaires" that were completed by men and women of all different types and ages. Her research concludes that a "pathfinder" is not some superhuman being, but one who is characterized by a sense of "well-being." The author explores the ten attributes of "well-being" including: creativity, the willingness to take risks, openness to love, and friendliness. She teaches the reader how be a "pathfinder" and how to internalize these traits in order to better solve life's problems.

333. *Risking.* **David Viscott, M.D. New York: Simon & Schuster, 1977. Hardcover. 220 pp.**

As a foundation for this book, Viscott uses the actual crisis experiences of his clients over the years. He stresses the vital importance of being willing to make hard choices in life. By courageously committing to taking a risk in our decision making process, Viscott feels we can greatly change and enhance the quality of our lives, provided the purpose is well-conceived and based on a solid understanding of our own needs. *Risking* gives practical, step-by-step advice for: facing the unknown, dealing with fear, clearly comprehending the elements of the risk, and developing the strength necessary to embrace the decision. The book also includes systematic guidance on how to make the process work most successfully whether on a personal, intimate, or business level.

334. *Shifting Gears: Finding Security in a Changing World.* **Nena O'Neill and George O'Neill. New York: M. Evans and Co., Inc., 1974. Hardcover. 255 pp.**

The focus of this book, which extends beyond marriage per se, is how to adapt to a world of continual social change and then incorporate this change into a personal life plan. Believing that life offers no guarantees, the authors present a positive, viable plan with specific guidelines for making good choices "in a world of futureshock." The O'Neills believe that a sense of helplessness and paralysis is inevitable in the fearful face of change unless individuals learn ways to develop sensible life strategies. Topics include: seven ways to manage one's life creatively, dealing with the "maturity myth," avoiding self-deprecation, using crisis productively, focusing on real needs, decision-making strategies, and the necessity of giving up mentors.

335. *Sudden Endings: Wife Rejection in Happy Marriages.* **Madeline Bennett. New York: Wm. Morrow, Inc., 1991. Hardcover. 240 pp.**

Bennett writes from her own traumatic experience. After 25 years of a seemingly happy marriage with no apparent danger signals or problems, her husband rejected her. The author has interviewed 25 women left by trusted and loved husbands to whom they fully supposed they would be married forever. An analysis of these women and the characteristics of their life scenarios led to the development of what Bennett calls the "Wife Rejection Syndrome," where a husband abandons his wife in order to "solve his own crisis of low self-esteem." One of the book's goals is to help women understand this process, not an uncommon one, and to realize that they are not alone. Another goal is to warn unsuspecting women of the possibility.

336. *'Til Divorce Do Us Part: A Fresh Look at Divorce.* **Dr. R. Lofton Hudson. New York: Thomas Nelson Inc. Publ., 1973. Hardcover. 132 pp.**

A conservative book based heavily on Scripture and fundamental Christian beliefs, this selection deals with the problems of actual individuals who are struggling with some of organized Christianity's biases against divorce and remarriage. Believing in the literal interpretation of the Scriptures, many of these individuals feel confused about their ability either to divorce or to remarry. From his long experience as a counselor, Dr. Hudson offers alternatives, compassion, and a view founded in the "reasonableness" of Christ and Christianity. The audience is intended to be those considering divorce or already divorced as well as their relatives and friends.

337. *Transitions: Making Sense of Life's Changes. Strategies for Coping With the Difficult, Painful and Confusing Times in Your Life.* **William Bridges. Reading, MA: Addison-Wesley Publishers, 1980. Paperback. 170 pp.**

It is Bridges' belief that most individuals cope with change poorly even though it occurs today at a rate much more rapid than ever before. He says this is especially true in the areas of marriage and work. His guide offers advice and valuable techniques that can be used to recognize and deal more effectively with the elements of transition. According to Bridges, making a change demands that we acknowledge an ending and then select an alternative path. He divides transition into "Endings, The Neutral Zone, and The New Beginning" with "disorientation and reorientation" as turning points. The book aims to make parting with the status quo less threatening and confusing and to make it a more predictable and acceptable rite of passage in life.

338. *Turning Points: How People Change Through Crisis & Commitment.* **Ellen Goodman. New York: A Fawcett Crest Book, 1979. Paperback. 295 pp.**

Goodman draws a picture of society in 1979. She discusses the multitude of confusing "dilemmas" new sex-role trends are causing in intimate and other types of relationships. Her book, based on 100 interviews with common people (housewives, husbands, young couples, and divorced people), examines: exactly "how we change," what happens within us during these dramatically evolving periods, and why we so often try to stop the process. The stresses and strains experienced during certain "passages" in our lives are analyzed as are the reasons we all view change in different ways. In addition, she considers how we react to and handle change. Other topics are: the effects of the women's movement, women working, and wives being abandoned by husbands.

339. *Turning Points: Self-Renewal at Midlife.* **Sol Landau with Joan M. Thomas. Far Hills, NJ: New Horizon Press, 1985. Hardcover. 181 pp.**

As a rabbi and president of the Midlife Services Foundation, Landau offers practical suggestions for making moments of crisis opportunities for reassessment and growth. The book observes that midlife frequently brings with it passages and problems in health, careers, and family. These can result in potentially traumatic outcomes, it notes, such as death, divorce, job loss, menopause, burnout, or serious illness. While the impact of such crises is not to be minimized, the authors believe that the way in which people handle each turning point affects whether or not their life and its relationships will deteriorate or actually be revitalized and renewed. Landau and Thomas use case histories to illustrate how readers can accomplish such renewal successfully.

340. *Uncoupling: The Art of Coming Apart. A Guide to Sane Divorce.* **Norman Sheresky and Marya Mannes. New York: The Viking Press, 1972. Hardcover. 208 pp.**

In clear terms, this guidebook analyzes the destructive psychological, social, and legal "warfare" associated with divorce. It outlines suggestions for surviving "with grace, tolerance, and good humor." Most helpful to those ending a marriage, it may also have value for those who are happily married and those who fear a potential uncoupling. The authors hope to educate the reader about using divorce and the courtroom only after exhausting all other avenues. They believe that, at that point, the divorce should be as amicable and sensible as possible. Sheresky and Mannes view adversarial divorce as "pathetically unnecessary." Their primary goal is just and fair treatment of the whole family unit. They say that lawyers, who are often personally motivated, should be avoided.

341. *Uncoupling: Turning Points in Intimate Relationships.* **Diane Vaughn. New York: Oxford University Press, 1986. Hardcover. 250 pp.**

Based on in-depth research, Vaughn's book studies the inner workings of deteriorating intimate relationships and the roles individuals play in the "leavetaking process." She guides the reader from the first indication of a breakup to the persistence of attachment long after the actual uncoupling itself. The book addresses reconciliation in addition to the ways in which partners deceive each other in the process. *Uncoupling* categorizes individuals into the "initiator" and "still loving" partner and analyzes them from the perspective of their ability to survive on their own. The audience consists of readers who fear a crisis or know one is occurring as well as those who seek a clearer grasp of what actually did happen during what can be a very rough transition.

342. *Women in Transition: A Feminist Handbook on Separation and Divorce.* **Women in Transition, Inc. New York: Charles Scribner's Sons, 1975. Hardcover. 538 pp.**

Women actually undergoing some form of transition put together this book. They created their group, a Philadelphia feminist collective, in order to offer support to women grappling with issues like separation and divorce. Their handbook is an extensive and comprehensive resource work containing detailed information as well as strategies. Much of the advice is derived from the members' personal experience in areas such as: emotional needs, children, lesbian mothers, the problems of welfare, alternative custody strategies, sexism in the workplace, beatings, rape and self-defense, legal matters, financial resources, property decisions, and continuing education.

343. *You Can Excel in Times of Change.* Shad Helmstetter. New York: Pocket Books, a Div. of Simon & Schuster, 1991. Hardcover. 258 pp.

Helmstetter complains that, although our handling of life's inevitable changes affects our futures immensely, no attention to understanding change is a formal part of our education or upbringing. This book is modeled on the author's successful workshops and strives to provide us the opportunity to work on change on our own. It offers concrete guidelines and exercises for: recognizing the need to change, understanding the seven most common types of change, developing a positive and creative attitude, determining the style to be used, making a plan and taking action, and evaluating the process. Stories illustrate successful strategies. The premise is that "taking charge" when change occurs will lead the reader to happier and more productive lives.

For additional help in "Breaking Up," see also book numbers:

- 6: *The Cinderella Complex*
- 10: *The Emotionally Abused Woman*
- 12: *The Female Stress Syndrome*
- 13: *Getting Unstuck*
- 14: *Golden Handcuffs*
- 15: *The Good Girl Syndrome*
- 19: *How to Be an Assertive (Not Aggressive) Woman in Life, Love and on the Job*
- 26: *Looking Out for #1*
- 37: *The Seashell People*
- 39: *Slay Your Own Dragons*
- 42: *Sweet Suffering: Woman As Victim*
- 49: *Unfinished Business: Pressure Points in the Lives of Women*
- 51: *What Smart Women Know*
- 56: *Why Women Worry*
- 60: *Women & Self-Esteem*
- 61: *Women & the Blues*
- 68: *Bad Guys*
- 69: *Being a Man*
- 93: *Men Who Hate Women and the Women Who Love Them*
- 103: *Some Men Are More Perfect Than Others*
- 116: *Husbands and Wives*

117: *The Kinsey Institute New Report on Sex*

119: *Marriage Divorce Remarriage*

120: *Marriage, Love, Sex and Divorce*

128: *The Art of Staying Together*

141: *Creative Marriage*

155: *How to Live With Another Person*

156: *How to Make Love All the Time*

163: *The Intermarriage Handbook*

177: *Love Is Letting Go of Fear*

195: *The Mirages of Marriage*

211: *Relationshift*

247: *How to Salvage Your Marriage or Survive Your Divorce*

248: *I Love You, Let's Work It Out*

277: *When a Mate Wants Out*

278: *When Love Goes Wrong*

290: *Every Other Man*

329: *Our Turn*

350: *The Day the Loving Stopped*

353: *Divorce and Your Child*

358: *A Grief Out of Season*

362: *Healthy Divorce*

365: *A Hole in My Heart: Adult Children of Divorce Speak Out*

368: *The Kids' Book About Single Parent Families*

379: *Surviving the Break-up*

380: *Talking About Divorce and Separation*

383: *What Should I Tell the Kids?*

384: *What's Going to Happen to Me?*

387: *Child Support*

393: *Dealing With Divorce*

394: *Divided Children*

396: *Divorce and Money*

397: *The Divorce Decision*

398: *The Divorce Decisions Workbook*

401: *Divorce Help Sourcebook*

407: *Divorcing*

411: *Getting Divorced Without Ruining Your Life*

428: *Winning Your Divorce*

434: *Crazy Time: Surviving Divorce*

436: *Divorce and New Beginnings*

439: *Divorced*

442: *Forgiveness*

443: *The Fresh Start Divorce Recovery Workbook*

446: *Guilt: Letting Go*

447: *Guilt Is the Teacher, Love Is the Lesson*

448: *How to Fall Out of Love*

453: *Letting Go*

456: *Life's Parachutes*

457: *Living and Loving After Divorce*

458: *Living Through Personal Crisis*

460: *Loveshock*

461: *Marital Separation*

462: *Necessary Losses*

470: *Staying On Top When Your World Turns Upside Down*

471: *Ten Days To Self-Esteem*

475: *Why Me • Why This • Why Now*

478: *The World of the Formerly Married*

479: *45 And Single Again*

484: *The Divorced Woman's Handbook*

485: *First Person Singular*

486: *Flying Solo*

487: *Formerly Married: Learning to Live With Yourself*

488: *Going It Alone*

496: *Loneliness*

504: *Single Again*

508: *Single Parents Are People Too*

511: *Singles: The New Americans*

512: *Singling*

514: *Suddenly Single*

515: *Survival Guide for the Suddenly Single*

522: *Choosing Lovers*

528: *Good Guys/Bad Guys*
552: *Why Love Is Not Enough*

8

The Impact of Divorce on Children

A hole in my heart

One of the primary concerns in considering the divorce option is what will happen to the children. Some couples fear potential emotional, psychological, or academic damage so much that they decide to endure an unsatisfactory marriage rather than risk any harm to their families. The question then becomes: how detrimental is an unhappy marriage to the child's development over the long-term?

The books chosen for this chapter focus on these complex issues in great detail. While most do not deny that the child's welfare should be of primary consideration and that this event can certainly be one of the most difficult for a child to manage, they do stress that careful and responsible handling of the transition can greatly reduce if not eliminate pain. A number of authors, who have studied the recovery of post-divorce families, record predictable effects in every phase of a child's life from infancy through adulthood. Many offer helpful strategies for parents who recognize the critical importance of remaining an involved, nonhostile parenting team. Authors help readers learn what trouble signs to look for, how to talk to their children about the divorce, and how it feels to be the affected child. They also enlighten the reader on the problems of losing touch with a father, being a victim of a custody dispute, or living with a single parent. Children themselves have written many of the books.

Caring parents will want to consult experts like these long before they need to address such sensitive issues with their children.

344. *Adult Children of Divorce: Breaking the Cycle and Finding Fulfillment in Love, Marriage and Family.* **Edward M. Beal, M.D. and Gloria**

Hochman. New York: Delacorte Press, Bantam Doubleday, 1991. Hardcover. 347 pp.

Beal and Hochman call their book the first designed for those who are still suffering or recovering from their parents' divorce. Case studies, interviews, counseling work, and research provide the basis for the book, which analyzes the impact of a breakup especially later in life as mature intimate commitments are sought. "Fears, resentment, and anger" often remain for years. The effects upon daughters as opposed to sons are also examined. The authors offer techniques to help: identify and understand birth-family relating styles (including divorce events), let go of damaging baggage from the past, heal the scars, and make the needed changes to break the cycle of divorce for both oneself and one's children.

345. *The Boys' and Girls' Book About Divorce: For Children and Their Divorced Parents—The First Book of its Kind.* **Richard A. Gardner, M.D. Northvale, NJ: Bantam Books, Jason Aronson, Inc., 1970. Paperback. 155 pp.**

Written for young children in simple language, large print, and with abundant illustrations, this book provides comforting answers to the basic emotional and psychological issues related to the divorce process. Gardner believes that children are far more strong than we think and thus his approach is straightforward and honest. His thesis is that parents should be "appropriately truthful" with their children. Topics include: anger, guilt, blame, parental love, fear of being left alone, professional counseling, and how to get along better with their separated mother, father, or stepparents. Children may read the book alone but Gardner feels it might be better to read aloud together as a springboard to conversation regarding specific issues.

346. *Children & Divorce: What to Expect; How to Help.* **Archibald D. Hart, Ph.D. Dallas, TX: Word Publishing, 1982, 1989. Paperback. 179 pp.**

Hart sees divorce as an immensely traumatic and painful disruption that requires children to use strengths they often do not possess. Writing from a Christian viewpoint as a child of divorce himself, he outlines what he views as the greatest dangers so that parents can minimize the most harmful consequences. While not anti-divorce, the book clearly emphasizes the gravity of the impact so that parents can make more informed decisions. Hart calls divorce the greatest "mental health crisis" for modern children. He urges parents to guard against letting their own battles scar these young victims. The book covers: mistakes often made by parents, watching for repressed "anger, anxiety, or depression," and nurturing the child's self-esteem.

347. *Children of Divorce*: *Developmental and Clinical Issues.* **Craig A. Everett, ed. New York: The Haworth Press, Inc., 1989. Hardcover. 348 pp.**

Aimed chiefly at professionals, this group of 18 articles studies the "developmental, structural, and interactional issues" surrounding children in divorcing families. They look at the full gamut of painful emotions from vulnerability and pain to anxiety, fear, hostility, and betrayal. The authors believe many of these feelings are made worse by adversarial divorce and can often persist into adult life. Aftereffects include doubts about the validity of relationships and problems with their own dating and mating patterns. Topics covered include: position of the child in the pre-divorce disintegrating unit, response patterns of siblings, post-divorce roles of children, and the child's view of it all.

348. *Children of Separation and Divorce.* **Irving R. Stuart and Lawrence E. Abt, eds. New York: Grossman Publishers, 1972. Hardcover. 313 pp.**

Stuart and Abt's book, composed of a compilation of articles, emphasizes numerous problems common to children in divorcing or separating families. A wide variety of professionals including social workers, lawyers, clergymen, and psychologists offer their views on such topics as: "the child as hostage," the adolescent, the child's adjustment to divorce, effects on education, religious issues, "economically and socially deprived children," and resources available. The focus is on reducing damaging and harmful effects on children by bringing parents to a deeper understanding of the consequences of this traumatic family event. In nontechnical language, the book discusses what should and should not be done.

349. *Daddy Doesn't Live Here Anymore*: *A Guide for Divorced Parents.* **Rita Turow. Matteson, IL: Great Lakes Living Press Ltd., 1977. Hardcover. 196 pp.**

Turow writes for those contemplating divorce as well as those who have already completed the legal steps. She covers many potential questions and problems, especially those relating to a child's reactions. Through fictional examples, interviews, and a specially designed parent survey, the author identifies common difficulties. The book provides help in dealing with the child's sense of guilt, sadness, hostility, and potential loneliness. It lists pertinent literature and agencies from which parents can obtain support. Topics also include: telling the children, custody, holidays, relatives, financial problems, getting professional help, reorganizing the family's life, the dangers of putting the child in the middle, and remarriage.

350. *The Day the Loving Stopped: A Daughter's View of Her Parents' Divorce.* **Julie Autumn List. New York: Seaview Books, 1980. Hardcover. 215 pp.**

Julie List's parents divorced and an "emotional tug of war" began. Approximately one month later, she started confiding her often confused feelings to a journal. It is this source, along with letters to her father, that provide the basis for her sensitive, personal account of one child's actual experiences with the entire divorce process. The book can be of use to parents as well as children in understanding the sorrow and anger of the period, the impact of the inevitable chaos, and the difficulty of remaining "loyal" to both parents. The spirit is positive in that Julie shows, no matter what happens, who was to blame, or where everyone lives, parent-child love can still survive.

351. *Dinosaurs Divorce: A Guide for Changing Families.* **Laureen Krasny Brown and Marc Brown. Boston, MA: Little, Brown & Co., 1986. Paperback. 32 pp.**

This award-winning children's book handles a variety of issues faced by families going through the process of divorce. It is aimed at very young readers and examines profoundly complex problems in a colorful, simple, and easy-to-understand manner. A dictionary of "divorce words" at the beginning of the book lays the fundamental groundwork. Topics include: reasons parents divorce, what happens during and after the divorce, visiting, having two homes, celebrating holidays, dealing with friends, meeting parents' new friends, and stepfamilies.

352. *Divided Families: What Happens to Children When Parents Part.* **Frank F. Furstenberg, Jr. and Andrew J. Cherlin. Cambridge, MA: Harvard University Press, 1991. Hardcover. 142 pp.**

Divided Families examines what happens during divorce and how to handle the subsequent disruption. The book outlines factors important for the healthy post-divorce survival of children: a soundly functioning mother as caretaker, consistency and "predictable routines" at home, the absence of parental conflict in the presence of children, and an ongoing closeness with their father. The authors blame divorce settlements that are financially unfair to women for seriously increasing a mother's dysfunction. They also analyze ways in which connections with the father can suffer once the mother no longer provides the "link" he depended upon. The book presents its theories via the study of a model couple's journey from separation through remarriage.

353. *Divorce and Your Child: Practical Suggestions for Parents.* **Sonja Goldstein, L.L.B. and Albert J. Solnit, M.D. New Haven, CT: Yale University Press, 1984. Paperback. 135 pp.**

Written by an attorney and a child psychiatrist, this book combines expert views on child-rearing and parenting for those in the process of divorce. While the audience is parents, the focus is on reducing pain and traumatic effects upon children. The goal is to make the disruptive changes constructive rather than destructive. Goldstein and Solnit's book looks at: reactions of children of different ages, handling "grief, anger, and guilt," the benefits of involving children throughout the process, and safeguarding a lasting bond with both parents. It offers practical advice on: financial matters, the effects of a parent moving out, telling the children, custody arrangements, "enforcing provisions of the divorce decree," and issues surrounding new marriages and stepfamilies.

354. *Divorce Without Victims: Helping Children Through Divorce With a Minimum of Pain and Trauma.* **Stuart Berger, M.D. Boston, MA: Houghton Mifflin Co., 1983. Hardcover. 194 pp.**

This handbook is designed to help parents become more aware of the highly detrimental side effects their actions and "gameplaying" can have on their children. The author/psychiatrist stresses the importance of providing children with "two genuinely loving parents" in order to assure that they survive the divorce process unharmed. He gives advice on how to maturely and sensitively handle the emotional difficulties that children inevitably experience. Topics include: discussing the divorce, custody issues, problems in "leaning on the opposite sex child," watching for hidden feelings, distinguishing between natural mourning responses and depression, knowing when to get professional help, potential remarriage, and stepfamilies.

355. *Divorced Kids: What You Need to Know to Help Kids Survive Divorce.* **Laureen Johnson and Georglyn Rosenfield. New York: Fawcett Crest, 1990. Paperback. 224 pp.**

These mothers believe all children need help in coping with divorce and that educated positive action by parents can spare kids pain and debilitation. Johnson and Rosenfield write with personal experience gained from their own "mistakes and victories." Although they are advocates for children, their handbook is full of practical strategies for parents. The underlying critical concept promoted by the book is that parents must instill in children a "strong emotional center" by nurturing their sense of self-esteem and by assuring them that they are loved. Topics include: communicating with ex-spouses, handling loss and mourning, forgiveness, visitation, support groups, children's anger, grandparents, teachers, household chores, the importance of consistent discipline, and stepfamily challenges.

356. *Divorced Parenting: How to Make It Work.* **Dr. Sol Goldstein. New York: E.P. Dutton, Inc., 1982, 1984. Paperback. 200 pp.**

Goldstein, a psychiatrist, believes that most children are strong enough to "survive divorce" psychologically intact. His research has shown, however, that the children who suffer most deeply are those whose parents have allowed the conflict-laden divorce process to get in the way of their being "caring and effective" parents. The author finds this destructive and unnecessary. His book offers practical guidelines that will enable ex-mates to participate in "constructive and healthy parenting" with their children's needs foremost in mind. Topics include: informing the children, defusing battles with the ex-spouse, rising "beyond mere survival" to building a rewarding relationship, coping with holidays and schooling, understanding the child's needs, and dealing with the issues of dating and stepfamilies.

357. *For the Sake of the Children: How to Share Your Children With Your Ex-Spouse in Spite of Your Anger.* **Kris Kline and Stephen Pew, Ph.D. Rocklin, CA: Prima Publishing, 1992. Hardcover. 250 pp.**

The mental and emotional health as well as the successful adjustment of both children and ex-spouses depend on the development of a post-divorce "situational peace," according to Kline and Pew. Their book presents readers with practical strategies for: interacting and talking about each other unjudgmentally, reducing stress levels, ridding oneself of destructive and deep-seated negative behavior patterns and resentments, eliminating game-playing, learning to relate in a "friendly manner," and arriving at an inner peace. In addition, the authors suggest new ways to communicate thereby minimizing conflict and unnecessary suffering in the children's lives. Case histories and techniques for surviving numerous difficult scenarios are also included.

358. *A Grief Out of Season: When Your Parents Divorce in Your Adult Years.* **Noelle Fintushel and Nancy Hillard, Ph.D. Boston, MA: Little, Brown and Company, 1991. Hardcover. 315 pp.**

This unique study, said to be the largest of its kind, examines the effects of late parental divorce on adult children, ages 18-46. When marriages over 20 years long break down, the authors find that the children, now adults, often have dramatic and disturbing reactions. Fintushel and Hillard suggest that in many cases, the children's marriages, which are frequently modeled after their parents' unions, seem in jeopardy. In other cases, loss, guilt, and hostility combine to affect the children deeply and may also cause them to align with one parent or the other creating serious stress. The authors' goal is to help readers cope with such a crisis and to assist with the long range recovery process for all victims. They give concrete guidelines to clarify feelings and help people deal with them.

359. *Growing Up Divorced: A Road to Healing for Adult Children of Divorce.* **Diane Fassel, Ph.D. New York: Pocket Books, Simon & Schuster, 1991. Hardcover. 194 pp.**

Fassel writes for adult children of divorce and for couples in the process of divorce who are concerned about the aftereffects of the breakup on their children. In layman's terms, the book outlines five kinds of divorce and discusses the relationship of a child's age at the time of the split to the type of reaction later experienced. While divorce can make children more capable of handling change, Fassel highlights predominantly negative effects. She discusses ten character traits some children display including: a feeling of powerlessness, a need to belong, fear of abandonment and conflict, the desire to be in control, and too great a sense of responsibility. *Growing Up Divorced* asserts that these children may also experience difficulties in their own intimate relationships in later years. The book offers help for successful recovery.

360. *Growing Up Divorced: How to Help Your Child Cope With Every Stage— From Infancy Through Teens.* **Linda Bird Francke. New York: A Fawcett Crest Book, Publ. by Ballantine Books, 1983. Paperback. 294 pp.**

This book is based on interviews with hundreds of children of all ages whose parents divorced. Its findings reveal that divorce can be a very threatening and disruptive event in the lives of children and that responses will differ according to their age and sex. Francke does not focus on specific individual problems but the child's overall state of emotional well-being. She gives guidance to parents on minimizing trauma and pain by helping them shepherd their children "from confusion to a renewed sense of security." The book discusses typical timetables for a child's most common responses to divorce. It also aids readers in detecting unexpressed or hidden feelings, "sleeper effects," and optimal times to divorce or remarry.

361. *Growing Up With Divorce: Helping Your Child Avoid Immediate and Later Emotional Problems.* **Neil Kalter. New York: A Fawcett Columbine Book, Publ. by Ballantine, 1990. Paperback. 416 pp.**

Kalter states that nearly half of today's children will watch their parents divorce. He writes a "practical guidebook" with strategies for minimizing the pain children go through because of the confusing range of emotions they will inevitably feel. Full of examples, the book teaches the reader how to: be aware of what kids feel, identify the impact of the "three universal stages of divorce" depending on their ages and sex, encourage the free expression of feelings, and spot markers of serious emotional problems. Kalter studies difficulties that can result from divorce, including: increased hostility, sadness and depression, diminished self-confidence, and problems with academics, social life, and future male-female intimacy."

362. *Healthy Divorce: For Parents and Children—An Original Clinically Proven Program for Working Through the Fourteen Stages of Separation, Divorce and Remarriage.* **Craig Everett and Sandra Volgy Everett. San Francisco, CA: Jossey-Bass Publishers, 1994. Hardcover. 187 pp.**

This counseling team believes strongly that couples who plan their divorce with explicit goals in mind can achieve a "constructive rather than destructive transition." Their "healthy" divorce is reached by attention to details and a decidedly positive attitude. The Everetts write for divorcing or divorced couples with children. They divide the disruptive process into 14 stages including the first doubts to "distancing," separation, "pseudoreconciliation," the actual decision, mediation, adversarial divorce, co-parenting, remarriages, and the "blending" of the new families. Knowledge of patterns is key, they propose, and cooperation in putting in the necessary effort is critical. Checklists, examples, practical advice and solutions to common problems are given along with lists of resources.

363. *Helping Children Cope With Divorce.* **Edward Teyber. New York: Lexington Books, Macmillan Inc., 1992. Hardcover. 221 pp.**

As a child-advocate, Teyber gives realistic help to parents for lessening a child's hardships during divorce. He presents the chronology of intense emotions that a child may experience. He also stresses the importance of guaranteeing the child a loving relationship with both parents after the divorce. Case histories illustrate potential problems and issues in the several year adjustment process. Sample dialogues as well as critical "parenting skills" are also analyzed. Topics include: sadness, "separation anxieties," shielding children from conflict, treating children like adults, age and gender response differences, reconciliation fantasies, defining needs, parental guilt, pain, and cooperation, custody and mediation, post-divorce discipline, and stepfamilies.

364. *Helping Children of Divorce: A Handbook for Parents and Teachers.* **Susan Arnsberg Diamond. New York: Schochen Books, 1985. Hardcover. 115 pp.**

Diamond's purpose is unique. She wishes to educate parents and school personnel in some practical procedures that help reduce the trauma, tension, and poor academic performance of students from divorced families. Using extensive interviews and her own personal experience as a dean of students, the author emphasizes revising existing procedures and standardized forms to better accommodate nontraditional families. The book gives constructive advice on: distinguishing between children's normal responses and behavior that needs therapy, activities that offer students ways to express their inner feelings, helpful services within the school system, and the elimination of "insensitive, unthinking actions and remarks" on the part of school personnel.

365. *A Hole in My Heart: Adult Children of Divorce Speak Out. For People Contemplating Divorce or Whose Parents Are Divorced: A Way to Recovery.* **Claire Berman. New York: Fireside, Simon & Schuster, 1991. Hardcover. 285 pp.**

This book studies 50 adult children of divorce, ages 20-60, whose parents had split earlier in their lives. Berman discusses their memories of past experiences, the character strengths the event gave them, and the resulting problems they later encountered in relationships. The author suggests that many of these "children" exhibit trouble with low self-esteem, sexuality, control issues, and commitment anxiety. She warns also that patterns of the past can be repeated in their own marriages unless they attempt to change. Her guidelines for such change include: releasing anger and dealing with conflict, finding support from others, and "forgiving" parents in order to reconcile with them.

366. *How It Feels When Parents Divorce.* **Jill Krementz. New York: Alfred A. Knopf, 1988. Paperback. 128 pp.**

Nineteen diverse children 7–16 years old reveal their feelings about the emotional, mental, and physical impact of divorce. Krementz is convinced that all children "pay the price" somehow. She believes that adults can balance negative effects, however, when they soften the upheaval by remaining an unmanipulative, sensitive, and nonhostile parenting team. The book discusses children's emotions ranging from a sense of guilt, hostility, pain, and contempt to total surprise, understanding, and even relief. Confusion is widely felt and exacerbated when kids are trapped in their parents' battle, it says. Topics include: telling friends, fears for their own future relationships, single parent and joint custody, parental dating and remarriage, and the issues of stepfamilies.

367. *How to Live With a Single Parent*: *Parents Without Partners, Inc.* **Sara Gilbert. New York: Lothrop, Lee & Shepard Books, a Div. of William Morrow & Co., 1982. Hardcover. 128 pp.**

This book is specifically written for the "millions of American teenagers who live with a single parent." Parents, however, will find a great deal of useful advice as well, suggests the author. Gilbert offers practical guidelines on coping with the variety of complex issues in a healthier and more enjoyable way. Her book is based upon personal experience and numerous conversations with teens and professional experts. Areas discussed include: conflict and stress at home, handling financial issues, the notion of the "broken home," "getting caught in the middle," problems with parents' lovers and friends, and possible responses to crisis situations.

368. *The Kids' Book About Single Parent Families: By Kids for Everyone.* **Paul Dolmetsch and Alexa Shih, eds. Garden City, NY: A Dolphin Book, Doubleday & Co., Inc., 1985. Paperback. 193 pp.**

Kids 11–15 years old actually wrote this unique text. It treats the full gamut of short- and long-term problems affecting children in families headed, for any reason, by a single parent. Its goal is to assist parents in developing a deepened awareness of their child's point of view, thereby creating a stronger family unit. The authors evaluate these families as distinctly different though "not inherently good or bad." While life may not be the same as it used to be, they say the attitude is positive and encouraging. Topics include: the immediate days, weeks, and months after the loss of the parent; the aftermath and future; discipline and family rules; problems with the working parent; stepfamilies; and overcoming "fear, anger, and guilt."

369. *The Kids' Book of Divorce*: *By, For & About Kids.* **The Unit at Fayerweather Street School. Eric Rofes, ed. New York: Vintage Books, a Div. of Random House, 1982. Paperback. 122 pp.**

The Kids' Book of Divorce is actually the product of 20 diverse young children (ages 11–14) whose parents either continually contemplated or actually did divorce. Evolving out of a support group designed to help them cope, the book took two years to complete. The children express their views candidly and offer advice. Some of their ideas are gleaned from books they read or from professionals they interviewed. Topics covered include: understanding the legal process, adapting to new living arrangements, dealing with visitation and holidays, obtaining professional help, being impartial to their parents, handling their parents' new social life, and stepfamily issues.

370. *The Kids' Guide to Divorce*. **John P. Brogan and Ula Maiden. New York: Fawcett Crest, 1986. Paperback. 164 pp.**

This book, aimed at kids themselves (ages 10–12+), was written by two experienced counselors who worked with hundreds of kids in the same predicament. Based on an extensive questionnaire answered by 200 kids, it reveals that most have a difficult time accepting and adjusting to this often painful event. The book's goal is to help children develop greater familiarity with what actually goes on during a divorce and thus improve their coping skills. Included is a "Loss Inventory" as well as information on why marriages end and what happens legally. Sample topics are: coping with shock, embarrassment, and guilt, strange parental behavior, parents' new romantic involvements, life style changes, being in a single parent house, and money problems.

371. *Long Distance Parenting*: *A Guide for Divorced Parents*. **Miriam Galper Cohen. New York: New American Library, a Div. of Penguin Books, 1989. Hardcover. 193 pp.**

Cohen offers practical advice for parents who are attempting to maintain satisfying connections with children when they are geographically separated by a considerable distance. She contends that while the relationship will inevitably experience changes, closeness and caring can grow and continue without harm to either parent or child. The book gives attention to: overcoming anxiety and loneliness, ways to answer the needs of everyone involved, understanding one's legal rights, little techniques to maintain regular contact, and methods of restoring lost contact. The guide is based upon the author's own personal experience along with information gleaned from 225 questionnaires and interviews with affected families.

372. *Mom's House, Dad's House: Making Shared Custody Work*. **Isolina Ricci. New York: Macmillan Publishing Co., 1980. Hardcover. 270 pp.**

Ricci writes for professionals, parents, and teachers. She advocates involving both parents in positive approach toward the creation of two homes for the children. Each adult can then participate in a "meaningful," "independent" parenting role, she says. The book covers the seven "stages of transition" that go from negotiating a "good divorce" to steps for providing children with "security and continuity." It discusses techniques for changing an intimate relationship with an ex-spouse into a working partnership and keeping the children out of the "middle." Checklists, surveys, suggested activities, sample "parenting agreements," and other aids are included. Case studies clarify crisis periods, distance problems, daycare, and the sharing of holidays.

373. *My Kids Don't Live With Me Anymore: Coping With the Custody Crisis.* **Doreen Virtue. Minneapolis, MN: CompCare Publishers, 1988. Paperback. 177 pp.**

The author temporarily surrendered custody of her children when she returned to school. Subsequent futile attempts to regain custody left her devastatingly depressed and angry. Thus she writes for other mothers and fathers suffering from such loss. Her book uses moving stories of real people to provide step-by-step guidelines for: regaining stability, healing the overwhelming pain, and "rebuilding" oneself as both a person and a parent. The goal is to provide solace, describe the emotional ramifications of the problem, and offer hope. Affirmations and concrete advice are included for: dealing with legalities, coping with anger and fear, resolving support issues, responding to friends' reactions, and overcoming the loss of "physical closeness."

374. *The Parent/Child Manual on Divorce for the Education of Children: A Book to Read Aloud Together.* **Maria Sullivan. New York: TOR, Tom Doherty Associates Inc., 1988. Paperback. 119 pp.**

Sullivan believes that divorce can be one of childhood's most painful experiences. Therefore, she urges parents to work diligently to ease this transition so they can communicate openly with the children, avoid asking kids to take sides, and help them survive unscarred. Her book cautions parents to watch for signs of self-blame, anger, and loneliness along with indications that children are burying their questions and fears. Its purpose is to create "informed" children by answering their questions through "lessons" in "dialogue form." Dealing with loss and grief is facilitated by parents and children reading aloud and discussing the 22 individual stories of other children in similar circumstances.

375. *The Parents' Book About Divorce: The #1 Guide for Concerned Parents Revised and Updated for Today's Needs.* **Richard A. Gardner, M.D. Toni Burbank and Jay Howland, eds. Rev. Ed, Cresskill, NJ: Creative Therapeutics, 1991. Paperback. 385 pp.**

Updated for the 90s, this book is a detailed guide with clear, practical suggestions. It is aimed at parents who are worried about the effects of divorce upon children and who would like to "ease the painful shock" of the transition. Written by a prominent child psychologist, it covers a comprehensive range of topics including: remaining married for the sake of the children, mediation, selecting the proper lawyer, custody, counseling, communication, understanding the child's needs, grief, anger, nurturing low self-esteem, detecting unspoken problems, keeping in touch with teachers, friends and neighbors, new relationships and remarriage, dealing with shame and guilt, avoiding blame, and adjusting to step-siblings.

376. *Planning a Wedding With Divorced Parents.* **Cindy Moore and Tricia Windon with Martha Giddens Nesbit. New York: Crown Publications, Inc., 1992. Paperback. 197 pp.**

Personal experience in trying to contend with divorced parents while planning a child's wedding gave rise to this handbook. A mother and wedding consultant have collaborated to produce a step-by-step guide and reference source for every conceivable concern and sticky issue. The authors feel conventional traditions simply do not work for the one of two couples who divorce. They furnish checklists, schedules, sample invitations, and announcements to smooth the way for their readers. Topics include: budgets and expenses, pre-parties, the ceremony, giving the bride away, photography, receptions, seating, and dancing. The book's objective is to provide a resource that will lessen tension, anxiety, and hostility through careful advance attention to details.

377. *Quality Time: Easing the Children Through Divorce.* **Melvin G. Goldzband, M.D. New York: McGraw Hill, 1985. Hardcover. 193 pp.**

Quality Time advises the reader on how to focus on the children's best interests and minimize pain during the emotion-fraught uncoupling process. The workbook, with exercises and questions, talks to parents about the negative impact of custody disputes and other battles over the children. It offers help in better understanding the roles of fathers, coping with guilt feelings, and avoiding thoughtless actions. Quality rather than quantity of time together is the emphasis. Goldzband also deals with such important matters as: kidnapping a child, sexual abuse, visitation conflicts, seeking outside support, the development of healthier relationships with the children, holidays, and dealing with stepfamilies.

378. *Second Chances: Men, Women & Children A Decade After Divorce. Who Wins, Who Loses and Why?* **Judith S. Wallerstein and Sandra Blakeslee. New York: Ticknor & Fields, 1989. Hardcover. 329 pp.**

These authors began, in 1971, what was to be a one year detailed study of the progress of individual family members after a divorce. In the process, they found that time alone does not reduce the effects of broken marriages and that often years later, continuing side effects can still be seen. Their book is the result of an extended ten year study that Wallerstein and Blakeslee say is the first of its kind. Second Chances observes the "complexities, tragedies, and opportunities inherent in divorce" and their effects upon adults and children. It portrays actual winners and losers in sections on specific families. The book tries to help readers minimize the traumatic financial and psychological impact of an event they view as "profoundly life-changing."

379. *Surviving the Break-Up*: *How Children and Parents Cope With Divorce.* **Judith Wallerstein and Joan Berlin Kelly. New York: Basic Books, Inc., 1980. Hardcover. 341 pp.**

In 1980, this was the first detailed examination of the "immediate and long term effects" of divorce upon children. Based on a study of 60 families over the five years following a divorce, the book looks at children from ages 3 to 18 and how they might be least scarred from this disruptive and life-changing event. The authors propose that the biggest factor in a child's successful recovery is the continuing ability of each parent to perform the appropriate parenting function. They also note that a child's healthy adjustment is impacted more by post-divorce than pre-divorce events. Other topics include: telling the children, reactions to be aware of, seeking help, staying close to the father, and the question of how long anger and longing for reconciliation will remain.

380. *Talking About Divorce and Separation*: *A Dialogue Between Parents and Child.* **Earl A. Grollman. Boston, MA: Beacon Press, 1975. Paperback. 87 pp.**

This book is unusual in that it deals with divorce and separation issues in three parts: first, a simple illustrated "read along section" for young children (probably ten years old and under) designed to be discussed with parents; second, a "Parents' Guide" to assist in the dialogue; and third, a bibliography and resource list. The author's express goal here is: to help families grow in their understanding of the issues, to develop more honest communication, and to assist everyone in coping more successfully with the often painful events and consequences of a divorce.

381. *Vicki Lansky's Divorce Book for Parents*: *Helping Your Children Cope with Divorce and Its Aftermath.* **Vicki Lansky. New York: A Signet Book, The Penguin Group, 1989. Paperback. 255 pp.**

This is a thorough step-by-step examination of all the stages of separation and divorce with "age-specific" practical help for the affected children. The book's goal is to help kids cope, survive, and even thrive through providing them ongoing reassurance that they are loved, will be cared for, and are not to blame. Lansky educates readers about various reactions to expect at each age and advises when to seek professional help. She warns parents that their own negative and angry behavior can be more damaging than divorce itself. Topics include: "preparing" the children, family adjustments, mastering "divorce speak" when discussing former spouses, reconciliation fantasies, "parenting partnerships," and custody and visitation issues.

382. *What Every Child Would Like Parents to Know About Divorce.* **Dr. Lee Salk. New York: Harper & Row Publishers, 1978. Hardcover. 149 pp.**

Salk writes from personal and professional experience as a spokesman for children involved in the emotionally stressful drama of divorce. He also shows sensitivity toward the distress of their parents. The book gives practical, constructive advice about likely danger spots and about lessening the pain for everyone involved. Its style resembles a private therapy session with parents but one focused on the children. As a well-known child psychologist, Salk is a proponent of making the child a real part of the divorce. He says that withholding facts can cause confusion, serious insecurity, and abandonment fears. The handling of child custody is seen as critically important along with being certain that the child is always confident of a parent's love.

383. *What Should I Tell the Kids? A Parent's Guide to Real Problems in the Real World.* **Ava L. Siegler, Ph.D. New York: Dutton, The Penguin Group, 1993. Hardcover. 324 pp.**

Siegler, a psychologist, treats the tough issues professionals or parents encounter with children. Concentrating on the emotional development of three to eleven year olds, the book counsels readers on communicating about such problems as: a child's "five basic fears;" hatred and violence; depression; separation, divorce and remarriage (Chapters 7-9, including the topics of gay, lesbian, mentally ill or abusive parents); incest, bigotry, AIDS and suicide; and illness and death. Sample dialogues help readers learn "protective parenting" techniques or how to channel the dialogue to provide the "cushion of safety" necessary for a child's sound development. Comments called "reparative narratives" accompany each dialogue and provide guidance for parents in understanding a conversation's "healing" elements.

384. *What's Going to Happen to Me? When Parents Separate or Divorce.* **Eda LeShan. New York: Four Winds Press, a Div. of Scholastic Magazine, 1978. Hardcover. 132 pp.**

Though designed especially for children (ages 8–10+), this easy-to-read book may also be useful to parents in dealing with the many problems that occur in separating, divorcing, and divorced families. It draws a picture of the conflicting emotions children feel ranging from relief to shock, guilt to fear, and anger to depression—all of which the author sees as very predictable reactions. LeShan encourages getting in touch with these feelings and expressing them as well as developing a better understanding of the process and the parents' situation as well. She offers answers to a multitude of commonly asked (or even unasked but pondered) questions.

385. *"Your Father's Not Coming Home Anymore": Teenagers Tell How They Survive Divorce.* **Michael Jackson and Jessica Jackson. New York: Richard Marek Publ., Inc., 1981. Hardcover. 320 pp.**

This book was actually written by two teens. It features 38 interviews with a diverse group of youths 13–21 years of age and their varied reactions to parental divorce. The Jacksons include consoling stories of continued faith and hope in life as well as alarming accounts of substance abuse, incest, hostility and violence, and feelings of being deceived and abandoned. Aimed at parents as well as children, it gives an "inside" report on the depth of children's feelings about divorce and the formidable impact the event can have on them. Financial insecurity is seen as one of the most pervasive sources of difficulty. There are positive notes including the fact that the majority of those studied still felt great love for their parents after all was said and done.

For additional help in understanding "The Impact of Divorce on Children," see also book numbers:

128: *The Art of Staying Together*
316: *The Divorce Experience*
320: *How to Get Out of an Unhappy Marriage Or an Unhappy Relationship*
321: *Learning to Leave*
329: *Our Turn*
342: *Women in Transition*
386: *Between Love & Hate: A Guide to Civilized Divorce*
388: *Child Support in America*
389: *The Child Support Survivor's Guide*
390: *Co-Parenting: Sharing Your Child Equally*
391: *The Complete Legal Guide to Marriage, Divorce, Custody and Living Together*
392: *The Custody Revolution: The Father Factor and the Motherhood Mystique*
393: *Dealing With Divorce*
394: *Divided Children*
395: *Divorce And Dissolution of Marriage Laws of the United States*
396: *Divorce and Money*

397: *The Divorce Decision*

401: *Divorce Help Sourcebook*

403: *Divorce Mediation,* Neumann

404: *Divorce Mediation,* Schneider & Schneider

405: *The Divorce Revolution*

406: *Divorce Yourself*

407: *Divorcing*

408: *The Dollars and Sense of Divorce*

409: *Don't Settle for Less*

410: *The Ex-Factor*

411: *Getting Divorced Without Ruining Your Life*

412: *Getting Your Share*

413: *Head and Heart*

414: *Mediate Your Divorce*

415: *Mothers and Divorce*

416: *Mothers On Trial*

417: *Our Money Our Selves*

418: *Parent Vs. Parent*

420: *Rematch*

421: *Sharing Parenthood After Divorce*

422: *Sharing the Children*

423: *The State-by-State Guide to Women's Legal Rights*

424: *Strassels' Tax Savers*

425: *The Survival Guide for Women*

426: *What Every Woman Should Know About Her Husband's Money*

427: *When Couples Part*

428: *Winning Your Divorce*

436: *Divorce and New Beginnings*

443: *The Fresh Start Divorce Recovery Workbook*

457: *Living and Loving After Divorce*

459: *Lost Lovers, Found Friends*

478: *The World of the Formerly Married*

479: *45 And Single Again*

483: *Coping*

484: *The Divorced Woman's Handbook*

486: *Flying Solo*

487: *Formerly Married: Learning to Live With Yourself*

488: *Going It Alone*

489: *How to Parent Alone*

490: *In Praise of Single Parents*

497: *On Our Own*

498: *One on the Seesaw*

500: *Parents Without Partners Sourcebook*

501: *Sex and the Single Parent*

502: *Single: Living Your Own Way*

504: *Single Again*

506: *The Single Mother's Book*

507: *Single Parenting: A Practical Resource Guide*

508: *Single Parents Are People Too*

511: *Singles, The New Americans*

513: *Solo Parenting*

515: *Survival Guide for the Suddenly Single*

520: *Beating the Marriage Odds*

541: *Making Remarriage Work*

544: *The Second Time Around*

549: *To Marry Again*

9

Legal and Financial Aspects of Divorce

The survival guide

Statistics show overwhelmingly that women can experience a dramatic decline in their standard of living after a divorce. Families existing at or below poverty levels frequently have single women as heads. While the causes can be debated, there is no question that inequitable divorce settlements, delinquent alimony and child support payments, and a job market that compensates males and females differently are all too often contributing factors. It is imperative that those involved in a divorce, especially women, be educated about their rights and be prepared to exercise them.

A number of books in this chapter cover potential courses of action in a practical, systematic fashion. Step-by-step support is provided on everything from hiring attorneys and avoiding expensive legal battles to mediation and the divorce laws in various states. Women can learn how to evaluate their budgets, make sound financial decisions, manage their money, and save on taxes. There is wide agreement on the necessity to limit hostility, act cooperatively, avoid custody battles at all costs, and keep everyone as whole as possible for optimum results. Some authors give clear guidelines for processing one's own divorce. Many stand squarely against the adversarial system, which is viewed as too often creating enemies of ex-spouses. Others give specific advice on negotiation skills, custody and visitation, and property division while offering words of caution on dating during the process.

Getting what one deserves, while preserving as much harmony as possible, demands thought and careful preparation, both of which can be greatly facilitated by referring to experts like the ones in this section.

386. *Between Love & Hate: A Guide to Civilized Divorce. How to Resolve Conflict, Improve Communication, and Avoid Costly Legal Battles.* **Lois Gold, M.S.W. New York: Plenum Press, 1992. Hardcover. 353 pp.**

Gold laments the damage caused to all in adversarial divorces. Her practical guide advocates using a more "humane" approach by avoiding court battles, handling the crisis "with dignity," and remaining civil. It stresses working together rather than trying to compete and praises mediation. Using actual cases, Gold provides advice about the entire "legal, financial, and emotional" process: preventing hostile and destructive separations; creating a cooperative parenting atmosphere to help children survive the changes unharmed; mastering new ex-spouse communication and joint decision-making skills; adopting "win-win" strategies to handle conflict with every family member intact; and "letting go" of the past to get on with our new and separate lives.

387. *Child Support: How to Get What Your Child Needs and Desires.* **Carole A. Chambers. New York: Summit Books, 1991. Hardcover. 283 pp.**

Among the worst inequities of divorce are the grave economic consequences for mothers and children. Chambers estimates that 30 percent of women never receive any support. Designed for women considering or involved in a divorce, this detailed book presents concrete guidelines for determining the amount of support that is needed and for getting it. Knowledge of the system is seen as a way to prevent "victimization" and to preserve control over one's life. Charts assist in creating expense budgets and in "validating" the children's present and future needs. Topics include: valuing assets; inflation; enforcing payments; "understanding the paperwork;" maintaining good records; working with lawyers, accountants, and the court; legislation; and emotional issues.

388. *Child Support in America: Practical Advice for Negotiating—and Collecting a Fair Settlement.* **Joseph I. Lieberman. New Haven, CT: Yale University Press, 1986. Hardcover. 122 pp.**

Senator Lieberman states that over 50 percent of husbands neglect mandated support payments, which frequently forces their ex-wives and children into poverty. He pleads for divorcing couples to cooperate in arriving at fair and workable divorce settlements in the first place to prevent this crime. His book is a guide. It offers solutions to protect women and children from being "victims" of a practice that Lieberman believes is having widely destructive effects upon American society. Writing for legal professionals as well as couples themselves, the author includes a comprehensive resource list of enforcement agencies. Other topics covered are:

determining needs and ability to pay, applying for increases, protecting children's rights, and suggested new laws.

389. *The Child Support Survivor's Guide: Practical Advice and Valuable Information for Enforcing Your Child Support.* **Barry T. Schnell. Salem, NJ: Consumer Awareness Learning Laboratory, 1984. Paperback. 96 pp.**

This guide is a realistic resource for parents involved in the difficult and often threatening area of child support decisions. Beginning with a general overview, Schnell emphasizes nonhostile cooperation between ex-spouses and the preservation of healthy relationships with the children. He also focuses on the stark realities of assuring satisfactory financial support as well as enforcing payment. Numerous do's and don'ts are included along with checklists and sample documents to help organize the process. Topics covered are: applying for support, methods of deciding on amounts, reasons parents are negligent, ways to bring about compliance, techniques to enforce rights, preparing for court appearances, and settling visitation disputes.

390. *Co-Parenting: Sharing Your Child Equally. A Source Book for the Separated or Divorced Family.* **Miriam Galper. Philadelphia, PA: Running Press, 1978. Paperback. 158 pp.**

Galper suggests that co-parenting (also known as "joint parenting, co-custody, shared custody or joint custody") is the ideal and only civilized situation for children. The major prerequisite is that parents be able to rise above their own, sometimes bitter, personal differences for the ultimate good of the child. Each parent spends equal time with the child and shares parenting duties jointly. This arrangement is seen as most beneficial in that it allows each parent to have a major role and a "pleasurable, ongoing, and intimate relationship" with the child. Galper is convinced that such working relationships between divorced spouses can and should be achieved and she shows how this can be done.

391. *The Complete Legal Guide to Marriage, Divorce, Custody and Living Together.* **Steven Mitchell Sack. New York: McGraw Hill, 1987. Hardcover. 325 pp.**

This noted legal expert gives us practical advice and techniques for protecting one's rights in situations where romance and emotion may cloud one's judgement. He covers a full range of issues but of special interest are the complex questions of custody, separation, and divorce. The goal is to reduce expenditures of time, worry, "money, and aggravation." Sack's book is a simple but comprehensive guide for lay people on how to prepare themselves well and "avoid mistakes." Full of strategies and checklists, it covers such areas as: what to do before contacting a lawyer, hiring the right private investigator or attorney, handling domestic disputes including violence, negotiating the separation or divorce, safeguarding our assets from our ex-mate, and tax considerations.

392. *The Custody Revolution: The Father Factor and the Motherhood Mystique. A New Approach to Child Custody After Divorce.* **Richard A. Warshak, Ph.D. New York: Poseidon Press, 1992. Hardcover. 272 pp.**

Warshak devoted 15 years of research to this topic. Seeing divorce as one of childhood's most serious crises, he supports keeping the individual child's needs a priority. The book identifies the "alienation" of the father and the overwhelming duties of the mother as two of the most "scarring" aspects of the divorce process. It argues that automatically awarding custody to mothers ("The Motherhood Mystique"), a long standing societal default, causes the problem. Warshak's research has revealed not only that fathers are truly capable of parenting well but, that male children, especially, often fare better under this arrangement. He advocates joint custody, at a minimum, if not full "father custody" when the needs of the child dictate.

393. *Dealing With Divorce.* **Robert K. Moffett and Jack F. Scherer, L.L.B., L.L.M. Boston, MA: Little, Brown & Co., 1976. Paperback. 248 pp.**

These authors have written a methodical, action-oriented handbook in layman's terms. It covers the "emotional, legal, financial, and social effects of divorce." The tone is positive and the goal is to lessen trauma and take away fear of the unknown. According to the authors, divorcing people can begin to see their way to a new and better future by familiarizing themselves with all facets of the often complex legal process. Moffett and Scherer encourage active participation. They increase the reader's knowledge with a glossary of divorce terms. Topics include: no-fault divorce, divorce laws by state, various contractual agreements, alimony, custody, visitation, credit rating issues, problems encountered in the realms of self-image and social life, and remarriage.

394. *Divided Children: A Legal Guide for Divorcing Parents.* **Michael Wheeler. New York: W.W. Norton & Co., 1980. Hardcover. 224 pp.**

Wheeler stands firmly against what he sees as abuses in the present adversarial system. He gives straightforward, positive advice based on "interviews with parents, children, judges, and lawyers." His book outlines the specifics of custody law and explores the legal problems that families face both during and after the divorce. *Divided Children* highlights the most common issues in an attempt to save individuals money and to prevent the anguish of a potential return to court. Topics included are: deciding who should have custody, determining the proper amount of support, and altering unworkable custody agreements. A checklist for parents considering divorce is included to prepare for the work of the process ahead.

395. *Divorce and Dissolution of Marriage Laws of the United States.* **Daniel Sitarz, Attorney-at-Law. Carbondale, IL: Nova Publishing, 1990. Paperback. 195 pp.**

Graphically organized subdivisions make this guide to United States divorce laws an easy reference book to use. Sitarz summarizes the statutes for each state and follows his review with the chapter or section number and title of his source. His book covers such areas as: residency requirements, grounds for divorce, property distribution, alimony and maintenance, custody and visitation, child support, mediation and counseling requirements, and post-divorce name changes. All 50 states and The District of Columbia are included.

396. *Divorce and Money: Everything You Need to Know About Dividing Property.* **Violet Woodhouse and Victoria Fenton-Collins with M.C. Blakeman. Berkeley, CA: Nolo Press, 1992. Paperback. (21 chapters & appendix.)**

This book is written by certified financial planners with special expertise in divorce and property matters. It tells first how to estimate the value of joint holdings and then how to work together with a spouse to arrive at a fair settlement. The authors treat the long-term financial impact rather than specific legal issues. Concise and simple charts, checklists, outlines, and lists of resources create a practical, systematic workbook approach. *Divorce and Money* delineates emotional issues, stresses, and decisions to be made in the first 30 days. Other topics include: selling the house, joint accounts and credit cards, tax problems, alimony and child support, dividing debts, reducing investment risk, avoiding hastily made decisions, and achieving a new financial independence.

397. *The Divorce Decision: The Legal and Human Consequences of Ending a Marriage.* **Richard Neely. New York: McGraw Hill, 1984. Hardcover. 207 pp.**

Drawing on personal experience, Neely has written a thorough and clear book describing all aspects of the dissolution process. Children, custody, financial matters, property issues, and palimony are covered. The author encourages couples to cooperate in reaching realistic voluntary agreements rather than entrusting their fate to the often inefficient and insensitive court system. He claims that the legal process can add fuel to an already problematic situation by delivering inappropriate or unenforceable decisions. His book, whose goal is to make everyone a "better bargainer," covers such topics as: using a lawyer, the dilemma of whether to go to court, enforce-ability of support and alimony, and understanding the aftereffects.

398. *The Divorce Decisions Workbook:* **A** *Planning and Action Guide with 55 FORM-ulas to Help You in the Four Key Decision Areas: Financial, Legal, Practical, Emotional.* **Margorie L. Engel and Diana D. Gould. New York: McGraw Hill, Inc., 1992. Paperback. (166 pp. + FORM-ulas.)**

This comprehensive and systematic workbook concentrates on the economic, social, and emotional challenges surrounding divorce. It helps spouses or professionals organize every conceivable aspect of what can be an extremely chaotic process. Practical solutions to countless problems and questions are proposed. Fifty-five charts or "FORM-ulas," covering every detail of the family and its assets, assist in: preparing documentation, arriving at fair financial decisions, easing transitions, and helping readers manage their own divorce thus reducing legal fees. The book is divided into three parts, "The Feel of Divorce, The Practical (Real) Divorce and the Legal Divorce," and covers the early problematic moments up through dissolution itself.

399. *Divorce Dirty Tricks.* **Joan M. Brovins and Thomas Oehmke. Hollywood, FL: Lifetime Books, Inc., 1993. Paperback. 270 pp.**

"Knowledge is power," say these attorneys. Their book is a comprehensive look at every item in a divorce proceeding and how to prepare shrewdly. To the authors, money is the name of this game and keeping as much as possible, the goal. The theory is that divorce attorneys are expensive; a spouse, therefore, should know the many "loopholes, pitfalls, and nasty surprises" before taking any action. The book handles each issue in an orga-nized fashion so that readers can have a ready reference to specifics. Sample stories of individuals, checklists, and sample judgements, injunctions and complaints help readers prepare. Topics include: annulments, abandonment, credit cards, mediation/attorneys, fees, trial, homes and personal property, alimony and custody, bankruptcy, business valuation, and college costs.

400. *The Divorce Handbook:* **Your Basic Guide to Divorce. James T. Friedman. New York: Random House, 1982. Paperback. 168 pp.**

Charts, checklists, work sheets, schedules, a glossary, a bibliography, and 227 questions with answers comprise this clear reference book. Issues occurring from the moment a spouse considers divorce to the final decree are covered. Friedman believes that knowledge and active participation can demystify the process, remove insecurity, and help one survive the frustrations. He sees organization and preparation as critical to the protection of rights. Topics include: dating during separation, bank accounts, hidden assets, credit, "living expense budgets," voluntary support, costs, lawyers, depositions, negotiating techniques, being a successful client, contested divorce, appeals, and decree modifications.

401. *Divorce Help Sourcebook.* **Margorie L. Engel. Detroit, MI: Visible Ink Press, 1994. Paperback. 419 pp.**

Advice, resource literature, addresses of counselors, support groups and hundreds of other pieces of information fill this book. Designed to help readers navigate the maze of complicated issues surrounding this often confusing time, the guide's five chapters open with essays by experts in the field and conclude with a list of helpful resources. The format is graphic and simple to follow and lends itself to a sourcebook motif. Topics include: the definition of divorce terms; the divorce process; mediation; the emotional impact; the history of divorce in America; and legal, financial and practical matters including custody, support, property settlements, pensions, credit and business valuation. Engel hopes to aid the reader in developing an organized plan to gain control of the situation.

402. *Divorce Mediation*: *A Rational Alternative to the Adversary System.* **Howard H. Irving. New York: Universe Books, 1980. Hardcover. 188 pp.**

In Irving's experience, the adversarial divorce process inflicts immense and unnecessary pain on all parties. His book explains the details of his preferred system of divorce mediation in layman's terms, simply and clearly. It provides case studies and practical guidelines for dealing with a divorce "in the least detrimental way to all parties involved." Irving sees mediation as a means to reduce the costs and pain of the process with the end result being open and realistic communication rather than a profusion of "legal documents." Unlike contested divorce, there are neither winners nor losers, Irving says, but an equitable settlement and workable structure for all family members.

403. *Divorce Mediation*: *How to Cut the Cost and Stress of Divorce.* **Diane Neumann. New York: Henry Holt & Co., 1989. Hardcover. 208 pp.**

Neumann cites $12,000 and one year as the routine cost and time span of the adversarial divorce vs. $1,000 and a couple of months for mediated divorces. She builds a strong case for a system that she sees as more sensible, healthy, and honest. The end result satisfies the needs of the whole family and minimizes the expense as well as the pain, her book concludes. While contested and hostile divorces are generally "win-lose" scenarios,

Neumann says that mediated divorce can be "win-win," which is always far more desirable. Her book gives concrete advice on how to benefit from the system and offers solutions to such problematic areas as: division of real estate, alimony, child support, visitation, insurance benefits, and parental responsibilities.

404. *Divorce Mediation: The Constructive New Way to End a Marriage.* **Karen L. Schneider and Dr. Myles J. Schneider. Washington, DC: Acropolis Books, Ltd., 1984. Hardcover. 208 pp.**

This book provides a step-by-step explanation of the mediation system as the most sensible, positive, and just way of ending a bad marriage. It suggests that this system enables ex-partners and their children to maintain: their pride, a sense of having their needs met, and the ability to preserve an ongoing civil relationship. The authors were divorced from each other through this process and thus speak from personal experience. They discuss the use of attorneys, therapists, or counselors as mediators as well as the process of defining areas of conflict and working them out one by one. The Schneiders believe that a win-win scenario is achieved when each individual is empowered through his or her own decision-making ability.

405. *The Divorce Revolution: The Unexpected Social and Economic Consequences for Women and Children in America.* **Lenore J. Weitzman. New York: Free Press, a Div. of Macmillan, Inc., 1985. Hardcover. 504 pp.**

Weitzman has created a resource for women who want to fight for what's due them and want to learn what could happen if they don't. It is based on ten years of detailed research into court records as well as interviews with legal professionals and divorced individuals. The book exposes the dire economic injustices women and children suffer in divorce settlements. It cites such hardships as: drastic declines in standards of living (as much as 73 percent), nonexistent or insufficient child support, and insecure future outlooks. Condemning no-fault divorce, the author accuses the courts of "disregarding" the wife's impaired earning power. Having frequently given more emphasis to homemaking than career, the woman may lose retirement benefits, health insurance, and job possibilities, she says.

406. *Divorce Yourself: The National No-Fault No-Lawyer Divorce Handbook.* **Daniel Sitarz. Carbondale, IL: Nova Publishing Co., 1990. Paperback. 315 pp.**

This is a detailed guide (including checklists, sample forms, and work sheets) for those who wish to prepare their own workable divorce agreement that will be legal in each of the 50 states. The author blames the adversarial divorce system for creating increased hostility between divorcing partners. As an experienced lawyer, Sitarz has written a step-by-step handbook for people who would like to spare themselves money and trauma by coming to agreement themselves. "Winning" is seen as possible only for the lawyers when couples declare war on each other. Topics covered include: an analysis of state laws, alimony, custody, and support, debts, taxes, name changes, and property issues.

407. *Divorcing*: *The Complete Guide.* **Melvin M. Belli, Sr. and Mel Krantzler, Ph.D. with Christopher S. Taylor. New York: St. Martin's Press, 1988. Hardcover. 434 pp.**

A famous attorney and leading divorce therapist pair up in this comprehensive handbook. In layman's terms, they strive to address all aspects of the divorce process: "legal, emotional, economic, and social." While unforeseen problems might seem threatening, these authors view the process as a "liberating opportunity" for finding out who we really are and for creating a far more fulfilling future. Areas discussed include: danger signs of a potential breakup, mourning, coping with fear, selecting an attorney who acts in our best interest, safeguarding our financial status, winning a just settlement, remaining unemotional during negotiations, redirecting hostility, effects upon children, custody, sexuality, and the legal implications of dating.

408. *The Dollars and Sense of Divorce*: *The Financial Guide for Women.* **Judith Briles. New York: Ballantine Books, 1988. Paperback. 330 pp.**

Written by a former stockbroker, financial advisor, and divorced mother, this guidebook helps women win in the divorce process both "mentally and financially." It is divided into two parts, I: "The Reality of Divorce" and II: "Profiting After Divorce." Stating that no-fault divorce has been directly responsible for escalating female poverty rates, Briles suggest women treat their future financial stability most seriously. She suggests that being smart not "nice" is imperative before, during, and after the divorce. Briles gives tested strategies for building financial security for mothers and children alike. Some topics covered are: support, custody, credit, lawyers, determining assets and expenses, mediation, court, property, taxes, and investments.

409. *Don't Settle for Less*: *A Woman's Guide to Getting a Fair Divorce and Custody Settlement.* **Beverly Pekala. New York: Doubleday, 1994. Hardcover. 272 pp.**

It is clear to this attorney that even a 50/50 divorce is unfair to women. Her book's goal is to provide women with the "ammunition" they need to be proactive, understand their rights, redistribute the power, and negotiate a solid settlement. Step-by step, Pekala takes readers from the first danger signs straight through the possibility of a postdecree. Topics include: domestic abuse; the importance of timing; selecting, paying, and firing a lawyer; filing; depositions; retirement benefits; "getting what you want;" trials; prenuptial agreements; cohabitation; and paternity. An appendix offers readers names of women's bar associations and battered women's shelters as well as examples of an income and expense affidavit, a real estate provision, and a visitation provision. Chapters conclude with references.

410. *The Ex-Factor*: *The Complete Do-It-Yourself Post-Divorce Handbook.* **Bernard Clair and Anthony Daniele. New York: Warner Books, 1986. Paperback. 313 pp.**

These authors write for those who feel helpless when faced with wrenching post-divorce conflict and who lack the expertise and funds to attack life's inequities. Clair and Daniele see their book as crucial because 24 percent of spouses receive no support after a divorce. An updated, simple and methodical, do-it yourself guide to reaching sensible solutions "without the expense of attorneys," the book is full of actual case histories. Checklists, examples of court papers, and summaries of state laws focus on preventing readers from becoming victims. The goal is to enable individuals to adjust or "enforce their legal rights" in the areas of money, property, visitation, custody, and alimony. Part I discusses financial issues and Part II, children.

411. *Getting Divorced Without Ruining Your Life*: *A Reasoned, Practical Guide to the Legal, Emotional and Financial Ins and Outs of Negotiating a Divorce Settlement.* **Sam Margulies, Ph.D., J.D. New York: A Fireside Book, Publ. by Simon & Schuster, 1992. Paperback. 318 pp.**

Margulies' book is a step-by-step guide to sensible, amicable, and fair divorce. It is complete with summaries, charts, solutions, and case studies. As a seasoned divorce attorney, the author wishes to empower the reader to gain control of the process rather than turning the settlement over to professionals. He sees mediation as the best method. Margulies feels, however, that conventional divorce procedures are acceptable if the goals are: 1) to answer sincerely the needs of the children and, 2) to allow everyone the "best possible standard of living" as well as a healthy start to a new beginning. Comprehensive advice is given on: reducing hostility, negotiating support, alimony and asset division, formulating budgets, and understanding all the economics.

412. *Getting Your Share*: *A Woman's Guide to Successful Divorce Strategies.* **Lois Brenner. New York: Crown Publishers, 1989. Paperback. 230 pp.**

As an attorney specializing in matrimonial law, Brenner gives realistic advice. She is convinced of its validity since she has previously tested her theories with many clients. Her book discusses a multitude of specific topics relating to the complex legal aspects of divorce such as: how to handle financial matters regarding savings and checking accounts, debts, determining and enforcing support and alimony payments, what happens if one party leaves home, and the pros and cons of a court trial. The book encourages women to participate in this process seriously since research into national statistics shows that a woman's financial standard of living could be lowered by as much as 73 percent after the divorce.

413. *Head and Heart: A Woman's Guide to Financial Independence.* **Susan Weidman Schneider and Arthur B.C. Drachne with Helene Brezinsky. Pasadena, CA: Trilogy Books, 1991. Paperback. 359 pp.**

Following women through life's many passages, this book discusses money issues involved at each stage and how women can make smarter decisions. The premise is that, traditionally, women have been reluctant to participate in financial decisions and thus they are less knowledgeable in these areas. Expertise will allow them to be more secure and independent as single or married people and will thus benefit any relationship they have, the authors believe. Chapter 9 discusses divorce issues such as: separating, selecting a lawyer, financial decisions, and custody. Other chapters cover: prenuptial agreements, investments, taxes and insurance, and home problems (buying, selling, renting etc.). The intent is to demystify the realm of money.

414. *Mediate Your Divorce: A Guide to Cooperative Custody, Property and Support Agreements.* **Joan Blades. Englewood Cliffs, NJ: Prentice-Hall, Inc., 1985. Paperback. 239 pp.**

Useful as a reference manual, this practical guide gives detailed outlines and analyses of the five different models of mediation. Blades' hope is that this will allow couples and professionals to decide if any of these variations could be appropriate for them. The author compares "public and private mediation, attorney and therapist mediation, co-mediation, and structural mediation." She analyzes adversarial divorce with respect to how it differs from the cooperative character of mediation. Her book sees the latter as superior in that it enables couples to retain more of their own decision-making powers. Blades provides transcripts of real mediations along with many examples of mediation forms, sample agreements, and effective techniques.

415. *Mothers and Divorce: Legal, Economic, and Social Dilemmas.* **Terry Arendell. Berkeley, CA: University of California Press, 1986. Hardcover. 221 pp.**

Arendell studies 60 divorced women and their responses to the many challenges encountered. In-depth interviews convinced the author that while society may glamorize divorce, the reality is often sadly different. She contends that the "central trauma" is financial rather than emotional. The book sees a severe decline in living standard, even poverty, as common in many cases. It shows how remedies are often unavailable with the burdens of child care, lack of support payments, and prejudices of the job market hurting women's earning power. In addition, the author observes, social status is downgraded and the chances of remarriage only about 33 percent. Arendell debunks seven assumptions concerning divorce, while painting a picture of women whose lives are often permanently and drastically changed.

416. *Mothers on Trial: The Battle for Children and Custody.* **Phyllis Chesler, Ph.D. San Diego, CA: Harcourt Brace Jovanovich, 1987. Paperback. 558 pp.**

Chesler exposes court discrimination that works against the rights of "good enough" mothers in custody fights. Fathers who battle for custody win 70 percent of the time, often, she laments, simply because they are rewarded for the caring that is part of a normal mother's routine day. The author's research revealed that mothers could lose custody and be "punished" for "crimes" such as working, being on welfare, committing "heterosexual adultery," or living with a man. The book falls into three parts: an overview of custody issues; crimes that "good enough mothers" commit to lose custody; and women dealing with the male establishment. It also shows that a great deal of work remains to be done in removing the "custody threat" from financial support issues.

417. *Our Money Our Selves: Money Management for Each Stage of a Woman's Life.* **Ginita Wall, C.P.A., C.F.P. and the Editors of Consumer Reports Books. Yonkers, NY: Consumer Reports Books, a Div. of Consumer's Union, 1992. Paperback. 247 pp.**

This book was designed for women by a female C.P.A. and financial planner, who believes that the chief cornerstone of independence is "financial responsibility." Wall proposes that this realm is often inadvisably left to the care of the man due to a woman's ignorance, naivete, or simply her disinterest. She claims that financial vicissitudes can seriously hurt a woman if she has not prepared herself well. The goal of her book is just that: to give women practical help for every financial matter they confront as they make their way through life. Topics covered include: jobs, budgets, setting goals, living together, prenuptial agreements, marriage, children, credit, investments, insurance, taxes, loans, bankruptcy, home buying, divorce, widowhood, and retirement.

418. *Parent Vs. Parent*: *How You and Your Child Can Survive the Custody Battle*. **Stephen P. Hermano, M.D. New York: Pantheon Books, 1990. Hardcover. 244 pp.**

As a child psychologist, Hermano urges parents to resist the destructive temptation to use their children as "bargaining chips" in their divorce. He stresses the importance of being "child-centered," keeping the children's interests foremost in a process that can be inordinately stressful to them. In the author's opinion, avoiding custody disputes is key if parents wish to prevent permanent damage. The book's three parts outline: the psychological impact of custody disputes and ways to avoid these battles, an overview of the complexities of the process, and the ramifications of the "custody decision" on everyone after the divorce. It offers examples to better inform parents of choices on the many issues and to help them understand children's responses more clearly.

419. *The Process of Divorce*: *How Professionals and Couples Negotiate Settlements*. **Kenneth Kressel. New York: Basic Books, Inc., 1985. Hardcover. 349 pp.**

Kressel proposes that how couples conduct "settlement negotiations" and the roles that professionals play in the process can determine how their families will be defined after the divorce, both psychologically and economically. He says, therefore, that it is most important for all those involved (couples, attorneys, mediators, and therapists) to promote "constructive" negotiating of conflict rather than hostility. The book's audience is professionals as well as families. It specifically explores different approaches and cites examples of actions that help and hurt. Kressel thinks that therapists are just as "critically" important as attorneys if they can help couples accept the divorce and move forward constructively. Kressel discusses some negatives of the mediation process as well.

420. *Rematch*: *Winning Legal Battles With Your Ex*. **Steven R. Lake with Ruth Duskin Feldman. Chicago, IL: Chicago Review Press, 1989. Paperback. 221 pp.**

The advice here may be useful to people weighing the possibility of divorce, in the process of divorce, or already divorced. The thesis is that final decrees are often not the last note. Knowing one's obligations, enforcing the orders, protecting all parties' rights, finding "remedies," and altering unworkable agreements can be problems for years, the authors feel. Their book stresses careful preparation and drafting of agreements to safeguard one's future and prevent expensive and emotionally disabling returns to the courtroom. It believes that such disputes will hurt the children most. Topics covered include: kidnapping, custody, visitation, child abuse, property issues, tax changes, "jeopardizing" actions, the legal system, avoiding document "omissions," and effects on "third parties."

421. *Sharing Parenthood After Divorce*: *An Enlightened Custody Guide for Mothers, Fathers, and Kids.* **Ciji Ware. New York: Viking Press, 1979. Hardcover. 349 pp.**

Believing that children deserve a close relationship with both their parents, Ware strongly advocates cooperative shared custody after divorce. This book is a highly detailed guide with checklists, sample agreements, and practical techniques for parents in: designing their own custody scenario, working together as partners in child rearing, and managing day-to-day life. While such cooperation may not always be easy to achieve, Ware feels it is well worth some solid effort since all parties will benefit immensely. The book sees contested divorce as the cause of much pain, especially to the child. It looks carefully at all the emotions involved and also offers suggestions for communicating with ex-spouses or lawyers and judges.

422. *Sharing the Children*: *How to Resolve Custody Problems and Get On With Your Life.* **Robert E. Adler, Ph.D. Bethesda, MD: Adler & Adler Publ., Inc., 1988. Paperback. 254 pp.**

Adler's research showed that divorced individuals were often seriously hurt by the traumatic process with the result that anger, struggles, and resentments seethed for years. "The custody minefield" emerged as a crucial area causing continued animosity and detrimental side-effects upon children emotionally, socially, and academically. To resolve these conflicts, Adler offers coping strategies for every phase of the dissolution process so that everyone involved can win. Case studies, "self-help checklists," and descriptions of U.S. custody laws are included. Adler believes that the keys to moving beyond conflict are a loving and realistic parent-child relationship on both sides and the ability to let go, release control, and build fulfilling independent lives.

423. *The State-by-State Guide to Women's Legal Rights.* **N.O.W./Legal Defense and Education Fund and Dr. Renee Chernow-O'Leary. New York: McGraw Hill, 1987. Paperback. 523 pp.**

The publisher describes this book as an "essential handbook for American women." It contains comprehensive and specific information on legislation that impacts women's lives in the four very significant areas of: domestic and family issues, education, the world of work, and the community at large. Potential problem areas are summarized in clear, layman's terminology. Pages 18–26 cover the general topic of divorce and separate state listings discuss in detail specific laws governing the areas of marital dissolution, child support, and custody.

424. *Strassels' Tax Savers*: *How to Hold on to More of What You Earn by Paying Less in Taxes for the Rest of Your Life.* **Paul N. Strassels and William B. Mead. New York: Time Books, New York Times Book Company, 1985. Hardcover. 308 pp.**

Strassels has written a comprehensive, detailed, and clear guide for saving money on taxes. It is personalized for each particular life situation, i.e., divorced, single, etc. The book updates all advice to cover changes enacted in the 1984 tax reform act. It includes a Tax Calendar and Taxpayers' Glossary. Strassels directs chapter 11 at divorced individuals and he includes such topics as: joint returns, settlements, child care, alimony and support, and altering divorce decrees. Chapter 5, for singles, discusses areas such as: refunds, expenses, IRA's, investments, underpayment penalties, home-buying, income averaging, and working for ourselves.

425. *The Survival Guide for Women: Single • Married • Divorced. Protecting Your Future.* **Renee Martin and Don Martin with Joan Scobey, ed. Washington, DC: Regnery Gateway, 1991. Paperback. (153 pp. + 65 work sheets.)**

Researched for three years, this reference book includes checklists and data sheets as well as 65 tear-out work sheets that become a permanent record of a woman's financial picture. The authors' experience showed that women tend to be ignorant and highly "disorganized" about their financial lives. This is a potential cause of numerous problems, even the loss of assets during crises. In simple layman's terms, the guide explains every financial detail and logs it for future use. Ensuring "peace of mind" is the goal. Topics covered include: keeping records, updating, budgeting, safeguarding personal assets and those of children, credit, loans, guardians, wills, trusts, probate, disability, illness, death, automobiles, careers, financial help, and legal matters.

426. *What Every Woman Should Know About Her Husband's Money.* **Shelby White. New York: Turtle Bay Books, a Div. of Random House, 1992. Hardcover. 262 pp.**

White writes about understanding, preserving, and protecting marital money. With high divorce rates and an 80 percent chance of widowhood, she considers deferring financial decisions to men unacceptable. Her book is called a "financial survival manual." It covers a woman's financial life in detail with special concern for such issues as: control; equality; balancing child-rearing, home and careers; and the ability to communicate about such sensitive topics. "Money mistakes" common to women are analyzed as are "Ten Financial Rules For a Marriage." Specific topics include: tax returns, homes, debts, pensions, death, protecting children, aging parents, prenuptial agreements, divorce, alimony and support, and pensions.

427. *When Couples Part*: *How the Legal System Can Work for You*. Judge Lawrence E. Kahn. New York: Franklin Watts, 1981. Hardcover. 208 pp.

Judge Kahn writes for couples in the throes of divorce. He offers layman's guidelines to help readers understand the legal process and to insure that it will work for them rather than against them. *When Couples Divorce* presents information on: how to reach workable financial solutions, hiring effective attorneys, handling the frustrations of the courtroom, and coping with an unexpected settlement. The approach is positive. Other topics discussed are: the effects of women's liberation, palimony issues, receiving alimony as a husband, no-fault divorce, child support and custody alternatives, taxes, concealing assets, developing a premarital contract, and related remarriage problems.

428. *Winning Your Divorce*: *A Man's Survival Guide*. Timothy J. Horgan. New York: Dutton, The Penguin Group, 1994. Hardcover. 196 pp.

While this attorney writes for men, women can learn much here about the legal tactics the competition may be contemplating. Horgan's contention is that, although society sees men as the typical winners in a divorce, this is often untrue. Men, he says, can lose their homes, suffer from unjust custody and visitation provisions, and lack say in the upbringing of the children or the way support payments are used. Step-by-step, the book intends to prepare men to survive monetarily and emotionally. Topics include: steps to take before and after selecting an attorney, issues surrounding the home, "motions for temporary relief," mens' rights groups, negotiating, custody and visitation, alimony and support, and trials. Chapters conclude with checklists. Horgan says his book is the first of its kind.

429. *A Woman's Legal Guide to Separation and Divorce in All 50 States*. Norma Harwood, J.D. New York: Charles Scribner's Sons, 1985. Paperback. 336 pp.

This book is based on hundreds of court cases and decisions in every state over a period of four years. It is a simple format designed for the laywoman who wishes to avoid financial disaster after a divorce and who wishes to be more informed about potential courses of action. Since poverty threatens many women after the dissolution of a marriage, they do not have the luxury of simply leaving their affairs in the hands of lawyers. Harwood offers comprehensive information on how to prevent financial inequities and ask the right questions. Topics included are: determining the need to use the courts, insurance and retirement benefits, and settlements for wives who have helped pay for their husband's education.

430. *Women, Divorce and Money.* **Mary Rogers. New York: McGraw Hill Book Co., 1981. Hardcover. 210 pp.**

Rogers has a tough, practical approach toward divorce. Her book acknowledges the plight of women who bought the happily-ever-after dream but are now are cast into the work force with no skills. She insists, however, that such challenges bring growth. To move on, she suggests women must forget the past. Her focus is on the critical need for step-by-step organized planning. The book maintains that the divorce process must work for women as "equal financial partners" while they create positive, independent new lives. It emphasizes obtaining "court ordered temporary support" as women learn new skills. Topics covered are: filing, attorneys, expense budgets, assets, selling the home, credit, wills, depositions, negotiating, careers, taxes, and insurance.

431. *You're Entitled: A Divorce Lawyer Talks to Women. Everything You Need to Know to Ensure Your Financial Security and Emerge a Winner.* **Sidney M. De Angelis. Chicago, IL: Contemporary Books, 1989. Hardcover. 300 pp.**

De Angelis gives a full and detailed analysis of every element of the divorce process including fees, time spans, and probable schedules of events. His goal is to encourage women to fight for and get what's due them in an informed, rational, organized, and "sophisticated" fashion. The book is not a "divorce yourself" manual. Carefully following a model family through the whole process, De Angelis uses his legal experience to expose ploys the husband's side may be devising. He leaves custody and visitation particulars for another book since maintaining power and financial stability require the most attention here. Keeping emotions in control and knowing how to deal with "the enemy" without giving in are discussed.

For additional help in understanding the "Legal and Financial Aspects of Divorce," see also book numbers:

 59: *Women & Money*

175: *Love and Money*

261: *Money Demons*

321: *Learning to Leave*

323: *Life Changes: How Women Can Make Courageous Choices*

325: *Living Through Your Divorce*

329: *Our Turn*
342: *Women in Transition*
349: *Daddy Doesn't Live Here Anymore*
352: *Divided Families*
353: *Divorce and Your Child*
354: *Divorce Without Victims*
362: *Healthy Divorce*
364: *Helping Children Cope With Divorce*
366: *How It Feels When Parents Divorce*
367: *How to Live With a Single Parent*
369: *The Kids' Book of Divorce*
370: *The Kids' Guide to Divorce*
371: *Long Distance Parenting*
372: *Mom's House, Dad's House*
373: *My Kids Don't Live With Me Anymore*
375: *The Parents' Book About Divorce*
376: *Planning a Wedding With Divorced Parents*
377: *Quality Time*
378: *Second Chances: Men, Women & Children a Decade After Divorce*
381: *Vicki Lansky's Divorce Book for Parents*
382: *What Every Child Would Like Parents to Know About Divorce*
385: *"Your Father's Not Coming Home Anymore"*
436: *Divorce and New Beginnings*
438: *Divorce Recovery*
443: *The Fresh Start Divorce Recovery Workbook*
457: *Living and Loving After Divorce*
461: *Marital Separation*
478: *The World of the Formerly Married*
480: *Alone—Not Lonely*
483: *Coping*
484: *The Divorced Woman's Handbook*
487: *Formerly Married: Learning to Live With Yourself*
489: *How to Parent Alone*
493: *The Joy of Being Single*
494: *Living Alone and Liking It*

497: *On Our Own*

500: *Parents Without Partners Sourcebook*

503: *Single After 50*

504: *Single Again*

506: *The Single Mother's Book*

508: *Single Parents Are People Too*

513: *Solo Parenting*

514: *Suddenly Single*

541: *Making Remarriage Work*

10

Recovering from Divorce

Smart cookies don't crumble

Surviving crisis and loss requires gradual healing, which involves rebuilding our lives while we regain strength. Regardless of the circumstances of a divorce, there will undoubtedly be a period of readjustment marked by such diverse emotions as sorrow, grief, anger, guilt, fear, depression, or even relief and elation. Since it is crucial that a parent remain functional in order to minimize any adverse effects upon the children, it is especially important to develop a support network at this time. Such a network can include counseling, friends and relatives, recovery groups, and books. This support system can help an individual open up and confide in others, a process invaluable to overall health.

This chapter's books recognize the pain of divorce. Certain authors concentrate first and foremost on self-nurturing and developing healthy self-esteem. Others present strategies for learning how to let go, get rid of self-pity or bitterness, break attachments to former spouses, and discover the benefits of forgiveness. Another group of authors surveys the qualities that characterize survivors in order to help readers learn by example. Predictable phases to expect are analyzed as are traps someone might fall victim to and mistakes that are commonplace.

Most of the resources encourage the newly divorced to be optimistic, to look at change as an opportunity, and to welcome the chance to grow through the unfolding of new behavior patterns.

432. *After You've Said Good-Bye*: *How to Recover After Ending a Relationship*. **Trudy Helmlinger. Cambridge, MA: Schenkman Publ. Co., Inc., Two Continents Publ. Group, Ltd., 1977. Hardcover. 273 pp.**

Aimed at victims of lost relationships, this book provides strategies for regaining strength and building self-esteem. It is practical and sometimes even humorous in nature. Helmlinger urges readers to free themselves of the past, "leave self-pity and self-doubt behind," and use their experience as a catalyst for growth. Experiments and exercises in each chapter assist both the leaver and the left in recovering. The author warns against harboring the need to define ourselves or our happiness in the context of a partner. Topics covered include: guilt, anger, and depression, "healthy ways to mourn," viewing the past rationally, weekends and anniversaries, resisting love on the rebound, dating, and avoiding dwelling on romantic memories.

433. *Coming Back: Rebuilding Lives After Crisis and Loss.* **Ann Kaiser Stearns. New York: Random House, 1988. Hardcover. 368 pp.**

Stearns examines her own "healing stories" and those of dozens of other men and women. The "triumphant survivors" she includes have been able to confront overwhelming crises and loss. In addition, these subjects have been able to transcend their difficulties to create even more fulfilling lives. This book studies some of the most notable personality traits and attitudes survivors share. From Stearns' examples, readers can learn what they must do to deal successfully with their own painful challenges. Concrete methods are suggested for: handling pain, allowing time for grief, watching for "turning points," and learning not only how to survive, but how to use the experience to bring greater meaning to life.

434. *Crazy Time: Surviving Divorce. A Step-by-Step Guide to Understanding the Predictable Emotional Passages of Men and Women After a Marriage Ends.* **Abigail Trafford. New York: Harper & Row, Publ., 1982. Paperback. 217 pp.**

Trafford, herself, survived a marriage that failed and then interviewed hundreds of divorced men and women across the country. Her study revealed regular patterns of "craziness" that almost every individual passed through from separation to recovery and the eventual reemergence into a new, even more rewarding life. The book sees divorce as a potentially traumatic emotional transition with feelings ranging from severe and debilitating depression to elation. It guides readers every step of the way, consoling them by comparisons to similar sufferings of others. The phases analyzed are: "Crisis (Deadlock and Confrontation), Crazy Time, and Recovery."

435. *Divorce and After: An Analysis of the Emotional and Social Problems of Divorce.* **Paul Bohannon, ed. Garden City, NY: Doubleday & Co., Inc., 1968, 1970. Hardcover. 301 pp.**

Select well-known experts in the fields of law, medicine, psychology, anthropology, and sociology write about the divorce process and its resulting "aftermath" in this book edited by Bohannon. The relationship between a husband and a wife, while it may be legally ended by a divorce decree, is seen as enduring in a "moral and emotional" sense. This, says the book, can present ongoing challenges to everyone involved. The contributors discuss: the varied reactions of friends and family, social and family relationships after the divorce, postmarital intercourse between ex-partners, multiple divorces, divorce in other cultures, and possibilities for "divorce reform."

436. *Divorce and New Beginnings: An Authoritative Guide to Recovery and Growth, Solo Parenting and Stepfamilies.* **Geneviev Clapp, Ph.D. New York: John Wiley & Sons, 1992. Paperback. 376 pp.**

This comprehensive self-help book guides readers through every detail and phase of the often painful divorce and recovery process. It is based on up-to-date research including over "400 studies, reports, and books." Action-oriented and practical, the book examines successful coping, forecasts future challenges, and instructs readers in skills aimed at mastering control of a new life. Cases illustrate emotional as well as day-to-day issues while checklists aid in areas such as development of goals. Topics include: anger, relaxation, letting go of emotions and conflict with regard to one's ex, depression, nurturing self-confidence, stress reduction, lessening the trauma of children, legal issues, dating, and stepfamilies.

437. *Divorce Hangover*: *A Step-by-Step Prescription for Creating a Bright Future After Your Marriage Ends.* **Anne N. Walther, M.S. New York: Pocket Books, a Div. of Simon & Schuster, 1991. Hardcover. 216 pp.**

Walther describes "divorce hangover" as a "crippling condition." Victims spend their time reliving resentments of the past instead of letting go and getting on with their lives, she contends. Her book views divorce as a distressing process often fraught with hostility, fear, and confusion. It proposes effective healing strategies that can: help us lay aside the baggage, teach us to react rationally, and guide us toward taking positive control of our lives. Exercises and assignments are offered to identify symptoms of anger and low self-esteem. In a step-by-step fashion, Walther shows how to take positive action to develop healthier and more generous methods of interaction.

438. *Divorce Recovery: The Help You Need to Heal the Pain.* **Allan J. Adler, M.D. and Christine Archambault. New York: Bantam Books, 1990. Paperback. 187 pp.**

Written by an experienced psychiatrist, this book gives concrete practical advice for people recovering from the "emotional, psychological, and financial" effects of divorce. The author presents tested techniques that he has used in divorce support groups and the Twelve Step Program used by Divorce Anonymous. Areas addressed include: rebuilding a weakened level of self-esteem, locating expert financial and legal advisors, dealing with fears of future rejection, understanding the responses of relatives and friends, and making it on one's own as a single person with the potential of new intimate relationships.

439. *Divorced*: *A Single Mother's Very Private Life*. **Nancy Wilkins with Mary Ellen Reese. New York: Wyden Books, Imprint of McKay, a Div. of Random House, 1977. Hardcover. 217 pp.**

Divorced is neither an analytical book nor a self-help guide. It is the emotional and personal story of one woman's struggle with a dying marriage, the "healing" process, and the frightening but also exhilarating quest for a new identity and new life. The authors write for those who might need inspiration for their own challenges. Wilkins, 34 years old "with no particular skills," brings us into her unraveling sheltered suburban life. Topics include: fear about financial stability for her family, worry about a job and a home, constant negative dealings with her ex-husband, anxieties about new men, sexuality, career problems in a largely male work force, and her "surge of confidence" as she discovers her own emotional and intellectual capabilities.

440. *The Ex-Wife Syndrome*: *Cutting the Cord and Breaking Free After the Marriage Is Over.* **(Newly titled: *Leaving Him Behind*) Sandra S. Kahn. New York: Random House, 1990. Hardcover. 248 pp.**

This book is based on the belief that the "Ex-Wife Syndrome" is an actual psychological state. "Self-destructive feelings" prevent large numbers of divorced women in this condition from beginning a full and satisfying new life, according to Kahn. Her book attributes most of these distressful feelings to a woman continuing to view herself as an ex-wife and thus somehow always connected to an ex-husband. It methodically outlines a "therapeutic process" for: coming to grips with emotions, breaking restrictive bonds with former husbands, finishing the divorce permanently, letting go of the past, "wiping the label of ex-wife from our vocabulary forever," and establishing new behaviors in order to move forward in life in a positive and independent fashion.

441. *Forgive & Forget*: *Healing the Hurts We Don't Deserve.* **Lewis B. Smedes. New York: Pocket Books, Harper & Row, 1984. Paperback. 192 pp.**

This work is an in-depth analysis of the meaning and complex dynamics of forgiveness. It explores: the nature of the act causing the pain, the three dimensional face of pain, and the four stages we all go through on our way to forgiveness. Smedes proposes that peace of mind and happiness cannot be achieved without letting go of the hurts of their past, such as infidelity, betrayal, abuse etc. He offers step-by-step strategies for taking the difficult but necessary steps toward healing. The book promises even greater rewards to the forgiver than to the forgiven. With his comforting advice, Smedes states that we can immediately begin to forgive ourselves and others of past or present sins.

442. *Forgiveness: How to Make Peace With Your Past and Get On With Your Life.* **Dr. Sidney B. Simon and Suzanne Simon. New York: Warner Books, 1990. Hardcover. 225 pp.**

The publisher defines this book as a "guide to spiritual healing." It is designed to help readers learn to let go of hard feelings and hostility (without forgetting) in order to reconcile themselves with hurts of the past. The Simons see holding grudges as most detrimental to the grudge-holder; this person may suffer from negative emotions such as jealousy, anger, insecurity, and resentment, which will lead nowhere. The authors are famous for their "Forgiveness Workshops." They have developed a six-stage system with exercises for understanding the origins of our injury and using the experience to aid recovery and growth. The Simons see forgiveness as an act of strength by which the forgiver, not the forgiven, receives the greatest benefit.

443. *The Fresh Start Divorce Recovery Workbook: A Step-by-Step Program for Those Who Are Divorced or Separated.* **Bob Burns and Tom Whiteman. Nashville, TN: Oliver Nelson, a Div. of Thomas Nelson Publ., 1992. Paperback. 302 pp.**

Grounded in the authors' experience with "Fresh Start Seminars," which they have successfully conducted, this book provides systematic and "healing Bible-based insights" for people in the throes of separation or divorce. It addresses all pertinent areas such as how individuals: make their way through the legal and financial process, understand themselves better, reconstruct their self-image, bolster their confidence after a perceived failure in marriage, develop a new post-divorce family identity, guide their children through the transition, let go of the past and hostile feelings, develop new and healthier patterns of relating, deal with their sexuality, and find comfort in a support network.

444. *Fresh Starts: Men and Women After Divorce.* **Elizabeth Cauhape. New York: Basic Books, Inc., 1983. Hardcover. 338 pp.**

Cauhape conducted research on "ordinary" career-oriented men and women. In the process, she discovered that solid recovery is possible for many of these divorced individuals. Her study analyzes the eight specific "divorce aftermaths" that are most prevalent. These are then further examined in three large categories depending upon how long transition from divorce lasts. The author states that each passage is ended by deliberate choice, when one has developed a new and workable social network and an acceptable self-concept. The book illustrates examples of happy and well-adjusted individuals (ranging from those who rush to remarry to those who never do), and discusses solutions to the numerous problems and challenges encountered.

445. *The Grief Recovery Handbook*: *A Step-by-Step Program for Moving beyond Loss*. **John W. James and Frank Cherry. New York: Harper & Row Publishers, Inc., 1988. Paperback. 175 pp.**

As cofounders of the Grief Recovery Institute, these authors have created a "proven" recovery program for people (currently or previously) afflicted with any type of loss. They encourage readers to mourn and express emotions openly. The failure to process all of the associated feelings, they warn, can lead to serious future problems. James and Cherry stress that we must bear responsibility for our own recovery and take positive action to achieve it. While friends might try to help, they say that the real work is accomplished within us or with the help of one confidante who acts as our partner. This handbook proposes that even greater levels of happiness are possible when we learn how to put our suffering behind us properly.

446. *Guilt: Letting Go*. **Lucy Freeman and Herbert S. Strean. New York: John Wiley & Sons, 1986. Hardcover. 270 pp.**

The types, origins (childhood and other), manifestations, and ways to overcome the effects of guilt are the subject of this book. Freeman and Strean propose that the bulk of one's conscious and unconscious guilt feelings are "irrationally" based. Their study notes the destructive effects of this emotion (e.g., addiction, depression, workaholism) and discusses how individuals can liberate themselves. The authors believe that by doing so, we will attain happiness in our personal lives and careers and will love both ourselves and others more fully. Eliminating perfectionism along with "unrealistic expectations" and adopting new behavior patterns will engender greater creativity and peace, they contend. The relationship of "anxiety, anger, and anguish" is also explored.

447. *Guilt Is the Teacher, Love Is the Lesson*. **Joan Borysenko, Ph.D. New York: Warner Books, 1990. Paperback. 239 pp.**

This book studies the destructive habit of blaming ourselves for perceived failings in relationships, careers, and even our own health. People can exaggerate these "failings," Borysenko says, by their perfectionist tendencies to please others. She bases her book on dramatic personal experience, case histories, and research in such fields as "science, philosophy, medicine, (and) psychology." With modern innovative solutions, the author enlightens the reader on the psychology of guilt. She explores the topic in depth to help us: recognize our wounds, heal ourselves, "free the child within us," and begin a healthier life. The book also offers instruction on developing serenity and a spiritual outlook in order to forgive ourselves and others.

448. *How to Fall Out of Love: How to Free Yourself of Love That Hurts—And Find the Love That Heals.* **Dr. Debora Phillips with Robert Judd. Boston, MA: Houghton Mifflin, 1978. Paperback. 135 pp.**

Phillips and Judd write for those readers who need healing while they attempt to overcome the pain of: losing a loving relationship, acknowledging a "dead-end affair" or destructive union, or coping with rejection by one who does not love them in return. The authors assist readers in dispelling jealousy and fear. They stress the importance of rebuilding self-esteem and confidence in order to move forward into a new and hopefully a healthier relationship. The book's theories are based on behavior therapy, which suggests that "all human behavior is learned" rather than purely instinctual.

449. *How to Forgive Your Ex-Husband (And Get On With Your Life): Working Through the Hurt So You Can Love Again.* **Marcia Hootman and Patt Perkins. New York: Warner Books, 1982. Paperback. 220 pp.**

This book's goal is to help women create independent new beginnings by redirecting their energy away from "revenge" to more productive and positive uses. Specifically, the authors suggest developing a realistic picture of former marriages and the characteristics and "destructive patterns" that existed there. This, they believe, will help readers better understand how to form healthier new pairings. Hootman and Perkins see resentment and hostility as impediments to positive living. Their book spends time teaching women how to: separate from their past, deal with their ex-husbands frankly, sensibly and unemotionally, and communicate with them honestly.

450. *How to Survive the Loss of a Love: A Clear and Simple Guide to Loss.* **Melba Colgrove, Ph.D., Harold Bloomfield, M.D. and Peter McWilliams. Los Angeles, CA: Prelude Press, 1976. Hardcover. 212 pp.**

A source of comfort and inspiration is what these authors hope to offer. Their revised and expanded handbook provides readers with step-by-step advice for every phase of the often formidable recovery process after the loss a special relationship. It is written in the format of 94 individual reflections on positive ways to regain strength and move forward in a healthy and constructive fashion. The authors deliver guidelines and suggestions in simple "bullet" form making it a quick and easy reference in time of need. Topics covered include: "acknowledging the loss," allowing oneself to feel and heal, the benefits of rest and comforting, seeking out mentors, dealing with fear, confiding in a journal, self-affirmations; and starting all over.

451. *If Love Is the Answer, What Is the Question?* **Uta West. New York: McGraw Hill, 1977. Hardcover. 227 pp.**

West poses questions regarding the meaning of love in the aftermath of the sexual revolution. Suggesting that a redefinition may be in order, the author widens our outlook on loving relationships. She gives more prominence to friendships, children, and the self. Her research covered rather unconventional individuals from 20-50 years old. It found that modern newly found freedoms frequently had the effect of removing the "refuges" that previously "sheltered" our lives, sometimes leaving us lost. West thinks that romantic love may have changed and men may often "have gone into retreat." Not pretending to be scientific, the book tries rather to facilitate a discussion of new meanings to alternatives in relating to one another.

452. *The Lessons of Love: Rediscovering Our Passions for Life When It All Seems Too Hard to Take.* **Melody Beattie. New York: HarperSanFrancisco, 1994. Hardcover. 225 pp.**

Beattie's life, while blessed with success as the author of several books including *Codependent No More*, was also traumatized by tragedy. The death of her 12 year old son in a ski accident so deeply depressed her that Beattie felt the "magic" of life was gone. This personal narrative, however, does not focus so much on her grief as the ways in which Beattie learned how to "see, touch, feel, and taste life's magic again." It is offered as an inspiration to others who may find it impossible to believe that their lost passion can ever be rekindled, much less thrive. The author encourages readers to develop a more open and trusting attitude and to reach deeply into the resources of their own hearts in order to conquer problems stemming from their pride and fears.

453. *Letting Go: A Twelve Week Personal Action Program to Overcome a Broken Heart.* **Dr. Zev Wanderer and Tracy Cabot. New York: A Dell Book, 1978. Paperback. 318 pp.**

These authors believe they have developed a reliable, even "proven," system for eliminating feelings of depression, hurt, and sadness after the often debilitating loss of a love. They claim recovery can occur in as short a time period as three months. Wanderer and Cabot propose that using their techniques will help readers make great strides towards: putting aside thoughts of the past, "regaining control of their feelings," breaking the sexual and romantic attachment to the old love, beginning to develop a new social network, and opening themselves up to other intimate relationships. *Letting Go* offers a methodical daily and weekly program to "short circuit" symptoms that can be overwhelming and to convert the pain and sense of victimization into more constructive anger.

454. *Life After Loss*: *A Personal Guide Dealing With Death, Divorce, Job Change and Relocation.* **Bob Deits. Tucson, AZ: Fisher Books, 1988, 1992. Paperback. 226 pp.**

Life's inevitable losses, such as divorce, bring with them their own particular pain and grieving, says Deits. His purpose is to assure readers that, despite the sadness, there is growth and "life after loss" if we approach each crisis with knowledge and care. His step-by-step action-oriented workbook is complete with case studies, exercises, and journal suggestions. It encourages readers to learn how to: know what to expect; allow themselves to grieve, cry, and talk; distinguish between "normal and distorted grief responses;" cope with angry or guilty feelings; deal with loneliness; care for their health and nutrition; create or join a support group; use their spiritual resources; nurture themselves; and "choose to live again."

455. *Life After Marriage: Love in an Age of Divorce.* **A. Alvarez. New York: Simon & Schuster, 1981. Hardcover. 269 pp.**

Focusing on marriage as well as divorce, this book avoids theory and statistical surveys since it seeks to prove nothing. It concentrates on the author's subjective fascination with the dozens of men and women he interviewed, his own divorce, and his own perception of what marriage should be. Suggesting that divorce brings with it sadness, depression, and many of the same stigma as does suicide, Alvarez covers such areas as: the confusions and contradictions suffered, the history of divorce, the negative impact of the early church on marriage, the mourning process, feelings of loneliness, the extended process of healing, and the exhilaration of new-found freedoms.

456. *Life's Parachutes*: *How to Land on Your Feet During Trying Times.* **Dr. Paul Coleman. New York: Dell Publishing, 1993. Paperback. 245 pp.**

Complete with stories, exercises and guidelines, this book seeks to give readers "gifts" or "parachutes" to hang onto when they face traumas like unhappiness, illness, job problems, divorce or death. Without crisis, true growth is not possible, Coleman feels, yet suffering remains undeniable. He sees determination, creative problem solving, self-awareness, tolerance, patience, decisiveness and forgiveness as "healing attitudes" that can be adopted to change negative feelings. Coleman emphasizes that a positive outlook toward change can empower our coping mechanisms and make all the difference. The book encourages us to detach ourselves, "make peace with the past," seek support and be grateful for whatever is left. It also stresses that failure to believe in ourselves is the most serious impediment to recovery.

457. *Living and Loving After Divorce.* **Catherine Napolitane with Victoria Pellegrino. New York: Signet Books, NAL, 1977. Paperback. 241 pp.**

Napolitane and Pellegrino have composed a systematic handbook to help divorced women start all over again in a new life. Topics include: eight predictable emotional phases all divorced people experience in the process; how to recognize and combat feelings of loneliness, hostility, and hurt; dangerous "games" couples play; how to widen our social circles and develop new relationships; dating and sex; legal questions including alimony; financial independence and jobs; the problems of single-parenting; taking advantage of therapy; and finally the possibility of remarriage. Ample case histories are included to aid in clarifying issues.

458. *Living Through Personal Crisis.* **Ann Kaiser Stearns. New York: Ballantine, 1985. Paperback. 175 pp.**

Stearns writes in straightforward terms for those feeling hurt and helpless due to the distressing effects of loss. Her book offers numerous case histories with sympathetic practical suggestions for: confronting the situation, taking the time to concentrate on it without ignoring or denying it, and finding peace again. Although human beings can't prevent themselves from being scarred, the trauma can provide a stepping stone to greater self-knowledge in the long run, Stearns says. She examines the types of stress signals associated with loss, namely: a sense of guilt; physical symptoms affecting eating, sleeping, and sexual habits; and worry, resentment, and anger. The book emphasizes the importance of nurturing ourselves, making a slow readjustment, and seeking help.

459. *Lost Lovers, Found Friends: Maintaining Friendship After the Breakup.* **Scott Nelson, Ph.D. New York: Fireside, Simon & Schuster, 1991. Paperback. 189 pp.**

While many people may believe that maintaining a friendship after a breakup is very unlikely, Nelson's interviews with 70 men and women who have succeeded at it show that definite advantages can be achieved. This is especially true if a future ongoing connection is necessary in work or through children and friends. The book gives advice on deciding whether such a "friendship" is appropriate. It contains quizzes for evaluating particular needs, lays out a program of exercises to "ease us through the transition," and suggests numerous alternatives for restructuring our relationships.

460. *Loveshock*: *How to Recover From a Broken Heart and Love Again.* **Stephen Gullo, Ph.D. and Connie Church. New York: Simon & Schuster, 1988. Hardcover. 189 pp.**

Gullo, a therapist, and Church, a victim of "loveshock," have joined together to provide viable, lifelong recovery skills for those who have suffered the painful loss of a love. Likening this trauma to a soldier's "shellshock," they provide practical guidance for understanding: why we hurt so badly; how we can survive; and how we can grow, "let go" and move forward to live and love once more. They outline six predictable stages in the process allowing readers to take solace in the fact that this pain is normal. They also forewarn the reader about the many potential "stumbling blocks" and "mistakes" likely to be made. The book gives advice on evaluating potential new lovers and using the knowledge of the past to make better decisions in the future.

461. *Marital Separation: Coping With the End of a Marriage and the Transition to Being Single Again.* **Robert S. Weiss. New York: Basic Books, Inc., 1975. Hardcover. 334 pp.**

This sociologist originated a successful program of "Seminars for the Separated." He bases his practical handbook on interviews with individuals undergoing the emotional trauma and "identity changes" related to divorce. His readers range from those suspecting marital breakdown to those already divorced. Weiss offers them potential guidelines for recovering and reorganizing their new lives and also gives them advice regarding the maintenance of a workable post-divorce relationship. His book stresses the fact that anyone in this situation should expect to be distressed. It examines such areas as: legal considerations, facilitating the transition, the ensuing social chaos, dealing with relatives, dating and sex, and changing roles.

462. *Necessary Losses*: *The Loves, Illusions, Dependencies and Impossible Expectations That All of Us Have to Give Up in Order to Grow.* **Judith Viorst. New York: Simon & Schuster, 1986. Hardcover. 447 pp.**

Viorst believes that understanding our own style of coping with loss has a tremendous impact on knowing who we are and how we can achieve happiness. Looking at life's passages and especially at the complexities of marriage, she examines losses of all types: intimate others, idealism and dreams, freedom, power, security, "impossible expectations," and youth. Her book is based on personal experience, interviews, literature, and "psychoanalytic theory." It stresses that each person grows by letting go of something and that there is thus a "bond between losses and gains." Loss is seen as a predictable and necessary by-product of investing ourselves deeply in something other than ourselves. The book stresses that loss cannot and should not be avoided in life.

463. *Opening Up: The Healing Power of Confiding in Others.* James W. Pennebaker, Ph.D. New York: William Morrow and Co., Inc., 1990. Hardcover. 251 pp.

Pennebaker's research on thousands of people tests how "inhibition" (suppressing thoughts and feelings) affects health. The results indicate overwhelmingly that "opening up" through writing or speaking has very salutary effects. His book offers people practical suggestions for coming to grips with "buried turmoil," thus improving their physical and mental well-being. Pennebaker shares his findings that "brain and immune function" are altered when people let go of pent-up feelings and thoughts that they have strenuously labored to hide. His work with a multitude of test cases reveals that the act of suppressing takes its toll on health. The book's case studies testify to the fact that mind and body are related and that relief is felt once confiding begins.

464. *Ordinary Women, Extraordinary Lives: How to Overcome Adversity and Achieve Positive Change in Your Life.* Marcia Chellis. New York: Viking, Publ. by The Penguin Group, 1992. Hardcover. 259 pp.

Having overcome her own crises with drinking and divorce, Chellis grew interested in exactly what enables some women to conquer adversity. Through interviews with many "ordinary" women, she developed her "self-empowerment" theory. She illustrates this theory with the real stories of eight women who survived against tremendous odds such as: drug and alcohol addiction, eating disorders, poverty, divorce, and devastating accidents and illnesses. Recovery patterns were noted to be the same. The victim first accepted outside support. Next, to "sustain the change," she took on a "survivor mission" and offered the same mentoring to others. The book's advice is based on this concept of giving and receiving. Chellis believes women can triumph over any problem by following her five-step plan.

465. *The Phoenix Factor: Surviving & Growing Through Personal Crisis.* Dr. Karl Slaikeu and Steve Lawhead. Boston, MA: Houghton Mifflin Co., 1985. Hardcover. 236 pp.

"The Phoenix Factor" is the theory that out of the remnants of the old can rise a "new and better order." In this book, a psychiatrist and a science fiction writer work together to assist those who have been assaulted by a serious life crisis either past or present. Their goal is to help readers achieve more than mere recovery. By adopting their techniques, Slaikeu and Lawhead contend people can channel these seemingly devastating moments into "turning points" and catalysts for overall growth. Their book shows how crises, natural events in the human condition, are able to be "conquered" when individuals: care for themselves; deal openly and effectively with grief, pain, guilt, and forgiveness; adapt a personal outlook; and organize their behavior.

466. *Rebuilding*: *When Your Relationship Ends*. **Bruce Fisher. San Luis Obispo, CA: Impact Publishers, 1991. Paperback. 214 pp.**

Written by a divorce therapist, this is a practical, down-to-earth handbook for healing pain and rebuilding a life after crisis or loss. It envisages stages of recovery as "building blocks" on a "mountain" that must be climbed (at the victim's own pace) to achieve full recovery and growth. Types of challenges include working through feelings such as denial, guilt, and grief to building friendship, trust, and self-esteem. The book assists readers in moving through these stages, developing new parts of themselves, and gaining self-understanding. It discusses what may be coming in the future, once recovery has been achieved. Fisher includes checklists and charts and encourages journal writing.

467. *Resilience*: *Discovering a New Strength at Times of Stress*. **Frederic Flach, M.D. New York: Fawcett Columbine, 1988. Hardcover. 270 pp.**

Case studies illustrate Flach's view that the natural life cycle is "disruption—giving in to stress— and reintegration." For humans, pain and change are inevitable, he says. The book reveals how those who temporarily crumble in the chaos actually have an advantage over those who don't. The author suggests that falling apart for some "reasonable period" allows individuals to respond creatively, put their lives into new perspectives, and emerge healthier, more focused, and better prepared to meet the next challenge. *Resilience* examines the kinds of personalities that survive crises by "learning, unlearning, and adapting." It defines the traits that enable people to take control of themselves and succeed, and it helps readers to develop inner problem-solving strength.

468. *Smart Cookies Don't Crumble*: *A Modern Woman's Guide to Living and Loving Her Own Life*. **Sonya Friedman. New York: G.P. Putnam's Sons, 1985. Hardcover. 252 pp.**

Friedman's belief is that it is never too late to begin to live a fulfilling, exciting, and meaningful life regardless of our age or previous history. Women can and should abandon unsatisfactory relationships and adopt healthier forms of interaction, she argues. Her book encourages readers to: put aside feelings of inferiority; strive to develop a clear sense of identity and purpose to motivate themselves; and move on to survive events like divorce or disappointment "without bitterness or alienation." Friedman shows that women are much more capable than many believe; they only need to learn to dream and embrace risks in order to take advantage of opportunities that can act as positive forces in their lives.

469. *The Sorrow and the Fury: Overcoming Hurt and Loss from Childhood to Old Age.* **Lucy Freeman. Englewood Cliffs, NJ: Prentice-Hall, Inc., 1978. Hardcover. 152 pp.**

Freeman has written a practical guide for coping more effectively with loss due to death, divorce or numerous other causes. She views these inevitable junctures in life, though "endless," as unusual opportunities for growth if handled creatively. The kinds of loss discussed here include the most common types involving jobs, material possessions, and loved ones. Every aspect of the process from "healthy and unhealthy mourning" through anger to recovery is a topic of discussion. Reasons for our reactions are also an area of concern. The book discusses patterns developed in our pasts as they relate to our present coping strategies. It emphasizes the healthful effects of developing new interests and relationships. *The Sorrow and the Fury* is based on case studies and conversations with professionals.

470. *Staying On Top When Your World Turns Upside Down: How to Triumph Over Trauma and Adversity.* **Kathryn D. Cramer, Ph.D. New York: Penguin Books, Penguin Group, 1990. Paperback. 332 pp.**

A stress psychologist, Cramer presents a four-step program to assist readers in "self-directed healing." She proposes that such healing builds inner resilience for confronting life's major and minor dilemmas. Her book notes that stress can lead to the development of inner strength. If people learn how to access their creativity, it states, they can use the stress as inspiration to move forward to higher levels. Cramer follows the sufferer through predictable stages from grief through acceptance to positive growth. She also studies the effects of trauma on health. Her book urges readers to commit their feelings to a diary that they can continually monitor and review. The diary will then provide the basis of a "mental conditioning program" for responding to stress in the future.

471. *Ten Days to Self-Esteem.* **David D. Burns, M.D. New York: Wm. Morrow, 1993. Paperback. 331 pp.**

Changing negative feelings is possible, proposes Burns, an expert on mood. His graphically designed workbook provides clear steps to: chart and test moods, inventory anxieties, weigh the costs and benefits of the way we feel, change "distorted thinking," evaluate "relationship satisfaction," and work at adding joy to our lives. The unique book is based on cognitive therapy which holds that our thoughts greatly affect our moods. Burns says that while some may require therapy, many of us can cure unhappiness ourselves if we commit to working actively on our outlook. His common sense methods were tested at the Presbyterian Medical Center in Philadelphia. Topics include: "healthy and unhealthy feelings," help for curing inferiority and depression, self-help assignments, and positive strategies for feeling good.

472. *When Bad Things Happen to Good People.* **Harold S. Kushner. New York: Schocken Books, 1981. Hardcover. 149 pp.**

This is a book of solace, comfort, and guidance for those who believe in God but find themselves distraught, discouraged, and angry. According to the author, these emotions are caused by pain in our lives which we feel we neither deserve nor understand. The book is written by a rabbi, who has experienced great suffering himself. It is directed at people who have been besieged by the events of a: death, serious illness or physical injury, personal or professional rejection, or any other major disappointment in life. The reader may be someone whose fundamental belief in God's goodness has been shaken and needs rebuilding. This book is not intended as a theology treatise but rather as a source of inspiration.

473. *When the Worst That Can Happen Already Has*: *Conquering Life's Most Difficult Times.* **Dennis Wholey. New York: Hyperion Publishers, 1992. Hardcover. 362 pp.**

Wholey has collected a series of "personal testimonials." Ordinary and famous individuals, who have survived and grown through major crises, speak to us. A reformed alcoholic himself, the author emphasizes the inevitability of suffering. He sees pain, however, both as a stimulus for personal growth and a teacher of new skills. If we learn from pain, he believes we can emerge stronger and more confident. Wholey maintains that we can greatly improve relationships when we redirect our life focus. Narratives from the likes of Betty Ford inspire the reader to have hope, dig deeper for sources of courage, and cope in healthier ways. Challenges such as "divorce, disability, illness, professional defeat, loneliness, and AIDS" are represented. Experts and clergy also give advice.

474. *Whoever Said Life Is Fair? Growing Through Life's Injuries.* **Sara Kay Cohen. New York: Charles Scribner's Sons, 1977. Hardcover. 117 pp.**

Having survived her own painful separation and divorce and having counseled patients for years, this psychotherapist knows firsthand that life is often unjust and unfair. Cohen's focus in this book is not on some dreamlike fantasy but on "dealing with life as it really is." Her approach allows readers to gain strength and self-knowledge through their experiences with tragedy and suffering. Cohen sees personal growth as directly related to an ability to cope with such trials, passages, and transitions. Individuals can discover joy and happiness in life again, she believes, if they learn how to regroup and rebuild themselves to the ultimate of their new capabilities.

475. *Why Me • Why This • Why Now*: *A Guide to Answering Life's Toughest Questions*. **Robin Norwood. New York: Carol Southern Books, 1994. Hardcover. 227 pp.**

Writing for women and men, Norwood has created a guide to help us "reframe" our crises so that we find answers to their deeper meaning. On one level, her book is deeply personal, having been completed after years of seclusion when Norwood was recovering from illness, divorce and career change. On another, it narrates the accounts of others who also have experienced great misfortune. Norwood's work with psychics and healers unveiled new realms of being to her such as "paranormal experiences," "subtle bodies," and "energy packages." Her conclusions are that we are far more than physical beings; our spiritual dimensions can allow us to penetrate human existence, becoming much more aware of and in tune with our destinies. Readers are to be healed here and enlightened about accepting what is rather than what "should have been."

476. *The Wife-In-Law Trap*: *Coping with the Pressures of Divorce and Remarriage, for Current and Former Wives—And the Husband Caught in the Middle*. **Ann Crytser. New York: A Pocket Star Book, a Div. of Simon & Schuster, 1990. Paperback. 237 pp.**

The "Wife-In-Law" is defined by Crytser as "a woman connected to another woman by marriage to the same man (at different times)." This is a condition that can create a problematic triangle of emotions especially when the point of contention is sex, the handling of children, or the allocation of finances. Based on the author's own experiences and illustrated with case histories, the book's intended audience is women in any phase of the divorce-remarriage cycle. Crytser covers potential areas of conflict as well as situations that can be rewarding to all parties. She also gives understanding counsel on what to expect and watch out for as well as what traits characterize a "good wife-in-law."

477. *Winning Life's Toughest Battles*: *Roots of Human Resilience*. **Dr. Julius Segal. New York: McGraw Hill, 1986. Hardcover. 157 pp.**

In this inspirational book, Segal wants to help readers survive life's most pressing crises—whether they be divorce, death, or other major traumas. He describes the experiences and spirit of average people (such as prisoners of war), who have become "triumphant survivors" against overwhelming odds.

These act as case studies on which to model one's attitudes. The author's purpose is not to present superficial techniques for "getting by." Instead he introduces fundamental strategies by which people can live their lives. Segal believes in the adaptability of the human spirit especially if it is empowered by the five important qualities that he elaborates upon: "communication, control of life, conviction, a clear conscience, and compassion for others."

478. *The World of the Formerly Married.* **Morton Hunt. New York: McGraw Hill Book Co., 1966. Hardcover. 326 pp.**

Hunt bases his book on a nationwide survey as well as real case histories. In it, he carefully studies hundreds of widely diverse people through the entire post-divorce transition and redefinition process. In many ways he sees them as misunderstood by, alienated from, and threatening to the largely married culture in which they almost secretly live. But he believes that these people have special challenges and joys. Hunt observes that moods can swing from ecstasy to deep depression. Topics include: the psychological impact of alimony and property disputes; effects of divorce on children; the "rediscovery of passion and emotion;" the pros and cons of sexual experimentation; the challenges of new love affairs; and the promise for greater success in a new marriage.

For additional help in "Recovering from Divorce," see also book numbers:

 4: *Bradshaw On:The Family*
10: *The Emotionally Abused Woman*
14: *Golden Handcuffs*
15: *The Good Girl Syndrome*
24: *Letters from Women Who Love Too Much*
27: *Lovesick: The Marilyn Syndrome*
33: *Passions*
34: *Perfect Women*
36: *Recovering from Co-Dependency*
37: *The Seashell People*
39: *Slay Your Own Dragons*
42: *Sweet Suffering: Woman As Victim*
49: *Unfinished Business: Pressure Points in the Lives of Women*
51: *What Smart Women Know*
53: *When Am I Going to Be Happy?*
56: *Why Women Worry*

60: *Women & Self-Esteem*
61: *Women & The Blues*
66: *Your Erroneous Zones*
93: *Men Who Hate Women and the Women Who Love Them*
177: *Love Is Letting Go of Fear*
247: *How to Salvage Your Marriage Or Survive Your Divorce*
297: *Love & Betrayal*
311: *Bailing Out*
312: *Between Marriage and Divorce*
314: *Coming Apart*
315: *Creative Divorce*
316: *The Divorce Experience*
319: *Growing Through Divorce*
320: *How to Get Out of an Unhappy Marriage Or an Unhappy Relationship*
321: *Learning to Leave*
323: *Life Changes: How Women Can Make Courageous Choices*
325: *Living Through Your Divorce*
327: *Nice Women Get Divorced*
328: *One Door Closes, Another Door Opens*
329: *Our Turn*
331: *Overwhelmed*
332: *Pathfinders*
334: *Shifting Gears*
336: *'Til Divorce Do Us Part*
339: *Turning Points*
340: *Uncoupling*
341: *Uncoupling: The Art of Coming Apart*
349: *Daddy Doesn't Live Here Anymore*
357: *For the Sake of the Children*
358: *A Grief Out of Season*
362: *Healthy Divorce*
372: *Mom's House, Dad's House*
373: *My Kids Don't Live With Me Anymore*
375: *The Parents' Book About Divorce*
378: *Second Chances: Men, Women & Children a Decade After Divorce*

379: *Surviving the Break-up*
380: *Talking About Divorce and Separation*
386: *Between Love & Hate: A Guide to Civilized Divorce*
393: *Dealing With Divorce*
404: *Divorce Mediation,* Schneider & Schneider
407: *Divorcing*
411: *Getting Divorced Without Ruining Your Life*
422: *Sharing the children*
479: *45 and Single Again*
482: *Breaking Out of Loneliness*
484: *The Divorced Woman's Handbook*
485: *First Person Singular*
487: *Formerly Married: Learning to Live With Yourself*
489: *How to Parent Alone*
499: *One's Company*
503: *Single After 50*
504: *Single Again*
505: *Single File*
508: *Single Parents Are People Too*
512: *Singling*
513: *Solo Parenting*
514: *Suddenly Single*
515: *Survival Guide for the Suddenly Single*
549: *To Marry Again*

11

Living Alone

Formerly married: Learning to live with yourself

Anxiety frequently troubles women early in this stage. Being on their own is something many have probably not experienced since they were much younger. Living without a man may appear both frightening and impossible. One day the woman realizes that almost every decision rests upon her shoulders, a prospect that brings with it tremendous responsibility but also, she soon finds out, an exciting degree of freedom as well. Some women will attempt to meet this challenge by trial and error. Others will look to resources like the ones in this chapter for practical advice and insight.

The books included here treat broad general issues as well as highly specific ones. A substantial number deal with the nitty-gritty aspects of day-to-day life such as home repair, safety, cars, finances, credit, insurance, taxes, and living arrangements. Handling the role of single parent while balancing social life, sexuality, dating, and career demands is another important topic. Many authors seek to differentiate between being alone and being lonely. They stress the fact that real happiness comes from within a person. Living for today rather than postponing her life until she meets the right person is emphasized, with particular attention given to developing new outlets, nurturing friendships, and having fun. Independence will enhance her ability to share a life with someone rather than impair it should she someday embark on a new relationship.

The personal stories of women who are alone and thriving reveal that a proactive approach and a positive attitude can have countless benefits.

479. *45 and Single Again.* Mildred Hope Witkin, Ph.D. with Burton Lehrenbaum. New York: Dembner Books, Publ. by Red Dembner Ent. Corp., 1985. Hardcover. 198 pp.

This book is for suddenly single older men and women. It gives advice on handling the traumas, predictable changes, and emotions that can occur. Most noticeable, the authors think, is a period of "regression" in which fearful insecurities may produce dependency needs. They see transition to a new, even better life ("with or without a long-term partner") as possible even though the painful effects of loss increase the older people grow. In practical terms and with case studies, the book examines all major issues involved including: responses such as "anger, humiliation, and shame," denial, difficult challenges to overcome, issues of sexuality, new economic demands, handling reactions of grown children, and being open to new opportunities for happiness.

480. *Alone—Not Lonely: Independent Living for Women Over Fifty.* Jane Seskin. Glenview, IL: American Assoc. for Retired Persons, Scott, Foresman & Co., 1985. Paperback. 228 pp.

Seskin's approach to living alone is a very positive and optimistic one. It stresses the rewards for women of gaining control of the physical, psychological, and financial aspects of their lives. Independence is seen as enriching and as a vehicle to reaching full potential. The book offers women practical guidance on day-to-day living and coping along with inspiration for: adjusting to their status, building self-esteem, overcoming loneliness and boredom, and reaching out for support, friendship, and entertainment. Seskin concentrates on improving physical appearance and health as well as on: continuing education, career goals, making sound financial decisions, understanding all the options, and issues of sexuality.

481. *Alone, Alive & Well: How to Fight Loneliness and Win.* Barbara Powell, Ph.D. Enmaus, PA: Rodale Press, 1985. Hardcover. 247 pp.

Powell shows how to find the rewarding fulfillment of solitude and overcome the frustrations, insecurity, and self-pity of wallowing in loneliness. She focuses on the positives of being alone such as independence, time for self-nurturing and creativity, and the benefits of being free of a negative relationship. Her book offers strategies for: the rebuilding of self-esteem, recognition and prevention of oncoming negative attitudes, developing friendships and a social network, and structuring routines and fulfilling activities. It also discusses the benefits of going back to school, becoming involved in church activities, and owning a pet for companionship.

482. *Breaking Out of Loneliness.* **Jerry A. Greenwald, Ph.D. New York: Rawson, Wade Publ. Inc., 1980. Hardcover. 228 pp.**

Greenwald states clearly that each of us is personally responsible for the loneliness we experience in our lives, even though it is a natural feeling and not to be considered a human failing. His theory is, therefore, that we all have the power to eliminate loneliness forever by developing a greater sense of self and "self-confrontation" skills. In the author's eyes, the job does not require special talent or numerous preparatory steps, even in a world where loneliness is very prevalent. Greenwald provides a tested program through "image therapy and role-playing exercises" that can be done at home. Topics include: developing a nurturing attitude, loneliness games, fears, living for today, examining childhood problems, and facing our enemies in order to forgive them and maintain a love for them.

483. *Coping***:** *A Survival Guide for Women Living Alone.* **Martha Yates. Englewood Cliffs, NJ: Prentice-Hall, Inc., 1976. Hardcover. 272 pp.**

This practical, common sense guide empathizes with the single woman living in a "couple-oriented" world—a world in which singles often make married people feel very ill at ease. Yates notes that the all-too-frequent result is that many social functions may eliminate singles. The author views being alone as a positive and fulfilling experience but one for which women need careful preparation if they are not to develop the characteristics of helpless victims. *Coping* covers such broad topics as: conquering loneliness, regaining self-confidence, emotional issues, sex, and helping children readjust. The book offers specific assistance for: establishing credit and dealing with finances, income tax, insurance and automobile problems.

484. *The Divorced Woman's Handbook***:** *An Outline for Starting the First Year Alone.* **Jane Wilkie. New York: Wm. Morrow, 1980. Hardcover. 172 pp.**

Wilkie's work with 40 divorced women reveals a wide range of fears and vulnerabilities. Many of these fears, she notes, go beyond the traditional "emotional trauma" to insecurities about handling day-to-day life by themselves. Her book, therefore, addresses psychological issues first and then progresses to every aspect of managing one's affairs. In an uncomplicated and informative style, Wilkie gives psychological advice on the emotional first year: healing, mood swings, and children. Then she offers practical suggestions on: bookkeeping, money matters, changing names, safety, home and car care, maintaining health, developing a social life, relocating, and jobs. Each chapter includes a chart to help in regaining control and prioritizing obligations.

485. *First Person Singular*: *Living the Good Life Alone*. **Stephen M. Johnson, Ph.D. New York: A Signet Book, New American Library, 1977. Paperback. 259 pp.**

Johnson's book follows the reader through the natural process of separating, coping as a single, and forming new relationships. As a clinical psychologist, he provides "tested techniques" for men and women to: leave each other in the bravest and least destructive manner, take on the varied challenges of change, and develop the ability to regain control of their lives. Understanding that living alone can make people insecure and lonely, Johnson shows how to: structure a support system and social network, approach new intimate relationships, and master the skills necessary to deal with the future in a mature and capable fashion. He also emphasizes the rewards and pleasures of living alone.

486. *Flying Solo*: *Single Women in Midlife*. **Carol M. Anderson and Susan Stewart with Sona Dimidjian. New York: W.W. Norton & Co., 1994. Hardcover. 309 pp.**

Readers will be surprised to learn that being single at midlife is a "new American life-style" not the "failure" many consider it. In fact, singles and unhappily marrieds may be inspired by the independent, rewarding, and creative lives of the individuals in this research. Ninety women, predominantly 40-45 years old, composed the study conducted from 1990-1992. Some had never married; others were divorced or widowed. The book considers all aspects of the subjects' lives from cultural pressures to marry to feelings on loneliness, practical logistics, goals and careers, bonds with friends, need for children, lives as single parents, thoughts on intimacy and dating, and the "challenges and triumphs" encountered. Readers can use these women as role models who not only survive but thrive on being on their own.

487. *Formerly Married: Learning to Live With Yourself.* **Marilyn Jensen. Philadelphia, PA: Bridgebooks, The Westminster Press, 1983. Hardcover. 116 pp.**

Jensen's sympathetic and practical book illustrates how to survive the variety of experiences that can overwhelm the newly single person. Based on interviews and personal experience, it is not a "how-to" book but rather a description of the natural course of events. The primary focus is on maintaining the ability to care for the children. Other topics covered are: coming to terms with loss and grief, getting professional help, learning to be in control of one's own life, careers, finances, dealing with the awkwardness and anxiety of being single, nurturing the self and finding time for fun, and embarking on new relationships. The book carries the reader from the painful period of grieving to the building of an independent new life.

488. *Going It Alone*: *The Family Life and Social Situation of the Single Parent*. **Robert S. Weiss. New York: Basic Books Inc., Publishers, 1979. Hardcover. 303 pp.**

The rapidly rising numbers of single parent families and the accompanying challenges led Weiss to address the special needs of these individuals. He bases his findings on 240+ interviews with parents and children. Four separate sections describe: 1) the shift from married to single life, 2) the ways households are structured, 3) the dynamics of social life, and 4) the advantages and disadvantages of this life-style. Topics include: child rearing problems; "establishing (oneself) in a community;" creating rewarding personal lives; balancing commitments to new partners, family and children; managing responsibilities and overload; and facing emotions such as "vulnerability," loneliness, and sexual needs.

489. *How to Parent Alone*: *A Guide for Single Parents*. **Joan Bel Geddes. New York: A Continuum Book, The Seabury Press, 1974. Hardcover. 293 pp.**

Written by a single parent for single parents, this book focuses on "parent care." It looks at the difficult tasks facing adults rather than the day-to-day demands of actual child rearing itself. Bel Geddes provides practical and positive suggestions for: recovering from grief; doing away with self-pity, guilt, and self-hatred; developing mature self-confidence; coping with the multitude of financial challenges; overcoming boredom; becoming decisive in all aspects of one's life; obtaining a good job and hanging on to it; creating a fulfilling social life to combat loneliness; and...balancing the whole act with the care of the children. The book emphasizes the rewards rather than the disadvantages of the situation.

490. *In Praise of Single Parents*: *Mothers and Fathers Embracing the Challenge*. **Shoshana Alexander. Boston, MA: Houghton Mifflin Co., 1994. Paperback. 404 pp.**

The stories of all kinds of single parents appear here: parents single by choice as well as parents single by circumstance. Alexander writes for the more than 10 million such individuals, 87 percent of whom she reports are women. Problems shared by them all as well as positive factors are topics. The author states that even though only 11 percent of American family units are traditional, single-parent families are still looked at somewhat askance. Her book examines how these parents became single, their guilt in trying to be perfect, their finances, how they deal with childcare, what occurs during dating, and finally how extended families operate. The outlook is positive especially regarding the rewarding, high quality relationships that can be formed with the children. Difficult, yes, says Alexander, but impossible no.

491. *In Search of Intimacy: Surprising Conclusions from a Nationwide Survey on Loneliness & What to Do About It.* **Carin Rubenstein and Philip Shaver. New York: Delacorte Press, 1982. Hardcover. 260 pp.**

Rubenstein and Shaver offer practical guidelines for dealing with loneliness, the normal human need for others. They state that sociological changes, which have removed the traditional safeguards against broken relationships, now give us no "guarantees" against facing life alone. Their book bases its detailed advice for coping on responses from thousands of questionnaires on a nationwide scale. It distinguishes the characteristics of loneliness from the acceptable and more voluntarily elected state called "solitude." The authors analyze causes of the condition from childhood through old age. Viewing loneliness as a "chronic condition," they feel that hope is possible since discussion of the topic is becoming much more common and open among those suffering.

492. *Intimate Connections: The New and Clinically Tested Program for Overcoming Loneliness Developed at the Presbyterian University of Pennsylvania Medical Center.* **David D. Burns, M.D. New York: Wm. Morrow, 1985. Hardcover. 333 pp.**

Intimate Connections offers a "hospital tested program" for sufferers from loneliness or lack of closeness to others. Based on cognitive therapy, the book proposes that our perceptions of reality greatly affect our feelings. It suggests that loneliness is a "state of mind" and that specific strategies can overcome it. Happiness originates within the individual and does not depend on a partner, Burns claims. He feels that what is most critical is "learning to like and love ourselves" through bolstering our self-esteem and eliminating negative thinking. His guide gives advice on how people can reach out to, accept, and love others and thus be more fulfilled. It contrasts "chronic" loneliness with "situational loneliness" and it presents specific questions to help us determine the degree to which we possess either kind.

493. *The Joy of Being Single: Stop Putting Your Life on Hold and Start Living.* **Janice Harayda. Garden City, NY: Doubleday & Co., Inc., 1986. Hardcover. 249 pp.**

Based on hundreds of interviews, this book stresses the absurdity of living in "suspended animation" until we become part of a marriage or relationship (the "real life"). While society is now more comfortable with singles, Harayda contends that the "pressure to marry" can still be a problem. She suggests, instead, that singlehood be viewed as a rewarding existence in and of itself, if it can be fully developed. Her book offers guidelines to the 33 percent of Americans living as singles on how to: foster love and close friendships; create a home; become financially independent; have fun; be proud of our independence; entertain; and in general, make the most of our life. The book proposes that marriage will occur more readily if we are happy and complete within ourselves first.

494. *Living Alone and Liking It: A Complete Guide to Living on Your Own.* **Lynn Shahan. New York: Stratford Press, Harper & Row, 1981. Hardcover. 189 pp.**

In 1981, Shahan stated that 21 percent of homes were composed of a single individual. As a single person herself and a counselor, teacher, and administrator, she possesses a positive outlook on this condition. Her book describes living alone as a way of life that requires complete self-sufficiency and one that can therefore result in great personal growth and fulfillment. Shahan teaches readers how they can live independently with genuine satisfaction. She addresses such issues as: conquering loneliness and depression, providing one's own entertainment, developing hobbies and pastimes, cooking, organizing a social life, finances and owning a home, reaching out to meet new people, and the pleasures of entertaining others.

495. *Living Single Successfully: How to Be Your Own Person—With or Without a Partner.* **Rolland S. Parker, Ph.D. New York: Franklin Watts, 1978. Hardcover. 182 pp.**

Employing numerous case histories, Parker focuses on the challenges and rewards of the single life. He does this in common sense, practical terms but with the expertise of a practicing psychologist. His book contends that understanding ourselves and leading a more fulfilling life are both possible if we achieve a balance between autonomy and intimacy with others. Parker discusses: dealing with feelings of loneliness and isolation, avoiding dependency or destructive relationships as a way out, becoming responsible for our own feelings and happiness, mastering the art of handling anger, and learning the fundamentals of forming sound relationships.

496. *Loneliness: The Experience of Emotional and Social Isolation.* **Robert S. Weiss. Cambridge, MA: The MIT Press, 1973. Hardcover. 236 pp.**

Designed chiefly for other professionals in the field, this book may also be useful for lay people who are suffering the effects of loneliness. Weiss sees this emotion not as a negative reaction but rather as a "natural response." His book analyzes loneliness in depth and examines the characteristic ways in which human beings act out the symptoms. Two specific types of loneliness are the targets: "emotional isolation," which occurs when a person loses an intimate relationship and "social isolation," which is the feeling of being divorced from a social network. Weiss uses case studies to describe the feelings of individuals and suggests techniques for effectively managing them.

497. *On Our Own*: *A Single Parent's Survival Guide.* **John DeFrain, Judy Fricke, and Julie Elman. Lexington, MA: Lexington Books, D.C. Heath and Co., 1987. Paperback. 282 pp.**

These authors base their study on years of family counseling and the experiences of approximately 1000 single parents who successfully reared children. Their book offers the advice of these parents and is positive in nature. DeFrain, Fricke and Elman provide encouragement for those who may fear that single parent families are somehow lacking. Topics in the book include: finding the most suitable custody arrangement; "good faith" negotiating; developing a healthy parenting partnership with an ex-spouse; learning how to build both parent and child "coping skills;" problems attached to finances, careers, dating, and visitation; creating necessary support networks; and improving individual parenting skills.

498. *One On the Seesaw*: *The Ups and Downs of a Single-Parent Family.* **Carol Lynn Pearson. New York: Random House, 1988. Hardcover. 205 pp.**

This book was written by a Mormon woman, divorced for ten years. Her former husband subsequently died. It is a personal narrative of the trials, tribulations, and often hysterical goings-on in a single-parent family of four children, two boys and two girls. Pearson's primary goal is "celebrating family" whether it be the traditional form or the increasingly common single-parent type. She highlights both the benefits and the challenges. While the tone is uplifting and encouraging for readers who may be looking for role models, the book does not overlook the numerous crises that can occur. Topics are covered in a non-self-help manner. They include: overload, aloneness, career, financial issues, attempts to "get rich," and raising an "old-fashioned family."

499. *One's Company*: *Reflections On Living Alone.* **Barbara Holland. New York: Ballantine Books, 1992. Hardcover. 255 pp.**

Holland, herself, is an expert in this area, having lived alone for years. She draws a balanced and optimistic picture of living alone stating that individuals can achieve exciting new levels of personal freedom and autonomy even though they must expect problems and challenges. With this practical handbook based on Holland's own personal philosophy, readers can learn everything from fixing things around the house to nursing themselves through illness. The book also discusses the larger issues of combating feelings of fear, depression, and loneliness. Topics include: widening social circles and forming new friendships, making career decisions, finding new outlets for fun, and developing fresh approaches for establishing new relationships.

500. *Parents Without Partners Sourcebook*: *The World's Largest Organization for Single Parents Gives You Positive, Practical Solutions to the Questions and Challenges of Single Parenting.* **Stephen L. Atlas. Philadelphia, PA: Running Press Book Publishers, 1984. Paperback. 192 pp.**

This is a book that allows readers to gain valuable assistance from individuals actually living and thriving in the single-parent situation. In it, Atlas discusses such topics as: legal rights and obligations, joint custody, sharing parenting responsibilities, visitation and support issues, finances, confronting divorce questions with children, dealing with teenagers and grandparents, making new friends, communicating cooperatively and nonhostilely with former spouses, conquering anxiety, dealing with loneliness, moving beyond hurt and lack of confidence, remarriage, stepparenting challenges, and single parents in military service. The sourcebook analyzes successful single-parent households as examples for readers to follow.

501. *Sex and the Single Parent.* **Jane Adams. New York: Coward, McCann and Geoghegan, Inc., 1978. Hardcover. 314 pp.**

Adams contends that most singles have been raised with the underlying moral premise that "sex is wrong without marriage." She notes that this belief generally causes them problems after a divorce. The intent of her book is to offer help in coping with the complex and often confusing question: how to fulfill commitments as parents while also satisfying one's needs as a sexual human being. Personal experience and interviews with children, parents, and lovers provide the basis. The book discusses: the challenges of privacy, living arrangements, partner demands, and the influence of parents' actions on children. Adams also includes the views of a variety of professionals in the field.

502. *Single: Living Your Own Way. A Lively Celebration of the Single Life that Shows How to Live Alone and Like It.* **Buff Bradley, Jan Berman, Murray Suid and Roberta Suid. Reading, MA: Addison-Wesley Publishing Co., 1977. Hardcover. 184 pp.**

These authors present a guide composed of short, concise chapters that address all the issues of living alone. Part I covers the real stories of 11 widely divergent single people and the ways they live their lives. Part II discusses the skills necessary to cope with common daily problems and challenges. Based on interviews and questionnaires, the book is positive and optimistic. It portrays singlehood as an exciting and fulfilling existence. In addition, there are reviews of 70 helpful and relevant books. Topics covered include: solitude, cooking, household chores, health, family and parenting, companionship, loving, sex, and careers. The book calls single people an "untapped national resource."

503. *Single After 50: How to Have the Time of Your Life.* **Adeline McConnell and Beverly Anderson. New York: McGraw Hill, 1978. Hardcover. 290 pp.**

This thorough and practical book is full of concrete techniques for embarking on an exciting new start in life regardless of age. It is based upon numerous interviews and a major questionnaire of actual individuals who have been suddenly left alone. McConnell and Anderson encourage a positive attitude, the elimination of worry, and the development of self-confidence and tranquility. This, they say, will break destructive life-style patterns. Topics discussed include: dealing with feelings of fear, guilt, and the effects of shock, financial stability, maintaining and finding jobs, safety, interactions with doctors and lawyers, cooking, developing new social circles, dating, sex, and remarriage.

504. *Single Again: The One Book That Will Help You Every Step of the Way if You Are a Newly Divorced or Widowed Man or Woman.* **Howard B. Lyman, Ph.D. New York: David McKay Company, Inc., 1971. Hardcover. 312 pp.**

Lyman has written a "basic crash course in self-preservation" for men and women. His book has a positive outlook drawn from his own experiences. Single Again offers advice on every step of the process beginning with the question of whether to divorce or not. It cautions against nurturing pain and harboring self-pity. There are practical guidelines on such topics as: damaged egos, lack of trust, detachment, communicating with the children, selecting the best attorneys, handling financial matters, in-laws and relatives, coping with the opinions of friends, developing new relationships, sex, and potential remarriage. Separate sections discuss issues pertaining to men and women.

505. *Single File: How to Live Happily Forever After With or Without Prince Charming.* **Susan Deitz with Anne Cassidy. New York: A Joan Kahn Book, St. Martin's Press, 1989. Hardcover. 317 pp.**

As the author of the widely-read column "Single File," Susan Deitz is an expert in helping single women stop stagnating in limbo and start living. She and Cassidy encourage women to set and to achieve specific goals toward an exciting life of their own instead of passively waiting for a man.

In a step-by-step proactive fashion, their book lays out practical exercises rather than theories. The building of self-esteem, competence, and confidence is a major goal. Independence is key to becoming interesting, vital, and happy—with or without a man, according to the authors. They urge readers to focus positively on themselves and deal decisively with choices. Topics include: interests, friends, money, career, study, meditation, entertaining, sex, and community.

506. *The Single Mother's Book: A Practical Guide to Managing Your Children, Career, Home, Finances, and Everything Else.* **Joan Anderson. Atlanta, GA: Peachtree Publishers, 1990. Paperback. 304 pp.**

This book offers answers, resource lists, and help for some of challenges most commonly experienced by single mothers. These challenges range from the broad issues of a life "game plan" to the smaller, specific, day-to-day traumas of fixing things around the house or burglar-proofing. Anderson believes that single living can be a positive experience, offering rewarding growth potential for women. Topics covered include: family issues revolving around children, teenagers, and stepfamilies; personal issues such as careers, self-nurturing, and developing new relationships; legal matters; financial issues related to insurance, establishing or maintaining credit, taxes, saving for retirement, and wills; and home repair information.

507. *Single Parenting: A Practical Resource Guide.* **Stephen L. Atlas. Englewood Cliffs, NJ: Prentice-Hall, Inc., 1981. Hardcover. 240 pp.**

Atlas uses the experiences of single parents to help other singles create successful family units. He says that such units should be "distinct and valid ways of life" not copies of two-parent families. Single-parent families are said to provide unusual benefits with greater opportunities for members to interact in a democratic way, building independence and strength. For children of divorce, the "sphere of influence" can be widened by having the lives of at least two adults serve as models, he believes. Atlas stresses sharing work loads and meeting the needs of all members. His book lists groups and resources that can provide support. Topics include: dealing with the non-single world, creating unique traditions, balancing work and family, discipline, and gay parents.

508. *Single Parents Are People Too: How to Achieve a Positive Self-Image and Personal Satisfaction.* **Carol Vejvoda Murdock. New York: Butterick Publishing Co., 1980. Hardcover. 192 pp.**

Murdock's guide is grounded in her work with hundreds of single parents and children. It provides advice on facing the problems and conflicting emotions prevalent among those who parent alone. Following the process of dissolution from the beginning to the end, the author describes the life-styles of these parents as well as their many demands and challenges. She offers specific solutions gleaned from leading experts in related fields. Topics included are: arriving at just settlements, custody and visitation, coping with the IRS, credit issues, problems of working parents, day care, nurturing ourselves, developing a new social network, and dealing with sexual challenges.

509. *Single Women, Alone and Together.* **Lucia H. Bequaert. Boston, MA: Beacon Press, 1976. Paperback. 256 pp.**

This book looks at single women of all types in an attempt to discover the techniques and support networks they use to survive as essentially "invisible women in married communities." Having interviewed 30 such females, Bequaert lets them tell for themselves how they deal with such issues as "sexuality, social life, counseling, religion, law, money, and careers." Setting a positive tone, the author discusses creative and "self-directed" approaches. Her book stresses the importance of knowing how to prepare for singlehood since so many will be in this position at some time. Topics include: the impact of feminism; women's groups; creating a life plan; and contending with "social barriers."

510. *Singled Out: A Civilized Guide to Sex and Sensibility for the Suddenly Single Man—or Woman.* **Richard Schickel. New York: The Viking Press, 1980. Hardcover. 115 pp.**

Singled Out is a personal reflection or "autobiographical essay" by a 47 year old middle class man. It makes an introductory statement that it is not a guide or survey nor is it based on any type of calculated scientific research. Instead, the book presents the views of a man who has personally passed through this awkward place in life and who wishes to share his reactions to the situations he encountered. Areas covered include: talking to women, accepting rejection, sexuality issues, learning to be "just friends," and developing the ability to recognize real love when it arrives.

511. *Singles: The New Americans.* **Jacqueline Simenauer and David Carroll. New York: Simon & Schuster, 1982. Hardcover. 399 pp.**

Simenauer and Carroll claim to have drawn the first nationwide "psycho-sexual portrait" of America's single men and women. Their study is based on a scientific survey designed to be representative of the whole country. It examines responses from 3000 subjects (ages 20-55) in 36 states regarding the "social, psychological, and sexual aspects of single life." The format presents questions first followed by findings, statistics, and then actual quotes from participants. Readers gain advice from a wide variety of the participants' answers on: divorce, marriage, parenting, careers, meeting people, dating, sex, and living arrangements. The book inventories advantages and disadvantages with freedom being the leading positive and loneliness, the most notable negative.

512. *Singling: A New Way to Live the Single Life.* **John R. Landgraf. Louisville, KY: Westminster/John Knox Press, 1990. Paperback. 202 pp.**

Landgraf states that 60 million adults are unmarried because of "death, divorce, delay, or design." As a professor of Theology, he sensed a need to offer practical survival advice learned from his own counseling experience. His guide provides basic strategies for surviving the transition to single life and developing an inner sense of wholeness without (or within, for that matter) a primary relationship. The author emphasizes becoming self-confident and "healthily single" as a whole person, inside and out. This, he says will be a key to attaining a satisfying and truly complete life. His book investigates a variety of common fears attributed to living alone and exposes them as unfounded.

513. *Solo Parenting: How to Find the Balance Between Parenthood and Personhood.* **Kathleen McCoy. New York: A Plume Book, New American Library, 1987. Paperback. 269 pp.**

Writing for the growing number of households run by a single parent, McCoy has concentrated on a positive outlook rather than on the distress of divorce. She has developed a sourcebook from her conversations with 100+ parents and involved professionals. Recognizing the weight and magnitude of the responsibilities, she offers strategies for coping and regaining control of one's life. Her emphasis is on self-nurturing as a vehicle for growth. Names, addresses, and phone numbers of helpful resource groups are included. Among topics covered are: child care, financial issues, seeking professional help, dealing successfully with guilt and depression, conquering loneliness, and making a new life.

514. *Suddenly Single: Learning to Start Over Through the Experience of Others.* **Joan Robertson and Betty Utterback. New York: Simon & Schuster, 1986. Hardcover. 233 pp.**

Suddenly Single is based on real experiences of numerous people who have suffered through the crisis of losing an intimate relationship. It offers psychological advice on understanding and coping with the stress, the desolation, and the regrouping that it sees as necessary if life is to go on productively and happily once again. The authors outline the entire process. They emphasize the new and frequently frightening "hard choices" that will be required both within our family and in our larger social network. Robertson and Utterback also delineate the effects of the decision-making process. Topics covered include: the end of a marriage, legal matters, recovery, being single as an older person, and developing new relationships.

515. *Survival Guide for the Suddenly Single.* **Barbara Berson and Ben Bova. New York: St. Martin's Press, 1974. Hardcover. 213 pp.**

Berson and Bova's handbook explores the personal experiences of a man and woman who have successfully made it through this often painful recovery and transition period. Chapters addressing a variety of issues alternate from the female to the male perspective. The book covers a full range of humorous, sad, and infuriating moments. There is positive emphasis on seizing the chance, even in the early weeks and months after a failed marriage, to develop oneself to the fullest. Increasing self-esteem, confidence, and maturity is the way to do it, they suggest. Topics for females include: the decline of financial status, keeping the ex out of the home, telling the children, new men and sex, fighting fear, and dealing with distant or smothering friends and relatives.

516. *The Woman Alone.* **Patricia O'Brien. New York: Quadrangle, The New York Times Book Company, 1973. Hardcover. 285 pp.**

O'Brien delves into questions surrounding the issues of loneliness and powerlessness for those who are single and live in a married world. She reveals how this world often misunderstands single women, discriminates against them and even regards them with suspicion. Drawing on personal knowledge and interviews, her book has a sensitivity to the needs of all single women. She sympathizes with their quest to be connected to rather than isolated from society at large. O'Brien also explores their sexual satisfaction and romantic relationships. While she may not give concrete answers per se, she reflects upon the many problems and conflicting emotions.

For additional help in "Living Alone," see also books numbered:

  6: *The Cinderella Complex*

  8: *The Crisis of the Working Mother*

14: *Golden Handcuffs*

15: *The Good Girl Syndrome*

26: *Looking Out for #1*

41: *The Superwoman Syndrome*

47: *The Type E Woman*

51: *What Smart Women Know*

53: *When Am I Going to Be Happy?*

54: *Where's My Happy Ending?*

55: *Why Do I Think I Am Nothing Without a Man?*

56: *Why Women Worry*

59: *Women & Money*

64: *Women's Burnout*

66: *Your Erroneous Zones*

103: *Some Men Are More Perfect Than Others*

130: *Born for Love*

254: *Living Together: Feeling Alone*

298: *Love Me Love Me Not*

310: *12 Steps to Mastering the Winds of Change*

311: *Bailing Out*

315: *Creative Divorce*

319: *Growing Through Divorce*

320: *How to Get Out of an Unhappy Marriage or An Unhappy Relationship*

321: *Learning to Leave*

322: *Leavetaking: When and How to Say Good-bye*

325: *Living Through Your Divorce*

329: *Our Turn*

340: *Uncoupling*

370: *The Kids' Guide to Divorce*

383: *What Should I Tell the Kids?*

413: *Head and Heart*

417: *Our Money Our Selves*

422: *Sharing the Children*

424: *Strassels' Tax Savers*

425: *The Survival Guide for Women*

430: *Women, Divorce and Money*

434: *Crazy Time: Surviving Divorce*

436: *Divorce and New Beginnings*

438: *Divorce Recovery*

439: *Divorced*
452: *The Lessons of Love*
454: *Life After Loss*
455: *Life After Marriage*
456: *Life's Parachutes*
457: *Living and Loving After Divorce*
468: *Smart Cookies Don't Crumble*
471: *Ten Days to Self-esteem*
473: *When the Worst That Can Happen Already Has*
474: *Whoever Said Life Is Fair?*
525: *Dare to Connect*
528: *Good Guys/Bad Guys*
530: *Haven't You Been Single Long Enough?*
553: *Why Women Shouldn't Marry*

12

Finding a New Relationship

When it's time to love again

At last we've made our way through the entire cycle. Years may have passed from the first doubts about the marriage to actual divorce and the desire for a fresh relationship. Or, the process might have been abbreviated and a new love blossoms almost instantaneously. Regardless of the sequence of events, it is possible for women to learn from their mistakes and to make their future choices better ones. With even higher divorce rates cited for second marriages than for first, it is essential that they exercise great caution, especially if children and remarriage are involved.

Too often the real question is how to find a man! Females may read that males are scarce, that women over 40 haven't a prayer of success, and that all the good ones are married. Loneliness appears to be rampant today and the demands and restrictions of careers add to the dilemma.

These authors counter with hope, creative methods, and "proven" strategies. Some are professionals and others write from personal experience. They discuss everything from becoming better candidates for romance by mastering the art of loving oneself to learning more about true compatibility, the inner desires of men, communication, unrealistic expectations, sexuality, men to avoid, and behavior patterns that should be changed. Making this search a "project" is often stressed. Dating services and personal ads are also explored. Certain authors describe how to blend new families; one even urges women never to marry at all.

Readers should note that many books listed previously, especially in chapters 2 and 4, can help in developing fulfilling relationships. It is my hope that women can gain enough knowledge from this sourcebook to prevent the divorce cycle from ever happening again.

517. *50 Ways to Find a Lover: Proven Techniques for Finding Someone Special.* **Sharyn Wolf with Katy Koontz. Holbrook, MA: Bob Adams, Inc., 1992. Paperback. 204 pp.**

While readers may doubt the viability of using a book to learn how to meet a man, these authors tout their own success rate. Having run seminars nationally and appeared on numerous TV shows, they have seen positive results when women decide to take action, develop skills, and change their lonely lives. Wolf and Koontz offer 50 separate strategies with an "action plan checklist" to review necessary steps. They address a wide range of readers through both "low and high-risk techniques." Tips include how to: improve desirability, polish communication skills, use humor, flirt and smile, widen friendships, accept some failure and rejection, resist snap judgements, and use mailing lists, personal ads, and dating services.

518. *Are You the One for Me? Knowing Who's Right & Avoiding Who's Wrong.* **Barbara De Angelis, Ph.D. New York: Delacorte Press, Bantam Doubleday Publ. Co., 1992. Hardcover. 353 pp.**

This compatibility study is chiefly for single and divorced women. It may also be of use to marrieds who wish to understand their couple differences and transcend them for greater fulfillment. Using simple graphic formatting with bold highlights, De Angelis concentrates on: why women select certain partners, qualities to search for and avoid, knowing if they made the wrong choice, and deciding if their "childhood programming" was a negative influence. Chapters have detailed exercises, checklists, and suggestions for analyzing: "sexual chemistry" and addictions, levels of commitment necessary for success, and the "wrong reasons" for falling in love. The book also discusses ten kinds of inferior pairings and five "deadly myths about love."

519. *At Long Last Love: Sage Advice and True Stories from America's Premier Matchmakers.* **John Wingo, Ph.D. and Julie Wingo, M.A. New York: Warner Books, 1994. Hardcover. 221 pp.**

Acclaimed matchmakers commanding as much as $25,000 per client, the Wingos share their practical techniques for finding truly satisfactory long-term relationships. Readers can follow the first encounter through commitment or to a breakup. Self-assessments, case studies, questionnaires, and guidelines appear throughout. The authors attempt to help readers discover their own true needs, values, interests and goals as well as evaluate exactly what they are looking for in a partner. They propose a balance between protecting oneself and being open and accessible. Topics include: ads, video dating, altering ineffective dating patterns, flirting, 20 attitudes that are impediments, respect vs. game-playing, "sexual etiquette," communication skills, how to spot a good potential, and signs of unhealthy relationships.

520. ***Beating the Marriage Odds*: *When You Are Smart, Single and Over 30*. Barbara Lovenheim. New York: Berkley Books, 1990. Paperback. 283 pp.**

Lovenheim writes a thoroughly modern and practical guide for those who would like to improve their chances of marrying the right man. While she agrees that there may be fewer unmarried men than women, the author shows with statistics that there is by no means a shortage. Her book stresses the importance of women understanding and liking themselves first as well as clearly knowing their own needs. It provides "active strategies" for: finding a spouse, identifying different types of men, dating, communicating about money issues, dealing with age differences, coping with sex and AIDS, and deciding on questions regarding children. The use of professional matchmaking services is also treated as is marrying after living alone for long periods of time.

521. ***Beyond Cinderella*: *How to Find and Marry the Man You Want*. Nita Tucker with Debra Feinstein. New York: St. Martin's Press, 1987. Paperback. 214 pp.**

Tucker and Feinstein have written a goal-oriented workbook complete with assignments. It suggests that finding a loving partner is not a matter of chance and that women should treat the task as legitimately as any respected "project" they undertake. The book contains "proven" techniques that have been successful for women enrolled in Tucker's seminars in "Connecting." Issues discussed are: changing attitudes, being open about the quest for a relationship, finding a supporting confidant, learning to approach attractive men, the myths about "chemistry," problems with sex, fears of rejection, doing away with problem men who are holding the woman back from the right ones, and knowing what to do with a good man when he is found.

522. ***Choosing Lovers*: *Ten Steps to a Happier Relationship*. Martin Blinder, M.D. with Carmen Lynch, M.S.W. New York: Avon Books, 1989. Paperback. 174 pp.**

Choosing Lovers outlines eight separate behavior patterns in intimate relationships that clarify why women select the lovers they do. An analysis of the inner dynamics of these pairings reveals why some relationships flourish and others are disastrously unhappy. Topics include: identifying early signs of men who are wrong so that women can restrain themselves from "sending signals" to attract them, understanding and eliminating tendencies to gravitate toward destructive unions, developing the ability to sense when relationships are not working, learning to recognize whether they are able to be repaired or not, ending a love affair properly, and how to "capture the magic of an enduring romantic relationship."

523. *Cold Feet*: *Why Men Don't Commit.* **Dr. Sonya Rhodes and Dr. Marlin S. Potash. New York: E. P. Dutton, 1988. Hardcover. 216 pp.**

Cold Feet is a resource book written for women. Its goal is to deepen their understanding of the causes and results of male "commitmentphobia." The authors describe three different types of men who suffer from this confusing problem. They then give advice on how to know if a potential partner is capable of commitment or not. The book examines the twin male fears of closeness and loneliness. It divides intimate behavior into "five levels of commitment," enabling women to evaluate the progress of relationships. Rhodes and Potash caution readers not to be misled by marriage, which may still not signify commitment for some men. They also give guidelines for improving partnerships or ending them if necessary.

524. *The Compatibility Quotient*: *If You're Thinking of Getting Married, Read This Book First.* **Sue Klavans Simring, D.S.W. and Steven S. Simring, M.D. with William Proctor. New York: A Fawcett Columbine Book, Ballantine Books, 1990. Paperback. 245 pp.**

Designed for single or married people, this book is useful for developing a more realistic understanding of ourselves and our partners. Such knowledge can determine both the compatibility and problem areas of our intimate relationships, the authors say. These two marriage counselors give detailed advice including a comprehensive questionnaire for analyzing the people and the relationship and predicting success or failure. They recommend regular use of the book since even compatible unions change and require constant adjustment. Their guide addresses the most significant issues in a marriage such as: sex, finances, personality differences, crisis points, goals, careers, impact of children, and life style preferences. Many case studies are included.

525. *Dare to Connect: Reaching Out in Romance, Friendship and the Workplace.* **Susan Jeffers, Ph.D. New York: Fawcett Columbine, 1992. Hardcover. 240 pp.**

This is a forthright book that studies the inner dynamics of relationships. It gives practical guidelines for having the kind of love people have always wanted. It is written for those who suffer from insecurity, loneliness, and isolation but who might subconsciously prefer to continue that way instead of suffering potential rejection. Jeffers emphasizes "compassion rather than blame" and the development of inner personal strength rather than "victim power." Topics discussed include: the building of self-assurance, honesty and open expression of views, the negative impact of competing, ways to turn new acquaintances into friendships, and techniques to combat inner loneliness by learning to be warm and open.

526. *Fit to Be Tied*: *Making Marriage Last a Lifetime*. **Bill & Lynne Hybels. Grand Rapids, MI: Zondervan Publ. House, a Div. of Harper Collins, 1991. Hardcover. 217 pp.**

Hybels, a pastor, and his author-editor wife do not claim to be marriage experts. They see their own personal experience in a "roller coaster marriage" and their desire to work to improve and enjoy their relationship, however, as more than satisfactory credentials for guiding others. Their book, based on "biblical principles," instructs readers in selecting appropriate mates and surviving for the long term. The authors' personal narrative has the male or female speaker identified in the margins with initials. The book provides practical checklists and quizzes for testing 1) compatibility before marriage, and 2) blocks to maintaining compatibility during marriage. It offers strategies for conflict resolution and building healthier relating patterns.

527. *Getting to "I Do."* **Dr. Patricia Allen and Sandra Harmon. New York: Wm. Morrow, 1994. Hardcover. 272 pp.**

Allen, a counselor with four marriages, and Harmon, a screenwriter and author, collaborate on this communication guide. They predict that women can go from dating to marriage in 12 months by following their tenets. The authors describe the "feminine and masculine sides" of both men and women, warning that certain male characteristics in strong women may threaten men, causing them to develop female traits. Part I helps women learn who they really are. It contrasts what men want from feminine women, what "masculine-energy women want from feminine-energy men," and equality vs. equity. Flirting is covered in Part II, the four stages of a one year relationship in Part III, and how to hang on to the Mr. Right in Part IV. Allen, the originator of successful seminars in Los Angeles, credits 2000 marriages to her systematic approach.

528. *Good Guys/Bad Guys: The Hite Guide to Smart Choices.* **Shere Hite and Kate Colleran. New York: Carroll & Graf Publ., Inc., 1991. Hardcover. 282 pp.**

This book is unlike many other handbooks on the market designed for the female audience, Hite and Colleran claim. They state that it is not based on the premise that women are "psychological wimps" who make mistake after mistake in love. The authors researched their topic for 15 years. They have written a book that probes emotional interactions in relationships and how women can make "smarter" decisions in their love lives. Subjects discussed include: new ways to deal with sexuality, a "new vocabulary" for strengthening communication and resolving conflicts, the positive aspects of being single, and determining when a problematic love affair should be ended.

529. *Guerrilla Dating Tactics: Strategies, Tips and Secrets for Finding Romance.* **Sharyn Wolf, C.S.W. New York: Dutton, The Penguin Group, 1993. Hardcover. 314 pp.**

Wolf proposes that dating in the nineties requires readers to dispose of old ideas and rules and be creative. As the originator of workshops by the same name, the author shows how to "find a good date, plan a good date, and be a good date." Her audience is "healthy" men and women who like each other and themselves but just can't find an appropriate partner. Though the title may appear militaristic, Wolf is quick to reject that as an approach. Her book is full of strategies for putting "fun and romance" into our lives. Stories and examples come from workshop participants as well as the author's own experience. Topics include: romantic myths, risking, safe sex, icebreakers, advice on eye contact, developing conversation skills, making dates, ads, gaining courage, game-playing, and finding new ways to look at ourselves.

530. *Haven't You Been Single Long Enough? A Practical Guide for Men or Women Who Want to Get Married.* **Milton Fisher. Green Farms, CT: Wildcat Publishing Co., Inc., 1992. Hardcover. 204 pp.**

Although he is an attorney and investment banker, Fisher's most compelling hobby is that of "dedicated matchmaker." He counts 29 marriages and numerous relationships in his 25-year track record. The goal of his book is to: examine good and bad relationships, analyze the nature of real love, discuss "how and where" to look, warn against using pretense to catch a mate, urge men and women to take risks, advise them to look for real rather than "fantasy lovers," teach people how to identify the winner, and encourage them to move on if their final selection doesn't wish to marry. Fisher believes that there is no need for loneliness. He claims there are "hundreds" even "thousands" of possible mates if men and women are real and outgoing, eager to receive love, and willing to throw out their "unrealistic criteria."

531. *Hot and Bothered: Sex and Love in the 90's.* **Wendy Dennis. New York: Viking, published by the Penguin Group, 1992. Hardcover. 276 pp.**

This bold and candid book's audience is mainly singles although married people may benefit from much of it as well. Dennis describes "contemporary sexual mores" and the confused feelings of hundreds of men and women in her admittedly unscientific exploration. Through comprehensive interviews, she has uncovered an "angst ridden" society, which often sees sex and the rules governing dating and mating as overwhelmingly complex. Dennis thinks that "politically correct" game-playing, AIDS, DINS, and career demands often prevent partners from honestly sharing their real dreams: comfort, intimacy, love, and perhaps even a return "to the way things were." Her book graphically delineates the rules of "sexual etiquette" in what the author calls an "erotic roadmap."

532. *How to Find Another Husband...By Someone Who Did: A Practical Guide to Dating and (Re)Mating.* **Rusty Rothman. Cincinnati, OH: Writer's Digest Books, 1985. Hardcover. 198 pp.**

Rothman writes from personal experience about the transition women make from being single to remarrying. While the passage may be difficult, she stresses the value and pleasures of the "in-between years." This is often the period when women begin to appreciate, nurture, and build themselves up to a solid level of self-confidence, Rothman says. Her book gives strategic advice on finding and meeting men, types to be sought, and "20 types of men to avoid." It provides lists of questions for analyzing former partners, new prospects, and "ideal" mates. "Tips" give readers an advantage on enhancing their appearance and fitness as well as revealing their best qualities. The book follows the whole cycle from dating through remarriage, and "blending" the new families.

533. *How to Find Romance After 40.* **Julia Grice. New York: M. Evans and Co., Inc., 1985. Hardcover. 288 pp.**

An ordinary woman herself, Grice offers "secrets" for other ordinary women who are seeking dates, relationships, or even marriage. She gives common sense suggestions with an emphasis on developing a self-confident, positive attitude rather than a perfect body and glamorous appearance. The book stresses a woman's choices and discourages reliance on mere chance and luck. Based on hundreds of interviews with men and women, it discusses: what men "really like about women over 40"; "five steps to meeting men;" and how to deal with "rejecting and being rejected." Topics include: different types of men, the importance of friendship, taking an active approach, "bedroom etiquette," joining groups, singles dances, ads, and dating services.

534. *How to Make a Man Fall in Love With You.* **Tracy Cabot, Ph.D. New York: A Dell Book, Dell Publishing Co., 1984. Paperback. 255 pp.**

Cabot has written a national best seller. It provides sensible, practical, and viable techniques for gaining a better understanding of exactly how a man looks at his world. The author tries to show women what really leads a man to fall in love with a particular woman. Her intent is to help women learn how to: master the skills of identifying the qualities in a man who is well-matched to them, answer needs that he is not even aware of, develop an atmosphere of trust, communication, and compatibility, and maintain this loving union for the rest of their lives. Cabot claims her ideas have been "scientifically tested and proven." A "Love Plan" will guide women who have not been receiving what they have been looking for in a relationship. Topics include: men as "visual, auditory, or feeling" types, "mirroring" strategies, and "anchoring" skills.

535. *How to Make Love to a Man.* **Alexandra Penney. New York: A Dell Book, Dell Publishing Co., 1981. Paperback. 154 pp.**

This is a book designed to dramatically improve a woman's love making and help her become what Penney says husbands or lovers have always wanted: a woman who makes love to them. Having interviewed hundreds of men about their deepest sexual needs and desires, this author shares her insights and offers simple techniques that she believes work. Her book discusses: how to be an active participant in love making, how to really enjoy the process, how to stimulate a man's senses like a professional, how to be "technically good," how to avoid being a woman who turns men off, how to feel sexy, how to talk about sex with men, and how to make love making full and enriching.

536. *How to Marry Super Rich: Or Love, Money and the Morning After.* **Sheilah Graham. New York: Grosset & Dunlap, 1974. Hardcover. 246 pp.**

Graham has written a unique "how-to" book. She sums up her purpose as: illustrating how various now wealthy and well-known men and women have improved their financial lot by carefully, strategically, shrewdly, and skillfully selecting their mates. Her book examines the lives and loves of a variety of American and British rich and famous people. In it, Graham tries to outline the techniques and strategies that have clearly worked to allow even some penniless individuals to "close the deal" with mates in upper financial brackets. It is designed for those who would like to run a similar search.

537. *How to Marry the Man of Your Choice: You Don't Have to Stay Single.* **Margaret Kent. New York: Warner Books, Inc., 1984. Paperback. 279 pp.**

Kent's best seller is comprised of easy-to-understand techniques that the author herself has tested. Her topic is: how to find, attract, and finally marry the "man of our choice" by digging ourselves out of the "rut of going nowhere relationships." The book offers concrete and practical suggestions for evaluating our own basic qualities, characteristics, and needs first. It then covers in detail such topics as: the desires and needs of the average man, 20 places where a woman can meet genuinely available men, 12 questions that will determine the suitability of a man, what to do about sex, and how to educate a man "to think like a husband."

538. *Keeping the Love You Find: A Guide for Singles.* **Harville Hendrix, Ph.D. New York: A Pocket Book, Simon & Schuster, 1992. Hardcover. 329 pp.**

This book is written for those who find themselves single again. It is a practical guide designed to show individuals how to develop healthy and fulfilling intimate relationships and nurture them for the long term. The book states that such capabilities are not a matter of chance but rather skills that must be studied. Hendrix believes that starting over again after a broken love affair or marriage can actually be an advantage. His guide allows readers to re-examine their previous behavior patterns, develop increased self-understanding, and alter their bothersome or unacceptable tendencies. All of this exploration can result in positive personal growth and improved future relating, the author contends.

539. *Learning to Love Again.* **Mel Krantzler. New York: Thomas Y. Crowell Co., 1977. Hardcover. 248 pp.**

Krantzler's self-help book is written from personal and professional experience. It is for those people who have never married, are divorced, or are widowed. In the book, the author has drafted specific guidelines for developing the ability to find a creative, fulfilling, and long-term new relationship. Based on his successful national "Creative Divorce/Learning to Love Again" Seminars, the techniques Krantzler offers provide answers for: meeting new people, learning to trust again, overcoming the anxiety of "making another mistake," learning to commit creatively, and building an exciting, deep partnership. Readers are taken through four stages in the process and learn skills illustrated by case histories.

540. *Love the Way You Want It: Using Your Head in Matters of the Heart.* **Dr. Robert Sternberg with Catherine Whitney. New York: Bantam Books, 1991. Hardcover. 177 pp.**

Sternberg specializes in the realm of love. He and Whitney have written a book of practical techniques designed to help readers develop more fulfilling, flexible, healthy, and long lasting intimate relationships. According to the book, these relationships should be based on soundly researched principles rather than on the romantic myth of being "in love" or "chemistry." Step-by-step, the authors teach readers how to: assess their "relationship intelligence" or "RI, understand their personal strengths and weaknesses in the area of romance, identify various roles they play which block intimacy, and most importantly, know the essence of real love. They say that school and work require entirely different skills from loving. Sternberg believes these skills can be learned, undesirable behaviors changed, and problem areas resolved.

541. *Making Remarriage Work.* **Jeanne Belovitch. Lexington, MA: Lexington Books, D.C. Heath & Co., 1987. Paperback. 208 pp.**

Statistics given in this book indicate that nearly 30 percent of today's marriages are remarriages (with 66 percent of those divorced trying it again) and that 60 percent of these will probably result in another divorce. The author, therefore, proposes to increase the probability of couples achieving happiness. Belovitch does this by outlining practical and easily understood principles for developing new skills. A collection of 70 articles by trained professionals, her book covers such topics as: the remarriage decision; excessive anxiety about repeating failure; stepparenting; custody and visitation; holidays, weekends and summers; splitting incomes with the other family; having another child; vasectomy reversals; mixed faith marriages; and weddings.

542. *Real Love: What It Is and How to Find It.* **Theodore Isaac Rubin. New York: Continuum Publishing Co., 1990. Hardcover. 219 pp.**

Rubin describes this unusual book as "a kind of photo album on one man's learnings on love" with "verbal snapshots of insights." He says readers can read in sequence or move around from one reflection to another. *Real Love* proposes that everyone has the potential to give and receive love. It sees this love as originating from within, as not depending on the actions of others, and as all-embracing. Impediments to the growth of mature, real love such as possessiveness, the need to control, and hidden agendas are exposed. The hope here is that it will be possible to develop the understanding, true unselfishness, enthusiasm, and commitment that are so necessary for love to thrive.

543. *Searching for Courtship: The Smart Woman's Guide to Finding a Good Husband.* **Winnifred B. Cutler, Ph.D. New York: Villard Books, 1993. Hardcover. 352 pp.**

As an authority on intimacy, Cutler bases her book on personal experience, stories and research. When she herself was single, the author handled her search for a new partner just as she did her work: deliberately and scientifically. The principles here are the same. Women can choose from many men if they: take charge of their lives, see their needs as "legitimate," devote concerted effort to their quest, and "empower" themselves by developing a "positive and powerful attitude." The core of Cutler's book is the 11 principles in her "Code of Courtship." Basing her ideas on a synthesis of psychology and biology, the author writes a guide for obtaining a long-term, committed relationship that is nurturing, sensual and loving. Topics include: planning, "politics of dating," first impressions, lust vs. love, orgasm, manners, and honesty.

544. *The Second Time Around: Why Some Second Marriages Fail While Others Succeed.* **Dr. Louis H. Janda and Ellen MacCormack. New York: A Lyle Stuart Book, Carol Publishing Group, 1991. Hardcover. 219 pp.**

Based on numerous interviews and extensive study, this book provides a comprehensive examination of second marriages and the challenges, hazards, and rewards to expect. The authors note that most divorced individuals expect a second marriage to rank far superior to their first because of the knowledge gained in the dissolution process. Eighty percent of their subjects, however, have been shocked to find even greater difficulties. Children and stepchildren can be the most obvious stumbling blocks, they say, but financial issues, dependency problems, and romantic delusions can also play a significant role. The authors' goal here is to offer practical solutions for creating a highly workable and fulfilling new experience.

545. *The Secret of Loving: How a Lasting Intimate Relationship Can Be Yours.* **Josh McDowell. Wheaton, IL: Living Books, Tyndale House Publ., Inc., 1985. Paperback. 332 pp.**

Written especially for singles, this book provides a new look at ways in which individuals can evaluate themselves, change negative behavior patterns, and thereby improve their love lives. The book is based on years of counseling experience. It offers readers guidelines for: learning to know themselves more fully, developing more successful listening and communication skills, learning how to give as well as to receive, identifying characteristics of "mature love," understanding the elements required for achieving personal growth, creative approaches to love, and "avoiding financial bondage." McDowell also emphasizes the necessity of individuals bearing responsibility for their own lives.

546. *Sexual Strategies: How Females Choose Their Mates.* **Mary Batten. New York: Jeremy P. Tarcher, G. P. Putnam's Sons Publ., 1992. Hardcover. 248 pp.**

This science journalist studies mating patterns in the animal kingdom in relationship to human behavior. She sees females, commonly described by others as "passive," weak, and uncompetitive as, in fact, the ultimate powers in mate selection and so also in the evolutionary process. Batten, an expert in the study of "female choice," believes that women control the process of reproduction and human development. They do this, she says, by nature of their ability to choose or reject characteristics of specific mates. She examines the tendency for women to be "attracted to wealthy, powerful men" as well as the differences in male-female mating behaviors. Batten states that increased happiness and fewer gender conflicts will result if women put aside "self-destructive" customs.

547. *Smart Women: Foolish Choices. Choices Women Make in the Men They Choose.* **Dr. Connell Cowan and Dr. Melvyn Kinder. New York: Clarkson N. Potter, Inc., 1985. Paperback. 283 pp.**

This book explores why some career-oriented and otherwise self-assured women, who seem committed to personal growth, are mysteriously drawn to the wrong men. Writing from a male vantage point, the authors give advice on how women can break their frustrating patterns in order to find real romance and happiness. These clinical psychologists give "insider's tips" on realistic techniques that work with men. Part I covers the causes leading to "frustration in romance" while Part II gives ideas for developing fulfilling relationships. Cowan and Kinder discuss the conflicting pull of traditional vs. modern expectations of women. They highlight the traditional total immersion in caring for others against the modern quest for an independent identity.

548. *Someone Right for You.* **Edward A. Dreyfus, Ph.D. Blue Ridge Summit, PA: Human Services Institute, TAB Books, 1992. Paperback. 215 pp.**

Someone Right For You is aimed at single people who are looking for a meaningful intimate relationship. It proposes that finding a mate, not a "playmate," requires serious work, strategizing, potentially radical changes of approach, careful self-exploration, and a whole new catalog of interpersonal relating techniques. Dreyfus devotes time to breaking the "repetitive, self-destructive cycle" that stands in the way of finding a suitable partner on a long-term basis. He believes that finding a lover should not be left to luck but the search should be treated like any other project requiring careful planning and study.

549. *To Marry Again: A Psychologist's Sensitive Guide to the Problems and Joys of Remarriage and Stepparenting.* **Joel D. Block, Ph.D. New York: Grosset & Dunlap, 1979. Hardcover. 186 pp.**

With a positive attitude toward remarriage, Block has written an easy-to-read, practical guide about "starting over" and making a new union truly work. Its audience is made up of those who are contemplating or currently struggling to balance former and new marriages with numerous challenges like: helping children through the transition, relatives, mixed feelings regarding roles, disentanglements, and "conflicts of loyalty." Offering constructive advice illustrated with case histories, the author covers such topics as: grieving for the former marriage, "reconciliation" with former mates, the influence of children on new partnerships, discipline, jealousy, seeking professional help, and the unique problems of working stepmothers.

550. *Were You Born for Each Other? Finding, Catching and Keeping the Love of Your Life.* **Dr. Kevin Leman. New York: A Dell Trade Paperback, Dell, 1991. Paperback. 259 pp.**

Dr. Leman writes about the critical importance of birth order (position among siblings) as the dominant factor in developing flourishing relationships. He considers this aspect more important than romantic chemistry or luck as perhaps popularly believed. His book's goal is to help those who are single find appropriate partners and those who are married to improve their current relationships. It maintains that individuals can accomplish this through developing an awareness of how birth order elements operate to define both their own personality and their partner's. The guide offers advice on determining compatibilities and transcending the many differences that are inevitable.

551. *What Has She Got? Women Who Attract Famous Men —And How They Did It.* **Cynthia S. Smith. New York: Donald I. Fine, Inc., 1991. Hardcover. 225 pp.**

Women who wish to marry rich or famous men will learn from this book. Smith examines the "motivations," characteristics, and behavior of 11 women (e.g., Mia Farrow, Wally Simpson, Jessica Lange) who have married two or more "powerful" men. She studies the patterns. Most noteworthy are such factors as: "ordinariness," lack of "memorable" traits, the absence of any forecasters of success, "total submergence of ego," a marked eagerness to please, and the ability to appear self-assured despite all of the above. Her book points out that, with these egotistical men focused on careers and needing continual "stroking," women devoted to playing an uncompetitive and supportive role succeed best. Smith states that once a woman latches onto her first famous man, she can be assured of chances for later similar pairings.

552. *Why Love Is Not Enough.* **Sol Gordon, Ph.D. Holbrook, MA: Bob Adams, Inc., 1988, 1990. Paperback. 155 pp.**

Aimed at singles searching for mates and marrieds hoping to work out problems, this book stresses that love alone is not sufficient to build fulfilling partnerships despite what modern mythology might suggest. Sound decisions have strong rational components and must be made carefully and maturely, Gordon says. He defines the ten most important traits in good unions with the goal of teaching readers how to make the best choices. The author also identifies people singles should walk away from before ever becoming involved. His book presents guidelines to facilitate the process. Topics also include: intimacy, improving image and desirability, learning "self-acceptance," sex, questions to ask a divorced prospect, the importance of "commitment to growth" and compromise, and letting go of harmful relationships.

553. *Why Women Shouldn't Marry.* **Cynthia S. Smith. Secaucus, NJ: Lyle Stuart, Inc., 1988. Hardcover. 223 pp.**

Smith sees only two compelling reasons for today's woman to marry: "sperm and support." She says that women are clearly not inadequate; they are fully able to care for themselves, earn a good income, and develop a satisfying life without the restrictions often inherent in marriage. Her book argues that choice is possible today if women allow themselves to break free of the old-fashioned "must marry" mentality. Remaining single allows a woman to focus completely on her own needs and live a more liberated life, she believes. Smith did her research by interviewing women single by choice, many of whom saw marriage as far less "central" to women's lives. Areas covered also include: legal and financial protection, wills, insurance, purchasing a home, and reasons widows should avoid remarriage.

For additional help in "Finding a New Relationship," see all books in chapters 2 & 11 and also book numbers:

 1: *The Agony of It All*
 2: *Being a Woman*
 5: *Career & Conflict*
10: *The Emotionally Abused Woman*
11: *Fascinating Womanhood*
17: *Having It All*
23: *The Late Show*
25: *Light His Fire*
27: *Lovesick:The Marilyn Syndrome*
28: *Men Are Just Desserts*
29: *My Enemy, My Love*
30: *My Mother, My Self*
32: *Opening Our Hearts to Men*

35: *The Pleasers…Women Who Can't Say No—
And the Men Who Control Them*
37: *The Seashell People*
38: *The Sensuous Woman*
39: *Slay Your Own Dragons*
43: *Too Good for Her Own Good*
44: *Too Smart for Her Own Good*
45: *Total Loving*
46: *The Total Woman*
48: *Type Talk* *
50: *The Wendy Dilemma*
51: *What Smart Women Know*
53: *When Am I Going to Be Happy?*
55: *Why Do I Think I Am Nothing Without a Man?*
58: *Women & Love*
62: *Women and Their Fathers*
63: *Women Who Love Too Much*
116: *Husbands and Wives*
120: *Marriage, Love, Sex and Divorce*
121: *The Marriage Premise*
123: *The Psychology of Love*
125: *The Age of Taboo*
126: *The Art and Practice of Loving*
127: *The Art of Loving*
131: *Centering and the Art of Intimacy*
134: *Conscious Loving*
138: *Courage My Love*
140: *Creating a Marriage*
145: *Do I Have to Give Up Me to Be Loved by You?*
146: *Equal Time*
150: *Getting the Love You Want*
151: *Going the Distance*
152: *Growing Together/Staying Together*
155: *How to Live With Another Person*
156: *How to Make Love All the Time*

162: *Inter-Cultural Marriage*

163: *The Intermarriage Handbook*

165: *Intimacy: The Need to Be Close*

167: *Intimate Partners* (Scarf)

168: *Intimate Strangers*

169: *Journey of the Heart*

171: *Lasting Love*

173: *Living, Loving & Learning*

174: *Love*

175: *Love and Money*

181: *Loving Each Other*

186: *Marital Choices*

188: *The Marriage Maintenance Manual*

193: *Men Are from Mars, Women Are from Venus*

194: *Men, Women and Relationships*

205: *Peer Marriage*

208: *Prescription for a Quality Relationship*

209: *The Psychology of Romantic Love*

210: *Rediscovering Love*

213: *The Road Less Traveled*

214: *The Road to Intimacy: Beyond Co-dependence*

217: *The Seven Marriages of Your Marriage*

221: *Struggle for Intimacy*

224: *The Triangle of Love*

226: *What Every Woman Ought to Know About Love & Marriage*

227: *What Love Asks of Us*

229: *Work and Love*

235: *Come Here/Go Away*

239: *False Love*

242: *Games People Play*

247: *How to Salvage Your Marriage Or Survive Your Divorce*

249: *If This Is Love, Why Do I Feel So Insecure?*

250: *The Incompatibility of Men and Women*

255: *Looking for Love in All the Wrong Places*

263: *Obsessive Love*

264: *One-Way Relationships*

265: *The Passion Paradox*

269: *The Stranger in Your Bed*

275: *We Can Work It Out*

280: *Why Did I Marry You Anyway?*

285: *All the Good Ones Are Married*

302: *The New Other Woman*

304: *A Passion for More*

311: *Bailing Out*

313: *Choices*

315: *Creative Divorce*

316: *The Divorce Experience*

317: *Get Rid of Him*

319: *Growing Through Divorce*

320: *How to Get Out of an Unhappy Marriage Or an Unhappy Relationship*

321: *Learning to Leave*

324: *Life Choices*

329: *Our Turn*

330: *Overcoming Indecisiveness*

333: *Risking*

336: *'Til Divorce Do Us Part*

349: *Daddy Doesn't Live Here Anymore*

354: *Divorce Without Victims*

356: *Divorced Parenting*

360: *Growing Up Divorced* (Francke)

366: *How It Feels When Parents Divorce*

367: *How to Live With a Single Parent*

369: *The Kids' Book of Divorce*

370: *The Kids' Guide to Divorce*

375: *The Parents' Book About Divorce*

383: *What Should I Tell the Kids?*

391: *The Complete Legal Guide to Marriage, Divorce, Custody and Living Together*

393: *Dealing With Divorce*

400: *The Divorce Handbook*

407: *Divorcing*

413: *Head and Heart*

417: *Our Money Our Selves*

426: *What Every Woman Should Know About Her Husband's Money*

427: *When Couples Part*

432: *After You've Said Goodbye*

434: *Crazy Time: Surviving Divorce*

436: *Divorce and New Beginnings*

438: *Divorce Recovery*

439: *Divorced*

443: *The Fresh Start Divorce Recovery Workbook*

449: *How to Forgive Your Ex-husband (And Get On With Your Life)*

451: *If Love Is the Answer, What Is the Question?*

453: *Letting Go*

457: *Living and Loving After Divorce*

460: *Loveshock*

461: *Marital Separation*

469: *The Sorrow and the Fury*

474: *Whoever Said Life Is Fair?*

476: *The Wife-in-law Trap*

478: *The World of the Formerly Married*

Epilogue

Remarriage and stepfamilies

As a separate and final stage in the life cycle of a divorced woman, the subject of remarriage, stepfamilies and even the reoccurrence of divorce is very important. The topic is so extensive, however, that it seemed outside the scope of this sourcebook. A specific chapter treating the issues surrounding remarriage has therefore been omitted from *Women on the Brink of Divorce*.

Many books which have already been summarized in previous chapters, however, explore a wide variety of meaningful issues relevant to this area. As a beginning, those readers who need help coping with the challenges of remarriage should refer to the following selections:

 69: *Being a Man*
 90: *Men and Marriage: The Changing Role of Husbands*
119: *Marriage Divorce Remarriage*
128: *The Art of Staying Together*
175: *Love and Money*
205: *Peer Marriage*
247: *How to Salvage Your Marriage or Survive Your Divorce*
280: *Why Did I Marry You Anyway?*
319: *Growing Through Divorce*
329: *Our Turn*
345: *The Boys' And Girls' Book About Divorce*
349: *Daddy Doesn't Live Here Anymore*
351: *Dinosaur's Divorce*

352: *Divided Families*

353: *Divorce and Your Child*

354: *Divorce Without Victims*

355: *Divorced Kids*

356: *Divorced Parenting*

360: *Growing Up Divorced*

362: *Healthy Divorce*

363: *Helping Children Cope With Divorce*

366: *How It Feels When Parents Divorce*

368: *The Kids' Book About Single Parent Families*

369: *The Kids' Book of Divorce*

375: *The Parents' Book About Divorce*

377: *Quality Time*

383: *What Should I Tell the Kids?*

393: *Dealing With Divorce*

420: *Rematch*

427: *When Couples Part*

436: *Divorce and New Beginnings*

457: *Living and Loving After Divorce*

476: *The Wife-In-Law Trap*

478: *The World of the Formerly Married*

488: *Going It Alone*

490: *In Praise of Single Parents*

500: *Parents Without Partners Sourcebook*

503: *Single After 50*

504: *Single Again*

506: *The Single Mother's Book*

532: *How to Find Another Husband....By Someone Who Did*

541: *Making Remarriage Work*

544: *The Second Time Around*

549: *To Marry Again*

About the Author

Cynthia David, a long-time resident of Madison, Connecticut, is a recent emigrant to Dana Point, California. She is the mother of two children, Kimberly, 23, and Miles, 20. Ms. David graduated from the College of New Rochelle and Fordham University with a B.A. and M.A. in classics. As an instructor of Latin, classics, and English, she taught on the college and private secondary school levels for fourteen years. A career change later led to seven years in the fields of insurance and commercial real estate sales. Ms. David's own separation in 1981 and subsequent divorce after a thirteen-year marriage introduced her to the benefits of psychotherapy and self-help reading, the latter of which she has pursued avidly since that time.

Title Index

A

Adult Children of Divorce   344
Adultery   282
Affair   283
Affair Prevention   284
After You've Said Good-Bye   432
Age of Taboo   125
Agony of It All   1
All the Good Ones Are Married   285
Alone —Not Lonely   480
Alone, Alive & Well   481
Anger   230
Anger Workbook   231
Angry Book   232
Are You the One for Me?   518
Art and Practice of Loving   126
Art of Loving   127
Art of Staying Together   128
At Long Last Love   519

B

Back from Betrayal   286
Bad Guys   68
Bailing Out   311
Beating the Marriage Odds   520
Being a Man   69
Being a Woman   2
Between Love & Hate   386

Between Marriage and Divorce   312
Beyond Affairs   287
Beyond Cinderella   521
Beyond the Male Myth   70
Binds That Tie   233
Bitches and Abdicators   3
Book for Couples   129
Born for Love   130
Boys' and Girls' Book About Divorce   345
Bradshaw On: The Family   4
Breaking Out of Loneliness   482

C

Career & Conflict   5
Casanova Complex   71
Case Against Divorce   234
Centering & the Art of Intimacy   131
Challenge of Marriage   132
Changing Him, Changing Her   133
Child Support   387
Child Support in America   388
Child Support Survivor's Guide   389
Children & Divorce   346
Children of Divorce   347
Children of Separation and Divorce   348
Choices   313
Choosing Lovers   522
Cinderella Complex   6

Note: Numbers used in all indexes identity books by book numbers that appear with each title, not by page number.

Classified Man 72
Co-Parenting 390
Codependent No More 7
Cold Feet 523
Come Here/Go Away 235
Coming Apart 314
Coming Back 433
Compatibility Quotient 524
Complete Legal Guide to Marriage,
    Divorce, Custody and Living
    Together 391
Conscious Loving 134
Coping 483
Couple Skills 135
Couples (Broderick) 136
Couples (Dym) 137
Courage My Love 138
Courtship After Marriage 139
Crazy Time 434
Creating a Marriage 140
Creative Divorce 315
Creative Marriage 141
Crisis of the Working Mother 8
Crisis Time 73
Custody Revolution 392

D

Daddy Doesn't Live Here Anymore 349
Dance Away Lover & Other Roles We
    Play in Love, Sex and Marriage 142
Dance of Anger 236
Dance of Intimacy 143
Dare to Connect 525
Day the Loving Stopped 350
Dealing With Divorce 393
Dinosaurs Divorce 351
Dirty Half Dozen 144
Divided Children 394
Divided Families 352
Divorce and After 435
Divorce and Dissolution of Marriage Laws
    of the United States 395
Divorce and Money 396
Divorce and New Beginnings 436
Divorce and Your Child 353
Divorce Busting 237

Divorce Decision 397
Divorce Decisions Workbook 398
Divorce Dirty Tricks 399
Divorce Experience 316
Divorce Handbook 400
Divorce Hangover 437
Divorce Help Sourcebook 401
Divorce Mediation (Irving) 402
Divorce Mediation (Neumann) 403
Divorce Mediation (Schneider) 404
Divorce Recovery 438
Divorce Revolution 405
Divorce Without Victims 354
Divorce Yourself 406
Divorced 439
Divorced Kids 355
Divorced Parenting 356
Divorced Woman's Handbook 484
Divorcing 407
Do I Have to Give Up Me to Be Loved
    by You? 145
Dollars and Sense of Divorce 408
Don Juan Dilemma 288
Don't Go Away Mad 238
Don't Say Yes When You
    Want to Say No 9
Don't Settle for Less 409

E

Emotionally Abused Woman 10
Equal Time 146
Erotic Silence of the American Wife 289
Every Other Man 290
Ex-Factor 410
Ex-Wife Syndrome 440

F

Faithful Attraction 291
False Love 239
Family Politics 147
Fascinating Womanhood 11
Female Stress Syndrome 12
50 Ways to Find a Lover 517
Fire in the Belly 74
First Person Singular 485
Fit to Be Tied 526

Flying Solo 486
For the Sake of the Children 357
Forgive & Forget 441
Forgiveness 442
Forgiving Marriage 240
Forgiving the Unforgivable 241
Formerly Married 487
40 to 60 Year Old Male 67
45 and Single Again 479
*Fresh Start Divorce Recovery
    Workbook* 443
Fresh Starts 444
From Conflict to Caring 148
From This Day Forward 149

G

Games People Play 242
Get Rid of Him 317
*Getting Divorced Without Ruining
    Your Life* 411
Getting the Love You Want 150
Getting to "I Do" 527
Getting Unstuck 13
Getting Your Share 412
Going It Alone 488
Going the Distance 151
Golden Handcuffs 14
Good Girl Syndrome 15
Good Guys/Bad Guys 528
Greatest Risk of All 318
Green-Eyed Marriage 243
Grief Out of Season 358
Grief Recovery Handbook 445
Growing Through Divorce 319
Growing Together/Staying Together 152
Growing Up Divorced (Fassel) 359
Growing Up Divorced (Francke) 360
Growing Up Firstborn 16
Growing Up With Divorce 361
Guerrilla Dating Tactics 529
Guilt 447
Guilt 446

H

*Have a Love Affair With Your Husband
    (Before Someone Else Does)* 292

*Haven't You Been Single Long
    Enough?* 530
Having It All 17
Head and Heart 413
Healthy Divorce 362
Hearts of Men 75
Helping Children Cope With Divorce 363
Helping Children of Divorce 364
His Needs Her Needs 293
Hole in My Heart 365
Homecoming 18
Hot and Bothered 531
How It Feels When Parents Divorce 366
How Men Feel 76
How Not to Split Up 244
*How to Be an Assertive (Not Aggressive)
    Woman in Life, Love and On the Job* 19
How to Fall Out of Love 448
*How to Find Another Husband...By
    Someone Who Did* 532
How to Find Romance After 40 533
*How to Forgive Your Ex-Husband (And
    Get On With Your Life)* 449
*How to Get Him Back from the Other
    Woman If You Still Want Him* 294
*How to Get Out of an Unhappy Marriage
    or an Unhappy Relationship* 320
How to Have a Happy Marriage 153
*How to Keep a Man in Love With You
    Forever* 154
How to Keep Love Alive 245
How to Keep Your Man Monogamous 295
How to Live With a Single Parent 367
How to Live With Another Person 155
How to Love a Difficult Man 246
*How to Make a Man Fall in Love
    With You* 534
How to Make Love All the Time 156
How to Make Love to a Man 535
*How to Make Love to the Same Person for
    the Rest of Your Life * and Still
    Love It* 157
How to Manage a Marriage 158
How to Marry Super Rich 536
How to Marry the Man of Your Choice 537
How to Parent Alone 489

How to Salvage Your Marriage or Survive
   Your Divorce 247
How to Survive the Loss of a Love 450
How to Win Back the One You Love 296
Husbands and Wives 116
Husbands and Wives 159
Husbands Wives & Sex 160

I

I Love You, Let's Work It Out 248
I'm OK –You're OK 20
If Love Is the Answer, What Is the
   Question? 451
If This Is Love, Why Do I Feel So
   Insecure? 249
In a Different Voice 21
In Defense of Marriage 161
In Praise of Single Parents 490
In Search of Intimacy 491
In Transition 22
Incompatibility of Men and Women 250
Inner Male 77
Inter-Cultural Marriage 162
Intermarriage Handbook 163
Intimacy (Crowther) 164
Intimacy (McAdams) 165
Intimate Connections 492
Intimate Enemy 251
Intimate Partners (Sager) 166
Intimate Partners (Scarf) 167
Intimate Strangers 168

J

Jealousy 252
Journey of the Heart 169
Joy of Being Single 493

K

Keeping the Love You Find 538
Keeping Your Family Together When the
   World Is Falling Apart 170
Kids' Book About Single Parent
   Families 368
Kids' Book of Divorce 369
Kids' Guide to Divorce 370
Kinsey Institute New Report on Sex 117

Knight in Shining Armor 78

L

Lasting Love 171
Late Show 23
Learning to Leave 321
Learning to Love Again 539
Leavetaking 322
Lessons of Love 452
Let's Have It Out 253
Letters from Women Who Love
   Too Much 24
Letting Go 453
Life After Loss 454
Life Changes 323
Life Choices 324
Life Mates 172
Life's Parachutes 456
Light His Fire 25
Living Alone and Liking It 494
Living and Loving After Divorce 457
Living Single Successfully 495
Living Through Personal Crisis 458
Living Together: Feeling Alone 254
Living, Loving & Learning 173
Loneliness 496
Long Distance Parenting 371
Looking for Love in All the Wrong
   Places 255
Looking Out for #1 26
Lost Lovers, Found Friends 459
Love & Betrayal 297
Love 174
Love and Addiction 256
Love and Money 175
Love Blocks 257
Love Busters 258
Love Cycles 176
Love Is Letting Go of Fear 177
Love Is Never Enough 178
Love Is the Answer 179
Love Knots 259
Love Me Love Me Not 298
Love Must Be Tough 260
Love Secrets for a Lasting
   Relationship 180

Love the Way You Want It 540
Love, Sex, and Aging 118
Loveshock 460
Lovesick 27
Loving & Leaving 326
Loving Each Other 181
Lucky in Love 182

M

Magic of Conflict 183
Making It Together As a Two Career Couple 184
Making Remarriage Work 541
Male Dilemma 79
Male Ego 80
Male Machine 81
Male Ordeal 82
Male Paradox 83
Male Stress Syndrome 84
Managing the Equity Factor 185
Manhood 85
Marital Choices 186
Marital Separation 461
Marriage Divorce Remarriage 119
Marriage Is for Loving 187
Marriage, Love, Sex and Divorce 120
Marriage Maintenance Manual 188
Marriage Map 189
Marriage Premise 121
Marriage Without B.S. 190
Married People 191
Masculine Dilemma 86
Masters and Johnson on Sex and Human Loving 192
Maybe He's Just a Jerk 87
McGill Report on Male Intimacy 88
Mediate Your Divorce 414
Men and Marriage 89
Men and Marriage 90
Men Are from Mars. Women Are from Venus 193
Men Are Just Desserts 28
Men Talk 91
Men Who Can't Be Faithful 299
Men Who Can't Love 92

Men Who Hate Women and the Women Who Love Them 93
Men, Women and Relationships 194
Mirages of Marriage 195
Mom's House, Dad's House 372
Money Demons 261
Monogamy Myth 300
More Than Just a Friend 301
Mothers and Divorce 415
Mothers on Trial 416
My Enemy, My Love 29
My Kids Don't Live With Me Anymore 373
My Mother/My Self 30
Myth of Male Power 94

N

Natural History of Love 122
Necessary Losses 462
New Male-Female Relationship 196
New Other Woman 302
New Suburban Woman 31
Nice Women Get Divorced 327
No Fault Marriage 197
Nobody's Perfect (Browne) 198
Nobody's Perfect (Weisinger) 199
Not With My Husband You Don't 303
Now That I'm Married, Why Isn't Everything Perfect? 262

O

Obsessive Love 263
On Our Own 497
One Door Closes, Another Door Opens 328
One on the Seesaw 498
One Question That Can Save Your Marriage 200
One to One 201
One's Company 499
One-Way Relationships 264
Open Marriage 202
Opening Our Hearts to Men 32
Opening Up 463
Ordinary Women, Extraordinary Lives 464
Our Money Our Selves 417

Our Turn 329
Overcoming Indecisiveness 330
Overwhelmed 331

P

Parent Vs. Parent 418
Parent/Child Manual on Divorce for the
   Education of Children 374
Parents Without Partners Sourcebook 500
Parents' Book About Divorce 375
Passages 203
Passages of Marriage 204
Passion for More 304
Passion Paradox 265
Passions 33
Passions of Men 95
Pathfinders 332
Peer Marriage 205
Perfect Husbands (& Other
   Fairy Tales) 96
Perfect Women 34
Peter Pan Syndrome 97
Phoenix Factor 465
Planning a Wedding With Divorced
   Parents 376
Pleasers... Women Who Can't Say No—
   And the Men Who Control Them 35
Pleasure Bond 206
Power of Unconditional Love 207
Prescription for a Quality
   Relationship 208
Private Lies 305
Process of Divorce 419
Psychology of Love 123
Psychology of Romantic Love 209

Q

Quality Time 377

R

Real Love 542
Rebuilding 466
Recovery from Co-Dependency 36
Rediscovering Love 210
Relationshift 211
Rematch 420

Resilience 467
Resolving Family and Other Conflicts 266
Return to Love 212
Risking 333
Road Less Traveled 213
Road to Intimacy 214
Romantic Jealousy 267

S

Searching for Courtship 543
Seashell People 37
Seasons of a Man's Life 98
Second Chances 378
Second Honeymoon 215
Second Time Around 544
Secret Loves 306
Secret of Loving 545
Secret of Staying in Love 216
Secrets About Men Every Woman
   Should Know 99
Secrets Men Keep 100
Sensuous Woman 38
Seven Basic Quarrels of Marriage 268
Seven Marriages of Your Marriage 217
Sex and the Single Parent 501
Sex Begins in the Kitchen 218
Sex, Lies and Forgiveness 307
Sexual Static 101
Sexual Strategies 546
Sharing Parenthood After Divorce 421
Sharing the Children 422
Shifting Gears 334
Single 502
Single After 50 503
Single Again 504
Single File 505
Single Mother's Book 506
Single Parenting 507
Single Parents Are People Too 508
Single Women, Alone and Together 509
Singled Out 510
Singles 511
Singling 512
Slay Your Own Dragons 39
Smart Cookies Don't Crumble 468
Smart Women 547

Snow White Syndrome 40
Solo Parenting 513
Some American Men 102
*Some Men Are More Perfect Than
    Others* 103
Someone Right for You 548
Sorrow and the Fury 469
*State-by-State Guide to Women's Legal
    Rights* 423
Staying in Love 219
*Staying On Top When Your World Turns
    Upside Down* 470
Staying Together 220
Straight Talk 104
Straight Talk to Men and Their Wives 105
Stranger in Your Bed 269
Strassels' Tax Savers 424
Struggle for Intimacy 221
Sudden Endings 335
Suddenly Single 514
Super Marriage 222
Superwoman Syndrome 41
Survival Guide for the Suddenly Single 515
Survival Guide for Women 425
Surviving Family Life 270
Surviving the Break-Up 379
Sweet Suffering 42

T

*Talking About Divorce and
    Separation* 380
Ten Days to Self-Esteem 471
That's Not What I Meant 223
*30 Secrets of Happily Married
    Couples* 124
'Til Divorce Do Us Part 336
To Marry Again 549
Together on a Tightrope 271
Too Good for Her Own Good 43
Too Smart for Her Own Good 44
Total Loving 45
Total Woman 46
Tough Marriage 272
Transition to Parenthood 273
Transitions 337
Triangle of Love 224

Turning Points (Goodman) 338
Turning Points (Landau) 339
*12 Steps to Mastering the Winds of
    Change* 310
Type E Woman 47
Type Talk* 48

U

Uncoupling (Sheresky) 340
Uncoupling (Vaughn) 341
Unfinished Business 49

V

Verbally Abusive Relationship 274
*Vicki Lansky's Divorce Book for
    Parents* 381

W

Warm Hearts & Cold Cash 225
We Can Work It Out 275
Wendy Dilemma 50
Were You Born for Each Other? 550
*What Every Child Would Like Parents to
    Know About Divorce* 382
*What Every Woman Ought to Know About
    Love & Marriage* 226
*What Every Woman Should Know About
    Her Husband's Money* 426
*What Every Woman Should Know About
    Men* 106
What Has She Got? 551
What Love Asks of Us 227
*What Men Really Think About Women,
    Love, Sex, Themselves* 107
What Men Really Want 108
*What Men Won't Tell You But Women
    Need to Know* 109
What Really Works With Men 110
What Should I Tell the Kids? 383
What Smart Women Know 51
What to Do When He Won't Change 276
*What Wives Wish Their Husbands Knew
    About Women* 52
What's Going to Happen to Me? 384
When a Mate Wants Out 277
When Am I Going To Be Happy? 53

When Bad Things Happen to Good
   People 472
When Couples Part 427
When Love Goes Wrong 278
When Someone You Love Is Someone
   You Hate 279
When the Worst That Can Happen Already
   Has: Conquering Life's Most Difficult
   Times 473
Where's My Happy Ending? 54
Whoever Said Life Is Fair? 474
Why Did I Marry You Anyway? 280
Why Do I Think I Am Nothing Without a
   Man? 55
Why Love Is Not Enough 552
Why Me * Why This * Why Now 475
Why Men Are the Way They Are 111
Why Men Can't Open Up 112
Why Men Don't Get Enough Sex and
   Women Don't Get Enough Love 228
Why Men Stray and Why Men Stay 308
Why Women Shouldn't Marry 553
Why Women Worry ...and How to Stop 56
Wife-In-Law Trap 476
Winning Life's Toughest Battles 477
Winning Your Divorce 428
Woman Alone 516
Woman Versus Woman 309
Woman's Legal Guide to Separation and
   Divorce in All 50 States 429
Woman's Worth 57
Women & Love 58
Women & Money 59
Women & Self-Esteem 60
Women & the Blues 61
Women and Their Fathers 62
Women in Transition 342
Women Men Love/Women Men Leave 113
Women Who Love Too Much 63
Women, Divorce and Money 430
Women's Burnout 64
Work and Love 229
Workaholics 114
Working It Out 65
World of the Formerly Married 478

Wrestling With Love 115

Y

You Can Excel in Times of Change 343
You Just Don't Understand 281
You're Entitled 431
Your Erroneous Zones 66
"Your Father's Not Coming Home
   Anymore" 385

Author Index

A

Abt, Lawrence E. 348
Ackerman, Diane 122
Adams, Jane 501
Adler, Allan J. 438
Adler, Robert E. 422
Alexander, Shoshana 490
Allen, Patricia 527
Alvarez, A. 455
Amodeo, John 297
Andelin, Helen 11
Anderson, Beverly 503
Anderson, Deborah 329
Anderson, Joan 506
Anderson, Walter 318
Andrews, Frank 126
Appleton, Jane 244
Appleton, William 244
Archambault, Christine 438
Arendell, Terry 415
Asterburn, Stephen F. 279
Astrachan, Anthony 76
Atlas, Stephen L. 500, 507

B

Bach, George R. 251
Baer, Jean 9, 19
Baker, Mark 107
Baraff, Alvin 91

Barbach, Lonnie 151
Bardwick, Judith M. 22
Barker, Robert L. 243
Barnes, Michael L. 123
Baroni, Diane 294
Barreca, Regina 96
Bartussis, Mary Ann 290
Batten, Mary 546
Beal, Edward M. 344
Beasley, Ruth 117
Beattie, Melody 7, 452
Beck, Aaron T. 178
Bel Geddes, Joan 489
Bell, Daniel H. 69
Belli, Melvin M., Sr. 407
Belovitch, Jeanne 541
Belsky, Jay 273
Bennett, Madeline 335
Bepko, Claudia 43
Bequaert, Lucia H. 509
Berg, Barbara J. 8
Berger, Stuart 354
Berkowitz, Bob 109
Berman, Claire 365
Berman, Jan 502
Berne, Eric 242
Berson, Barbara 515
Betcher, William 268
Bilodeau, Lorrainne 231

Note: Numbers used in all indexes identity books by book numbers that appear with each title, not by page number.

Blades, Joan 414
Blakeslee, Sandra 378
Blau, Melinda 329
Blinder, Martin 522
Block, Joel D. 171, 549
Bloomfield, Harold 172, 180, 450
Bohannon, Paul 435
Borysenko, Joan 447
Botwin, Carol 299
Bova, Ben 515
Bradley, Buff 502
Bradshaw, John 4, 18
Braiker, Harriet B., 47
Branden, Nathaniel 209, 227
Braudy, Susan 312
Brecher, Edward M. 118
Bregman, Alice Miller 292
Brenner, Lois 412
Bridges, William 337
Briles, Judith 408
Broder, Michael S. 128
Broderick, Carlfred 136
Brodsky, Archie 249, 256
Brogan, John P. 370
Brothers, Joyce 226
Brovins, Joan M. 399
Brown, Helen Gurley 17, 23
Brown, Laureen Krasny 351
Brown, Marc 351
Browne, Joy 198
Bruns, Bill 284
Buck, Craig 261, 263
Burns, Bob 443
Burns, David D. 471, 492
Buscaglia, Leo F. 130, 173-174, 181

C

Cabot, Tracy 154, 453, 534
Carey, Art 161
Carpineto, Jane 288
Carroll, David 511
Carter, Steven 51
Cassidy, Anne 505
Cauhape, Elizabeth 444
Chambers, Carole A. 387
Chellis, Marcia 464

Cherlin, Andrew J. 119, 352
Chernow, Renee 423
Cherry, Frank 445
Chesler, Phyllis 416
Church, Connie 460
Clair, Bernard 410
Clapp, Geneviev 436
Cohen, Betsy 40
Cohen, Miriam Galper 371
Cohen, Sara Kay 474
Coleman, Paul 124, 240, 456
Colgrove, Melba 450
Colleran, Kate 528
Conway, Jim 277
Conway, Sally 277
Cowan, Connell 113, 159, 547
Cramer, Kathryn D. 470
Creighton, James L. 238
Crowther, C. Edward 164
Crum, Thomas F. 183
Crytser, Ann 476
Cutler, Winnifred B. 176, 543

D

Daniele, Anthony 410
Davidson, Joy 1
De Angelis, Barbara 156, 518
De Angelis, Sidney M. 431
DeFrain, John 497
DeGrave, Louise 149
Deits, Bob 454
Deitz, Susan 505
Delis, Dean C. 265
Dennis, Wendy 531
Derenski, Arlene 125
Diamond, Jed 255
Diamond, Susan Arnsberg 364
Dobson, James 52, 260
Dolesh, Daniel J. 298
Dolmetsch, Paul 368
Donovan, Mary Ellen 60, 257
Dowling, Colette 6, 34
Drachne, Arthur 413
Dreikurs, Rudolf 132
Dreyfus, Edward A. 548
Driscoll, Richard 233

Druck, Ken 100
Dunaway, Diane 228
Dunne Harry P. 200
Dyer, Wayne 66
Dym, Barry 137

E

Earle, Ralph 235
East, Julius 250
Ehrenreich, Barbara 75
Ells, Alfred 264
Elman, Julie 497
Emerson, Gloria 102
Engel, Beverly 10
Engel, Margorie L. 398, 401
Eskapa, Shirley 309
Evans, Patricia 274
Everett, Craig 347, 362
Everett, Sandra Volgy 362

F

Fanning, Patrick 135
Farrell, Warren 111
Fassel, Diane 359
Fasteau, Marc Feigen 81
Fay, Allen 208
Feinberg, Gloria 322
Feinberg, Mortimer R. 322
Feinstein, Debra 521
Feldman, Ruth Duskin 420
Fensterheim, Herbert 9
Fenton-Collins, Victoria 396
Fezler, William 15
Fintushel, Noelle 358
Fisher, Bruce 466
Fisher, Milton 530
Fitzgibbons, Patricia 5
Flach, Frederic 467
Flanigan, Beverly 241
Forward, Susan 93, 261, 263
Fowler, Richard 271
Francke, Linda Bird 360
Freeman, Lucy 446, 469
Freudenberger, Herbert J. 64
Fricke, John 497
Friday, Nancy 30, 252

Friedman, James T. 400
Friedman, Sonya 28, 306, 468
Fromm, Erich 127
Furstenberg, Frank F., Jr. 352

G

Galper, Miriam 390
Gardner, Richard A. 345, 375
Gathorne-Hardy, Jonathan 120
Gaylin, Willard
Gaylin, Willard 210
Gilbert, Sara 367
Gilder, George 90
Gilligan, Carol 21
Glenn, Michael L. 137
Gold, Lois 386
Goldberg, Herb 77, 108, 196
Goldstein, Sol 356
Goldstein, Sonja 353
Goldstine, Daniel 142
Goldstine, Hilary 142
Goldzband, Melvin G. 377
Good, Nancy 39, 246
Goodman, Ellen 338
Gordon, Lori Heyman 259
Gordon, Sol 552
Gould, Diana D. 398
Graham, Sheilah 536
Grant, Toni 2
Gray, John 193-194
Greeley, Andrew M. 291
Greenwald, Jerry A. 482
Greteman, James 140
Grice, Julia 533
Grollman, Earl A. 325, 380
Gullo, Stephen 460

H

Handly, Jane 56
Harayda, Janice 493
Hardie, Marion 266
Harley, Willard F., Jr. 258, 293
Harmon, Sandra 527
Harris, Thomas A. 20
Hart, Archibald D. 346
Harwood, Norma 429

Hatfield, John D. 185
Hayes, Christopher L. 329
Helmering, Doris Wild 160
Helmlinger, Trudy 432
Helmstetter, Shad 343
Hendricks, Gay 131, 134
Hendricks, Kathlyn 131, 134
Hendrix, Harville 150, 538
Hermano, Stephen P. 418
Hersey, Brook 68
Heyn, Dalma 289
Hillard, Nancy 358
Hindy, Carl G. 249
Hite, Shere 58, 528
Hoffman, Susanna M. 72
Holland, Barbara 499
Hootman, Marcia 449
Horgan, Timothy J. 428
Hornstein, Harvey 78
Horton, Martha 37
Hough, Arthur S. 253
Houston, Julie 328
Hudson, R. Lofton 336
Hunt, Berenice 316
Hunt, Morton 283
Hunt, Morton 316
Hunt, Morton 478
Huseman, Richard C. 185
Hybels, Bill & Lynne 526

I

Irving, Howard H. 402

J

"J." 38, 45
Jackson, Don D. 195
Jackson, Jessica 385
Jackson, Michael 385
James, Jennifer 61
James, John W. 445
James, Muriel 187
Jampolsky, Gerold G. 177, 179
Janda, Louis H. 544
Jeffers, Susan 32, 525
Jensen, Marilyn 487
Johnson, Catherine 182

Johnson, Laureen 355
Johnson, Stephen M. 485
Johnson, Virginia E. 192, 206
Jones, Ann 278
Judd, Robert 448

K

Kahn, Lawrence E. 427
Kahn, Sandra S. 440
Kalter, Neil 361
Kargman, Marie 158
Katz, Stan J. 239
Keen, Sam
Kelly, Betty 294
Kelly, Joan Berlin 379
Kent, Margaret 303, 537
Keyes, Ken, Jr. 207
Kiev, Ari 245
Kiley, Dan 50, 97, 254, 276
Kinder, Melvyn 113, 159, 547
Kingma, Daphne Rose 314
Klagsbrun, Francine 191
Kline, Kris 357
Kohl, Susan 292
Kolodny, Robert C. 192
Koontz, Katy 517
Kramer, Jonathan 228
Krantzler, Mel 141, 217, 315, 407, 539
Kreidman, Ellen 25
Kreitler, Peter 284
Krementz, Jill 366
Kressel, Kenneth 419
Krestan, Jo-Ann 43
Kristy, Norton F. 219
Kroeger, Otto 48
Kushner, Harold S. 472

L

Lake, Steven R. 420
Landau, Sol 339
Landgraf, John R. 512
Landsburg, Sally B. 125
Lansky, Vicki 381
Larner, Katherine 142
Lasswell, Marcia 146, 197
Lawhead, Steve 465

Lawson, Annette 282
Lederer, William J. 186, 195
Lehmann, Sherelynn 298
Leman, Dr. Kevin 16, 35, 170, 218, 550
Lennox, Jason Hatch 323
Leonard, Frances 59
Lerner, Harriet Goldhor 143, 236
LeShan, Eda 384
Levine, Judith 29
Levine, Karen 44
Levine-Shneidman, Conalee 44
Levinson, Daniel J.
Lieberman, Joseph I. 388
Lieberman, Mendel 266
List, Julie Autumn 350
Liu, Aimee E. 239
Livsey, Clara G. 188
Lobsenz, Norman M. 146, 197, 199
Lovenheim, Barbara 520
Lubetkin, Barry 311
Lyman, Howard B. 504
Lynch, Carmen 522

M

Macavoy, Elizabeth 27
MacCormack, Ellen 544
Mace, David and Vera 153
Machlowitz, Marilyn 114
Maiden, Ula 370
Mannes, Marya 340
Margulies, Sam 411
Martin, Don 425
Martin, Renee 425
Masters, William H. 192, 206
Matthews, Arlene Modica 280
McAdams, Dan P. 165
McConnell, Adeline 503
McCoy, Kathleen 513
McDowell, Josh 545
McGill, Michael E. 67, 88, 133
McGinnis, Tom 301
McKay, Matthew 135
Mead, William B. 424
Medved, Diane 234
Meltsner, Susan 235
Mickey, Paul A. 272

Miller, Gordon Porter 324
Millman, Marcia 225
Minirth, Frank and Mary Alice 204
Moffett, Robert K. 393
Mooney, Elizabeth C. 77
Moore, Cindy 376
Morgan, Marabel 46
Morical, Lee 54
Murdock, Carol Vejvoda 508

N

N.O.W./Legal Defense and Education
    Fund 423
Nagler, William 144
Naifeh, Steven 112
Napolitane, Catherine 457
Neely, Richard 397
Nelson, Scott 459
Neumann, Diane 403
Newton, Tanist 247
Nolen, William A. 73
North, Gail 64
Norwood, Robin 24, 63, 475
Notarius, Clifford 275

O

O'Brien, Patricia 220, 516
O'Connor, Dagmar 157
O'Neill, George 202
O'Neill, George 334
O'Neill, Nena 121, 202, 334
Oehmke, Thomas 399
Olesen, Erik 310
Olshan, Neal H. 14
Osherson, Samuel 115
Oumano, Elena 311

P

Page, Susan 262
Paleg, Kim 135
Parker, Rolland S. 495
Paul, Jordon and Margaret 145, 148
Peacock, Richard 321
Pearson, Carol Lynn 498
Peck, M. Scott 213
Peele, Stanton 256

Pekala, Beverly 409
Pellegrino, Victoria 457
Pennebaker, James W. 463
Penney, Alexandra 295, 308, 535
Perkins, Patt 449
Perrett, Kathryn Dale 211
Petsonk, Judy 163
Pew, Stephen 357
Phillips, Debora 448
Pietropinto, Anthony 79, 116
Pine, Arthur 328
Pines, Ayala M. 267
Pittman, Frank 305
Pogrebin, Letty Cottin 147
Porter, Sylvia 175
Potash, Marlin S. 523
Powell, Barbara 481
Powell, John 216
Prather, Hugh and Gail 129
Proctor, William 272

R

Rabkin, Brenda 326
Rabkin, Richard 326
Reese, Mary Ellen 439
Reichman, Rosalie 269
Reinisch, June M. 117
Remsen, Jim 163
Rhodes, Sonya 215, 270, 523
Ricci, Isolina 372
Richardson, Laurel 302
Ringer, Robert J. 26
Ripps, Susan 304
Robertson, Joan 514
Rochlin, Gregory 99
Rock, Maxine 189
Rofes, Eric 369
Rogers, Mary 430
Rohrlich, Jay B. 229
Romano, Dugan 162
Rosen, Carol 75
Rosenfield, Georglyn 355
Ross, John Munder 97
Rothman, Rusty 532
Ruben, Harvey L. 222
Rubenstein, Carin 491

Rubin, Lillian B. 168
Rubin, Nancy 31
Rubin, Theodore Isaac 201, 232, 330, 540
Russell, Anne 5
Russianoff, Penelope 53, 55
Ryan, William P. 257

S

Sack, Steven Mitchell 391
Sager, Clifford J. 166
Salk, Lee 382
Sams, Marjorie L. 325
Sanford, Linda Tschirhart 60
Scalia, Toni 3
Scarf, Maggie 49, 167
Schechter, Susan 278
Scherer, Jack F. 393
Schickel, Richard 510
Schlossberg, Nancy K. 331
Schneider, Jennifer P. 286, 307
Schneider, Karen L. and Myles J. 404
Schneider, Susan 215
Schneider, Susan Weidman 413
Schnell, Barry T. 389
Schwartz, Pepper 205
Schwarz, Conrad J. 249
Schweitz, Rita 271
Secunda, Victoria 62
Segal, Julius 477
Seskin, Jane 480
Shaevitz, Marjorie Hansen 41, 184
Shaevitz, Morton H. 101, 184
Shahan, Lynn 494
Shain, Merle 103, 138
Shainess, Natalie 42
Shapiro, Judith Hatch 323
Shapiro, Stephen A. 85
Shaver, Philip 491
Sheehy, Gail 203, 332
Sheresky, Norman 340
Shih, Alexa 368
Siegler, Ava L. 383
Simenauer, Jacqueline 116, 511
Simmons, James C.
Simon, Sidney B. 13, 442
Simon, Suzanne 442

Simring, Steven S. 296
Simring, Sue Klavans 524
Sitarz, Daniel 395, 406
Skjei, Eric 82
Slaikeu, Karl 465
Smedes, Lewis B. 313, 441
Smith, Cynthia S. 551, 553
Smith, Gregory White 112
Smoke, Jim 319
Sokol, Julia 51
Solange, Catherine 214
Solnit, Albert J. 353
Sprankle, Judith K. 65
Stearns, Ann Kaiser 433, 458
Steinmann, Anne 93
Sterling, A. Justin 110
Sternberg, Robert J. 123, 224, 540
Stewart, Susan 486
Stoop, David A. 279
Strassels, Paul N. 424
Strean, Herbert S. 446
Stuart, Irving R. 348
Sugarbaker, Geneva 327
Suid, Murray and Roberta 502
Sullivan, Maria 374

T

Tannen, Deborah 223, 281
Tarrant, John J. 322
Tavris, Carol 230
Teyber, Edward 363
Thomas, Joan M. 339
Thuesen, Janet M. 48
Trachtenberg, Peter 71
Trafford, Abigail 434
Triere, Lynette 321
Tucker, Nita 521
Turow, Rita 349

U

Utterback, Betty 514

V

Vaughn, Diane 341
Vaughn, James and Peggy 287
Vaughn, Peggy 300

Vedrai, Joyce L. 317
Vettese, Sirah 172
Viorst, Judith 462
Virtue, Doreen 373
Viscott, David 155, 248, 333

W

Walder, Eugene 320
Wall, Ginita 417
Wallerstein, Judith 378, 379
Walther, Anne N. 437
Wanderer, Zev 453
Ware, Ciji 421
Warshak, Richard A. 392
Weber, Eric 296
Weiner-Davis, Michele 237
Weisinger, Hendrie 199
Weiss, Jonathan B. 36
Weiss, Laurie 36
Weiss, Robert S. 461, 488, 496
Weitzman, Lenore J. 405
Welwood, John 169
West, Uta 451
Wheeler, Michael 394
White, Shelby 426
Whiteman, Tom 443
Whitney, Catherine 540
Wholey, Dennis 473
Wilkie, Jane 484
Wilkins, Nancy 439
Willi, Jurg 152
Williamson, Marianne 57, 212
Wilson, Josleen 270
Windon, Tricia 376
Wingo, John 519
Wingo, Julie 519
Witkin, Georgia 12, 33
Witkin, Mildred Hope 479
Witkin-Lanoil, Georgia
Woititz, Janet G. 221
Wolf, Sharyn 517, 529
Women in Transition, Inc. 342
Woodhouse, Violet 396
Wyden, Peter 251

Y

Yates, Martha 483

Z

Ziglar, Zig 139
Zola, Marion 285
Zuckerman, Shirley 142

Subject Index

A

A Course in Miracles
    Return to Love 212
abusive behavior
    *Men Who Hate Women and the Women
        Who Love Them 93*
abusive relationships
    Emotionally Abused Woman 10
    Getting Unstuck 13
    When Love Goes Wrong 278
    *When Someone You Love Is Someone
        You Hate 279*
academic performance
    Helping Children of Divorce 364
addictions
    Agony of It All 1
    Bradshaw On. The Family 4
    Love and Addiction 256
adjustments
    For the Sake of the Children 357
adultery
    Adultery 282
adventure
    Agony of It All 1
adversarial divorce
    Between Love & Hate 386
    Children of Divorce 347
    Divorce Mediation 402
    Divorce Mediation 403

Uncoupling 340
adversity
    *One Door Closes, Another Door Opens
        328*
    *Ordinary Women, Extraordinary Lives
        464*
affair prevention
    Affair Prevention 284
affairs
    Not With My Husband You Don't 303
    Passion for More 304
affairs with married men
    New Other Woman 302
age differences
    Age of Taboo 125
aging
    Love, Sex, and Aging 118
    Unfinished Business 49
aging parents
    *What Every Woman Should Know
        About Her Husband's Money 426*
agreements
    What Every Woman Sho
alcoholism
    Codependent No More 7
alternative life-styles
    Marriage Divorce Remarriage 119
anger
    Anger 230
    Anger Workbook 231

Note: Numbers used in all indexes identity books by book numbers that appear with each title, not by page number.

259

Angry Book 232
Dance of Anger 236
My Mother/My Self 30
appeals
Divorce Handbook 400
assertiveness
Don't Say Yes When You Want to Say No 9
How to Be an Assertive (Not Aggressive) Woman in Life, Love and On the Job 19
attitudes, effect of
Love Secrets for a Lasting Relationship 180

B

bad relationships
Bailing Out 311
behavior modeling
My Mother/My Self 30
behavior patterns
Keeping the Love You Find 538
Secret of Loving 545
behavior therapy
How to Fall Out of Love 448
behavioral styles
Intimate Partners 166
best friends
New Male-Female Relationship 196
betrayal
Love & Betrayal 297
Bible-based insights
Fresh Start Divorce Recovery Workbook 443
Biblical principles
Fit to Be Tied 526
birth order
Were You Born for Each Other? 550
blame-free living
Nobody's Perfect 198
blending families
Healthy Divorce 362
buddy love
In Defense of Marriage 161
burnout
Women's Burnout 64

C

careers
Career & Conflict 5
Woman's Worth 57
change, affecting positive
You Can Excel in Times of Change 343
change, dealing with
12 Steps to Mastering the Winds of Change 310
character traits
How to Love a Difficult Man 246
childcare
In Praise of Single Parents 490
childhood
Homecoming 18
child-rearing
Divorce and Your Child 353
children as hostages
Children of Separation and Divorce 348
Christian beliefs
Children & Divorce 346
'Til Divorce Do Us Part 336
co-dependency
One-Way Relationships 264
Recovery from Co-Dependency 36
Struggle for Intimacy 221
commitment
Men Who Can't Love 92
Women Men Love/Women Men Leave 113
commitment, fear of
Cold Feet 523
Hearts of Men 75
communication
Centering & the Art of Intimacy 131
Courtship After Marriage 139
I Love You, Let's Work It Out 248
Love Is Never Enough 178
Men Are from Mars. Women Are from Venus 193
Men Talk 91
RelationShift 211
Secret of Staying in Love 216
Sexual Static 101

Talking About Divorce and
  Separation 380
That's Not What I Meant 223
What Men Really Want 108
Why Men Are the Way They Are 111
communication skills
  How to Make a Man Fall in Love With
    You 534
  30 Secrets of Happily Married Couples
    124
compatibility
  Are You the One for Me? 518
  Compatibility Quotient 524
  How to Make a Man Fall in Love With
    You 534
  How to Make Love All the Time 156
  How to Marry the Man of Your Choice
    537
  Smart Women 547
  Were You Born for Each Other? 550
  What Every Woman Ought to Know
    About Love & Marriage 226
  Why Love Is Not Enough 552
compromise
  How to Live With Another Person 155
compulisive lovers
  Casanova Complex 71
compulsive disorders
  Codependent No More 7
conflict
  What Wives Wish Their Husbands
    Knew About Women 52
conflict, positive aspects
  How to Keep Love Alive 245
  Magic of Conflict
conflict resolution
  Book for Couples 129
  Changing Him, Changing Her 133
  Couple Skills 135
  Don't Go Away Mad 238
  Getting the Love You Want 150
  How to Manage a Marriage 158
  Let's Have It Out 253
  One Question That Can Save Your
    Marriage 200
  Resolving Family and Other Conflicts
    266

Seven Basic Quarrels of Marriage 268
constructive agression
  Intimate Enemy 251
constructive interaction
  Love Is the Answer 179
co-parenting
  Healthy Divorce 362
coping skills
  Coping 483
  Divorce and After 435
  Divorced Kids 355
  Divorced Woman's Handbook 484
  How to Fall Out of Love 448
  Letting Go 453
  Life After Loss 454
  Life's Parachutes 456
  Marital Separation 461
  Overwhelmed 331
  Sorrow and the Fury 469
  Suddenly Single 514
  Turning Points 338
  Wife-In-Law Trap 476
coping with loss
  Necessary Losses 462
counselors
  Divorce Help Sourcebook 401
courtship
  Searching for Courtship 543
  What Every Woman Ought to Know
    About Love & Marriage 226
crises
  Coming Back 433
  Leavetaking 322
  Living Through Personal Crisis 458
  Pathfinders 332
  Phoenix Factor 465
  Risking 333
  Suddenly Single 514
  Super Marriage 222
  When the Worst That Can Happen
    Already Has 473
  Why Me • Why This • Why Now 475
custody
  Custody Revolution 392
  How It Feels When Parents Divorce
    366

Mothers on Trial 416

My Kids Don't Live With Me Anymore 373

custody disputes

Parent Vs. Parent 418

Quality Time 377

custody laws

Sharing the Children 422

cycles of intimate relationships

Couples 137

D

dating

Divorced Parenting 356

Guerrilla Dating Tactics 529

Hot and Bothered 531

How to Find Another Husband...By Someone Who Did 532

Searching for Courtship 543

dating services

How to Find Romance After 40 533

decision-making

Choices 313

Divorce Decisions Workbook 398

Good Guys/Bad Guys 528

How to Get Out of an Unhappy Marriage or an Unhappy Relationship 320

How to Salvage Your Marriage or Survive Your Divorce 247

Life Choices 324

Overcoming Indecisiveness 330

decree modifications

Divorce Handbook 400

defense mechanisms

Love Knots 259

democratic partnerships

Challenge of Marriage 132

dependency

Women Who Love Too Much 63

depression

Divorce Without Victims 354

Women & the Blues 61

Women's Burnout 64

destructive relationships

Women Who Love Too Much 63

discord in marriages

His Needs Her Needs 293

dissatifaction in marriage

What Wives Wish Their Husbands Knew About Women 52

divorce--causes

How Not to Split Up 244

divorce--negative aspects

Case Against Divorce 234

Divorce Busting 237

Divorce Anonymous

Divorce Recovery 438

divorce decree

Divorce Decision 397

divorce laws

Dealing With Divorce 393

Divorce and Dissolution of Marriage Laws of the United States 395

Woman's Legal Guide to Separation and Divorce in All 50 States 429

divorce proceedings

Divorce Dirty Tricks 399

divorce process

Divorce Decisions Workbook 398

Divorcing 407

Living Through Your Divorce 325

divorce rates

Husbands and Wives 116

divorce reform

Divorce and After 435

divorce settlements

Child Support in America 388

Don't Settle for Less 409

Getting Divorced Without Ruining Your Life 411

Mediate Your Divorce 414

Process of Divorce 419

divorce speak

Vicki Lansky's Divorce Book for Parents 381

divorced parents

Boys' and Girls' Book About Divorce 345

dysfunctional childhoods

Sex, Lies and Forgiveness 307

dysfunctional lovers
Casanova Complex 71

E

economic injustices
Divorce Revolution 405

emotional independence
Why Do I Think I Am Nothing Without a
Man? 55

emotional problems
Growing Up With Divorce 361

emotional satisfaction
No Fault Marriage 197

emotional workouts
Life Mates 172

emotions
Anger Workbook 231
Angry Book 232
Dance of Anger 236

envy
Jealousy 252
Snow White Syndrome 40

evaluating marriage
Marriage Without B.S. 190

extended family
In Praise of Single Parents 490

extramarital affairs
Affair 283
More Than Just a Friend 301
Woman Versus Woman 309

ex-wife syndrome
Ex-Wife Syndrome 440

F

family life
Surviving Family Life 270

father-daughter relationships
Women and Their Fathers 62

fear of abandonment
Growing Up Divorced 360

fear of commitment
Hearts of Men 75
Men Who Can't Love 92

fears of children
What Should I Tell the Kids? 383

female affairs
Erotic Silence of the American Wife 289

female personality
In a Different Voice 21

feminine roles
From This Day Forward 149

femininity
Being a Woman 2
Fascinating Womanhood 11

feminism
Being a Woman 2
Where's My Happy Ending? 54

fidelity
Faithful Attraction 291
Private Lies 305

financial dependence
Golden Handcuffs 14

financial issues
Dollars and Sense of Divorce 408
Head and Heart 413
Love and Money 175
Mothers and Divorce 415

financial planning
Our Money Our Selves 417
Survival Guide for Women 425
What Every Woman Should Know
About Her Husband's Money 426
Women, Divorce and Money 430

financial problems
What Every Woman Ought to Know
About Love & Marriage 226

financial security
Women & Money 59
You're Entitled 431

firstborns
Growing Up Firstborn 16

forgiveness
Forgiveness 442
Forgiving Marriage 240
Forgiving the Unforgivable 241
Growing Through Divorce 319
How to Forgive Your Ex-Husband (And
Get On With Your Life) 449
Love Is Letting Go of Fear 177
When Someone You Love Is Someone
You Hate 279

friendship
Lost Lovers, Found Friends 459
fulfillment
Secret Loves 306

G
gambling
Money Demons 261
game-playing
Games People Play 242
gender differences
Men Are from Mars. Women Are from
Venus 193
genderlect
You Just Don't Understand 281
geographic separation
Long Distance Parenting 371
good girl behavior
Too Good for Her Own Good 43
grief .
Grief Out of Season 358
Lessons of Love 452
Life After Loss 454
When Bad Things Happen to Good
People 472
grief recovery
Grief Recovery Handbook 445
guilt
Guilt 446
Guilt Is the Teacher, Love Is the
Lesson 447
Nice Women Get Divorced 327

H
happiness
Total Loving 45
healing
Growing Up Divorced 359
household responsibilities
What to Do When He Won't Change
276
Working It Out 65
human sexuality
Masters and Johnson on Sex and
Human Loving 192

humor
Why Did I Marry You Anyway? 280

I
image therapy
Breaking Out of Loneliness 482
immaturity
Seashell People 37
impact of divorce
Second Chances 378
incompatibility
Coming Apart 314
Incompatibility of Men and Women 250
independence
Cinderella Complex 6
Formerly Married 487
Joy of Being Single 493
Living Single Successfully 495
Single After 50 503
Why Women Shouldn't Marry 553
independent living
Alone—Not Lonely 480
Living Alone and Liking It 494
One's Company 499
Single 502
individual freedom
Family Politics 147
inferiority
Smart Cookies Don't Crumble 468
infidelity
Beyond Affairs 287
Love Me Love Me Not 298
Men Who Can't Be Faithful 299
Private Lies 305
inner child
Homecoming 18
insecurities of children
What Every Child Would Like Parents
to Know About Divorce 382
intension therapy
Do I Have to Give Up Me to Be Loved
by You? 145
inter-cultural marriages
Inter-Cultural Marriage 162
Intermarriage Handbook 163

interdependence
Road to Intimacy 214
interpersonal skills
Challenge of Marriage 132
intimacy
Art of Staying Together 128
Dance of Intimacy 143
Intimacy 164
McGill Report on Male Intimacy 88
Men Are Just Desserts 28
Opening Our Hearts to Men 32
Sex Begins in the Kitchen 218
intimacy, fear of
Why Men Can't Open Up 112
intimacy--patterns
Intimate Partners 167
intimacy paradox
Come Here/Go Away 235
intimacy quotients
Stranger in Your Bed 269
intimate relationships
Art and Practice of Loving 126
Choosing Lovers 522
Going the Distance 151
Journey of the Heart 169
Keeping the Love You Find 538
Love the Way You Want It 540
Secret of Loving 545
Someone Right for You 548
Uncoupling 341
Why Men Don't Get Enough Sex and
Women Don't Get Enough Love 228
Women & Love 58
intimate strangers
Intimate Strangers 168

J
jealousy
Green-Eyed Marriage 243
Romantic Jealousy 267
joint custody
Co-Parenting 390
Custody Revolution 392

K
kidnapping
Quality Time 377
Rematch 420

L
language styles
You Just Don't Understand 281
lawyers
Divorce Handbook 400
leave-taking
Learning to Leave 321
legal issues
Getting Your Share 412
When Couples Part 427
legal rights
Complete Legal Guide to Marriage,
Divorce, Custody and Living
Together 391
Ex-Factor 410
Rematch 420
lesbian mothers
Women in Transition 342
lesbians
When Love Goes Wrong 278
life cycles
Creating a Marriage 140
Creative Marriage 141
Passages 203
life plans
Shifting Gears 334
living alone
First Person Singular 485
Our Turn 329
loneliness
Alone—Not Lonely 480
Alone, Alive & Well 481
Born for Love 130
Breaking Out of Loneliness 482
In Search of Intimacy 491
Intimate Connections 492
Life After Marriage 455
Living Together 254
Loneliness 496
Love Blocks 257

Woman Alone 516
loss inventory
Kids' Guide to Divorce 370
love
Art of Loving 127
Born for Love 130
*If Love Is the Answer, What Is the
    Question? 451*
Living, Loving & Learning 173
Love 174
Natural History of Love 122
Psychology of Love 123
Real Love 542
Triangle of Love 224
What Love Asks of Us 227
love cycles
Love Cycles 176
love-hate relationships
*When Someone You Love Is Someone
    You Hate 279*
lovesickness
Lovesick 27
loving relationships
Couples 136
From Conflict to Caring 148

M

male anxieties
Masculine Dilemma 86
male behavior
Fire in the Belly 74
How Men Feel 76
Male Paradox 83
*What Every Woman Should Know
    About Men 106*
male characteristics
*Some Men Are More Perfect Than
    Others 103*
male classification
Classified Man 72
male crises
Seasons of a Man's Life 98
male ego
Male Ego 80
male immaturity
Peter Pan Syndrome 97

male intimacy
McGill Report on Male Intimacy 88
male middle years
Crisis Time 73
male roles
Male Ego 80
Male Ordeal 82
Men and Marriage 90
Passions of Men 95
*Perfect Husbands (& Other Fairy
    Tales) 96*
Some American Men 102
*Straight Talk to Men and Their Wives
    105*
male self-esteem
*What Men Won't Tell You But Women
    Need to Know 109*
male sexuality
Male Machine 81
male-female communication
Men Talk 91
man-hating
My Enemy, My Love 29
marital conflict
We Can Work It Out 275
marital forecasting
Marital Choices 186
marital happiness
Lucky in Love 182
marital property
Women & Money 59
marital scenarios
Marriage Premise 121
marital stages
Marriage Map 189
marriage skills
Loving Each Other 181
masculinity
Being a Man 69
Fire in the Belly 74
Male Paradox 83
Manhood 85
Secrets Men Keep 41
Straight Talk 104
matchmakers
At Long Last Love 519

*Haven't You Been Single Long
    Enough?* 530
mate selection
    Sexual Strategies 546
    What Really Works With Men 110
mediation
    Between Love & Hate 386
    Divorce Mediation 402
    Divorce Mediation 403
    Divorce Mediation 404
    *Getting Divorced Without Ruining Your
        Life* 411
    Healthy Divorce 362
    Learning to Leave 321
    Parents' Book About Divorce 375
men's legal rights
    Winning Your Divorce 428
men's sexuality
    Beyond the Male Myth 70
menopause
    Unfinished Business 49
midlife
    Flying Solo 486
mid-life crisis
    Crisis Time 73
miracles
    Return to Love 212
mistresses
    All the Good Ones Are Married 285
misunderstandings
    Love Is Never Enough 178
money
    Warm Hearts & Cold Cash 225
money conflicts
    Money Demons 261
monogamy
    How to Keep Your Man Monogamous
        295
    Monogamy Myth 300
    Why Men Stray and Why Men Stay 308
mothering men
    Wendy Dilemma 50
mourning
    Divorce Without Victims 354
mourning process
    Life After Marriage 455

moving on
    Get Rid of Him 317
Myers-Briggs Type Indicators
    Type Talk 48

N

negative behavior patterns
    Binds That Tie 233
    For the Sake of the Children 357
    Power of Unconditional Love 207
    Women Men Love/Women Men Leave
        113
negative thinking
    Slay Your Own Dragons 39
    When Am I Going To Be Happy? 53
new relationships
    Dare to Connect 525
    Learning to Love Again 539
no-fault divorce
    Dealing With Divorce 393
    Divorce Yourself 406
nonhostile parenting
    How It Feels When Parents Divorce
        366

O

obsessive attachments
    *If This Is Love, Why Do I Feel So
        Insecure?* 249
obsessive love
    Obsessive Love 263
open marriage
    Open Marriage 202

P

palimony
    Divorce Decision 397
    When Couples Part 427
parental divorce
    Adult Children of Divorce 344
parenthood
    Transition to Parenthood 273
parenting
    Divorce and Your Child 353
    Surviving the Break-Up 379

parenting skills
Helping Children Cope With Divorce
363
Parents Without Partners
Parents Without Partners Sourcebook
500
parents without partners
How to Live With a Single Parent 367
partnerships
Conscious Loving 134
How to Have a Happy Marriage 153
Peer Marriage 205
passages of marriage
Passages of Marriage 204
passions
Passions 33
peer marriage
Peer Marriage 205
perfectionism
Pleasers... Women Who Can't Say
No 35
Superwoman Syndrome 41
Type E Woman 47
personal growth
Creative Divorce 315
personality types
Husbands Wives & Sex 160
One to One 201
pertnerships
New Male-Female Relationship 196
positive criticism
Nobody's Perfect 198
positive relationships
Love Is the Answer 179
post-divorce conflict
Ex-Factor 410
post-divorce transition
World of the Formerly Married 478
prenuptial agreements
Love and Money 175
What Every Woman Should Know
About Her Husband's Money 426
preserving marriage
Growing Together/Staying Together
152
How to Get Him Back from the Other
Woman If You Still Want Him 294

Marriage Maintenance Manual 188
Married People 191
Mirages of Marriage 195
Second Honeymoon 215
Staying Together 220
When a Mate Wants Out 277
Why Did I Marry You Anyway? 280
pressure points
Unfinished Business 49
problem-solving
Resilience 467
property settlement
Divorce and Money 396

R

realistic love
Courage My Love 138
reality discipline principles
Keeping Your Family Together When
the World Is Falling Apart 170
reconciliation
Uncoupling 341
reconciliation fantansies
Vicki Lansky's Divorce Book for
Parents 381
recovery
Divorce Recovery 438
Forgive & Forget 441
How to Survive the Loss of a Love 450
Living and Loving After Divorce 457
Loveshock 460
Rebuilding 466
Whoever Said Life Is Fair? 474
recovery strategies
Lovesick 27
reinventing marriage
Staying in Love 219
rejection
Dare to Connect 525
Sudden Endings 335
relationship addiction
Letters from Women Who Love Too
Much 24
relationship dynamics
Seven Marriages of Your Marriage 217

relationship problems
What Really Works With Men 110
relationship-enhancement inventory
Lasting Love 171
religious issues
Children of Separation and Divorce 348
remarriage
Beating the Marriage Odds 520
Beyond Cinderella 521
Making Remarriage Work 541
To Marry Again 549
resilience
Staying On Top When Your World Turns Upside Down 470
Winning Life's Toughest Battles 477
revenge
Obsessive Love 263
revitalization (of marriage)
Total Woman 46
rich and famous people
How to Marry Super Rich 536
What Has She Got? 551
risk taking
Greatest Risk of All 318
roles
Loving & Leaving 326
roles & role theory
Dance Away Lover & Other Roles We Play in Love, Sex and Marriage 142
romance
Courtship After Marriage 139
How to Find Romance After 40 533
Light His Fire 25
romance, male illusions
Knight in Shining Armor 78
romantic love
False Love 239
Love Busters 258
Marriage, Love, Sex and Divorce 120
Psychology of Romantic Love 211
Rediscovering Love 210

S
salvaging relationships
How to Win Back the One You Love 296

sane divorce
Uncoupling 340
second marriages
Second Time Around 544
security
Shifting Gears 334
self-counselling
No Fault Marriage 197
self-destructive behaviors
Come Here/Go Away 235
Your Erroneous Zones 66
self-development
Life Changes 323
Self-Directed Marriage
Husbands and Wives 159
self-esteem
After You've Said Good-Bye 432
Getting Unstuck 13
Hole in My Heart 365
Looking Out for #1 26
Men, Women and Relationships 194
Secret of Staying in Love 216
Sweet Suffering 42
Ten Days to Self-Esteem 471
What Men Won't Tell You But Women Need to Know 109
When Am I Going To Be Happy? 53
Women & Self-Esteem 60
self-gratification
In Transition 22
self-image
What Smart Women Know 51
self-preservation
Single Again 504
self-renewal
Turning Points 339
self-sacrifice
One-Way Relationships 264
sense of identity
Intimacy 165
separation
Divorce Experience 316
How to Get Out of an Unhappy Marriage or an Unhappy Relationship 320
Talking About Divorce and Separation 380

sex
  Hot and Bothered 531
  How to Make Love to a Man 535
  Sex and the Single Parent 501
sex addiction
  Sex, Lies and Forgiveness 307
sex life
  How to Make Love to the Same Person
    for the Rest of Your Life 157
  Secrets About Men Every Woman
    Should Know 99
sex roles
  Inner Male 77
  Men and Marriage 89
sex-addiction
  Back from Betrayal 286
  Don Juan Dilemma 288
  Looking for Love in All the Wrong
    Places 255
sexism in the workplace
  Women in Transition 342
sexual abuse
  Quality Time 377
sexual equality
  Pleasure Bond 206
sexual freedom
  Sensuous Woman 38
sexual intimacy
  Marriage Is for Loving 187
sexual movement
  Sexual Static 41
sexual revitalization
  Have a Love Affair With Your Husband
    (Before Someone Else Does) 292
sexual revolution
  Equal Time 146
  Innter Male 77
  Male Dilemma 79
  Passions of Men 95
sexual revolution, effects of
  How Men Feel 76
sexual roles
  Equal Time 146
sexuality
  Kinsey Institute New Report on Sex 117
  Love, Sex, and Aging 118

shared custody
  Co-Parenting 390
  Mom's House, Dad's House 372
  Sharing Parenthood After Divorce 421
single life
  Singled Out 510
  Singles 511
  Singling 512
single mothers
  Single Mother's Book 506
single older men and women
  45 and Single Again 479
single parent families
  Going It Alone 488
  Kids' Book About Single Parent
    Families 368
  One On the Seesaw 498
single parenting
  Divorce and New Beginnings 436
  Divorced 439
  Parents Without Partners Sourcebook
    500
  Single Parenting 507
  Solo Parenting 513
single parents
  How to Live With a Single Parent 367
  How to Parent Alone 489
  In Praise of Single Parents 490
  On Our Own 497
  Sex and the Single Parent 501
  Single Parents Are People Too 508
single women
  Single Women, Alone and Together 509
  Woman Alone 516
social networks
  Alone, Alive & Well 481
social trends
  Marriage Divorce Remarriage 119
spiritual growth
  Road Less Traveled 213
spritual psychotherapy
  Return to Love 212
stages of divorce
  Growing Through Divorce 319
  Growing Up Divorced 359

stepfamilies
Divorce and New Beginnings 436
Divorced Parenting 356
stepparenting
To Marry Again 549
stress
Female Stress Syndrome 12
Green-Eyed Marriage 243
Male Stress Syndrome 84
Masculine Dilemma 86
Men, Women and Relationships 194
Resilience 467
Together on a Tightrope 271
stress resolution
Prescription for a Quality Relationship 208
submissive women
Sweet Suffering 42
substance abuse
Ordinary Women, Extraordinary Lives 464
Struggle for Intimacy 221
suburban life
New Suburban Woman 31
success
Having It All 17
success in the workplace
Too Smart for Her Own Good 44
superwoman syndrome
Superwoman Syndrome 41
support
Child Support 387
Child Support Survivor's Guide 389
support groups
Divorce Help Sourcebook 401
support networks
On Our Own 497
One Door Closes, Another Door Opens 328
Single Women, Alone and Together 509
surveys of marriage
Husbands and Wives 116
surving infidelity
Every Other Man 290
sustaining love
How to Keep a Man in Love With You Forever 154

T
taxes
Strassels' Tax Savers 424
teachers
Parents' Book About Divorce 375
teenagers
"Your Father's Not Coming Home Anymore" 385
tension reduction
Dirty Half Dozen 144
therapy
Helping Children of Divorce 364
tough love
Love Must Be Tough 260
Tough Marriage 272
transactional analysis
I'm OK—You're OK 20
transition
Crazy Time 434
Fresh Starts 444
Parents' Book About Divorce 375
Survival Guide for the Suddenly Single 515
Transitions 337
Women in Transition 342
trust
Love & Betrayal 297
two-career couples
Making It Together As a Two Career Couple 184

U
unconditional love
Power of Unconditional Love 207
unequal feelings
Passion Paradox 265
unrealistic expectations
Now That I'm Married, Why Isn't Everything Perfect? 262
unsatisfactory relationships
Agony of It All 1

V
verbal abuse
Verbally Abusive Relationship 274

victim mentality
Opening Our Hearts to Men 32
visitation
Dinosaurs Divorce 351
Kids' Book of Divorce 369

W
weddings and divorced parents
Planning a Wedding With Divorced Parents 376
women's movement
Being a Woman 2
Inner Male 77
Sexual Static 41
work and love
Work and Love 229
workaholics
Workaholics 114
working mothers
Crisis of the Working Mother 8
working women
Working It Out 65
worrying
Why Women Worry ...and How to Stop 56

Y
younger men
Age of Taboo 125

ATHENS REGIONAL LIBRARY SYSTEM

3 3207 00339 6126